American Chestnut

American Chestnut

The Life, Death, and Rebirth of a Perfect Tree

Susan Freinkel

UNIVERSITY OF CALIFORNIA PRESS

Berkeley   Los Angeles   London

University of California Press, one of the most distinguished university presses in the United States, enriches lives around the
world by advancing scholarship in the humanities, social sciences,
and natural sciences. Its activities are supported by the UC Press
Foundation and by philanthropic contributions from individuals
and institutions. For more information, visit www.ucpress.edu.

University of California Press
Berkeley and Los Angeles, California

University of California Press, Ltd.
London, England

Library of Congress Cataloging-in-Publication Data
Freinkel, Susan, 1957–
    American chestnut : the life, death, and rebirth of a perfect
tree / Susan Freinkel.
        p.   cm.
    Includes bibliographical references and index.
    ISBN 978-0-520-24730-7 (cloth : alk. paper)
    1. American chestnut.   I. Title.
    SD397.A48F74   2007
    634.9'724—dc22   2007007769

Manufactured in the United States of America

16   15   14   13   12   11   10   09   08   07
10   9   8   7   6   5   4   3   2   1

For Eric,
who always has the right words

What can turn us from this deserted future, back into the sphere of our being, the great dance that joins us to our home, to each other and to other creatures, to the dead and the unborn?

Wendell Berry

I see again, as one in vision sees,
The blossoms and the bees
And hear the children's voices shout and call
And the brown chestnuts fall.

Henry Wadsworth Longfellow

CONTENTS

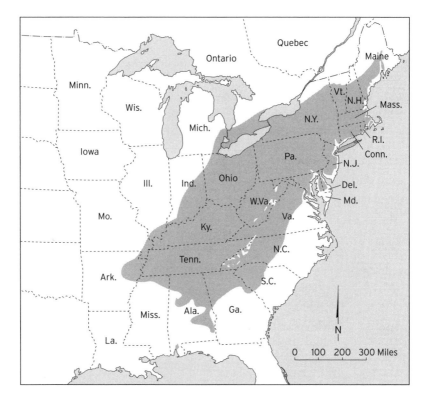

Distribution of the American chestnut, 1938. The native range of the American chestnut sprawled across the eastern United States, though the heart of chestnut country was along the steep slopes of the southern Appalachians. By the time this map was published, however, the blight had demolished most mature chestnuts in the tree's northern range and was laying waste to those in the South. (Source: E. N. Munns, *The Distribution of Important Forest Trees of the Eastern United States* [Washington, D.C.: USDA, 1938].)

Introduction

In the spring of 2006, a wildlife biologist hiking a little-used trail near Pine Mountain in Warm Springs, Georgia, made a startling discovery. Not far from the trail he spotted a small stand of American chestnuts—living examples of a tree that had become all but extinct half a century before. The biologist had never seen an American chestnut, but as soon as he spied one among the gnarly oaks, he knew at once what he had found. "It was just shining there, almost impossible to miss." The find made headlines around the country. As one news report pointed out, what the fabled ivory-billed woodpecker is to birders, the American chestnut is to tree lovers: a vanquished species that continues to haunt their dreams.

A century ago, the American chestnut was one of the country's most populous and important trees, a soaring tower of wood that ruled the East Coast forests from Georgia to Maine. Many considered it the "perfect tree," for chestnut had a value and versatility unmatched by any other hardwood. And nowhere were those qualities better appreciated than in southern Appalachia, where generations of impoverished mountain farmers had depended on the chestnut for food, lumber, and livelihood. "Chestnut defined the region," says Charlotte Ross, a folklorist at Appalachian State University, in North Carolina. "If ever a region was associated with a tree, then the chestnut was *our* tree."

But in the early twentieth century, the chestnut met its perfect foe: a brutally efficient and virulent pathogen that came to be known as the chestnut blight. On its home turf in Asia, the blight fungus is relatively harmless. But after it was unwittingly imported to this country, it spread with unprecedented ferocity. Over the course of a single generation, the blight rampaged across the Atlantic seaboard, destroying billions of American chestnut trees and devastating communities that had come to rely on them. In the space of two generations, America's perfect tree was teetering on the brink of extinction. It was one of the worst blows to the continent's ecosystem since the Ice Age.

You'd think such an environmental and social catastrophe would be as well known as the disappearance of the dodo. Yet I had never heard of the chestnut blight until I began researching a magazine article about another potentially devastating forest disease that was killing thousands of oak trees in the San Francisco Bay Area, where I live. At the time, no one knew how serious sudden oak death might turn out to be. All the experts I talked to shared the same nightmare vision—that this outbreak would be another chestnut blight, a pandemic with the potential to obliterate an entire species, or even several species. I tried to imagine what the Bay Area's hillsides would be like without those familiar lollipop-shaped clusters of coast live oaks. How would their disappearance change the look and feel of this place? What would the impact be on the dozens of animals and insects that depend on various species of oaks for sustenance and shelter? What does it mean when a beloved species vanishes? I began looking into the story of the American chestnut to see how earlier generations had grappled with these questions.

Much to my surprise, I found that outside the scientific literature, relatively little had been written about the chestnut, especially prior to the blight. The American elm, also the victim of a decimating disease, has been the subject of poems and paeans for centuries. The wealth of post-blight eulogies makes it clear that the chestnut was a highly esteemed tree, so I didn't understand why so little written documentation of that esteem existed, compared to that for the elm, until I read a perceptive history of the elm tree titled *Republic of Shade: New England and the American Elm.* The elm, as author Thomas Campanella explains, was a town tree; indeed, it was the perfect town tree. Planted in countless New England town squares, elms became a signal part of the middle-class landscape and an ever-present feature in the lives of the people who write history. The chestnut, on the other hand, was a country tree. Its life in the forest and its dramatic demise took place in view of relatively few human witnesses. Those who did bear witness to the tree's disappearance—those to whom the chestnut tree was most important—were the rural poor, people whose stories were passed down through oral rather than written accounts. Such stories endure only so long as they are told, one person to another, until they pass into legend . . . or oblivion.

As I began listening to chestnut stories and the melancholia that often accompanies them, I found myself transported to a time very different from our own and yet disturbingly familiar. How astonishing to think that a "perfect tree" could dominate so much of this continent, suffer utter collapse in the space of a human lifetime, and then slip from historical memory as if it had never existed. What did it mean to the people who had loved and lost the tree, and what meaning could there be for people today in a world where so much that we love is in danger of being lost?

The chestnut blight arrived at a time when Americans were just starting to recognize that the country's natural bounty had limits. The last passenger pigeons had been shot from the sky, the vast bison herds hunted to near extinction. And in 1907—just a few years after the chestnut blight was first reported—President Teddy Roosevelt declared that decades of frenzied logging had so depleted the nation's forests that "the country is unquestionably on the verge of a timber famine which will be felt in every household in the land." These early intimations of vulnerability and loss are the anxious roots of modern environmental consciousness. Chestnut blight, though not the first imported plant pathogen, revealed the seriousness of the problem of human-facilitated invasive species and foreshadowed the rapid decline of biodiversity the planet is witnessing today. The chestnut catastrophe may have passed from public view, but the specter of catastrophe increasingly haunts any informed view of industrial civilization and its brute impact on the world. And so the chestnut can instruct us about the terrible fragility of even the mightiest species, including our own.

Unlike so many environmental stories today, the chestnut's demise is not simply a tale of loss. A stubborn cadre of the tree's devotees has refused to let it go. Successive generations of dedicated scientists and ardent amateurs have fought for nearly a century to save this species so well matched to our own. They have pledged to help the chestnut outwit its mortal enemy. Their efforts are no less fervid today than they were in the blight's earliest days, even though none of today's chestnut crusaders has ever experienced the "perfect tree" in its historical setting. Instead, they draw inspiration from stories handed down, from a desire to right an ecological wrong, and from a powerful, if nameless, affinity for a fellow species.

I confess that affinity is not something I felt myself, as strange as that may sound coming from someone who has spent three years thinking about a tree. I can't name more than a handful of trees in the park where I walk my dog, and houseplants wilt when my shadow passes over them. But something in the chestnut's desperate dance with extinction riveted me. I was moved by the deeply personal ways in which people in Appalachia experienced the loss of the chestnut tree, and in which they still grieve its demise decades after the last chestnut forests disappeared. I was intrigued by the spirit animating current efforts to bring the chestnut back—a devotion that persists beyond all logic. In many ways, that deep sense of affinity for a tree is what I set out to understand.

It's been called chestnut fever, and even "chestnuttiness" (though that term makes chestnut fans cringe). By whatever name, it's a genuine phenomenon. If anyone was ever in its thrall, it was the late Barney Barnhart, a wealthy Pennsylvania businessman whose head-over-heels love for the tree led him to accumulate the world's largest—and probably only—collection of American chestnut tchotchkes. It started, as do many collections, innocently enough. When Barnhart was in his mid-sixties and recuperating from an illness, he started spending time in a wooded area near the family's home in Roaring Springs. Chestnuts had once flourished in this part of central Pennsylvania, and Barnhart began finding vestiges of the tree: huge stumps and corrugated husks of old logs.

One day he brought home a twisted hunk of wood. "This is beautiful," he told his wife, Charlotte. "We have to clean this up." Sure enough, when they scrubbed away the encrusted dirt and soft rotten wood, a lovely sinuous shape was revealed. Soon Barnhart was hauling home chestnut relics every day, drafting his dumbfounded teenage children into helping him clean and sort the growing piles of chestnut wood. "He'd point and say, 'Look at the wormholes, look at the blond and the dark.' He'd be so fascinated by it," his daughter Charlene recalls. "I'd be thinking, 'Yeah, it's a piece of wood.'" For the life of her, Charlene couldn't see what her father saw. "I can only equate it to being colorblind," she says. Barnhart eventually filled three industrial-size buildings with chestnut odds and ends.

While his chestnut fervor started with the dead wood, Barney soon became interested in efforts to bring the tree back to life. He was a leading figure in one of the foremost chestnut restoration programs, the American Chestnut Foundation. When I began working on this book, various members of the group repeatedly told me, "You *have* to visit Roaring Springs." In the spring of 2005, I finally did. I spent a day touring Barnhart's collection, and that night his widow, Charlotte, was kind enough to let me stay in one of the guest log cabins at the family's "farm," a piece of property on which Barnhart had built a half-size golf course for his employees and where much of his chestnut collection is stored. The course is decorated not only with an old chestnut split-rail fence, but also with gigantic metal animals Barnhart picked up at an auction somewhere.

My cabin was a cozy space, with braided rugs on the floor and chestnut paneling on the bedroom walls. I woke early the next morning and lay in the antique brass bed for a while, looking at the chestnut wainscoting at the end of the bed, trying to see it through Barney's eyes. There was an incredible variety among the boards. One board had a dark-eyed knot; another was corrugated with deep ridges. The grain on one rippled down like the rain on a windowpane. This board was a dull brown; that one, warm amber. Each piece, I now saw, was utterly unique, as individual as a fingerprint.

Without my glasses, the room was pleasantly blurred, and it didn't seem such a stretch to pretend that I was back in the nineteenth century. The sun was rising and I watched the first rays play across the honey-colored pine ceiling. I tried to ignore the hum of the refrigerator and the electric light on the nightstand. If I didn't look out the window, if I didn't think about the eighteen-foot metal rooster on the golf course below, I could almost transport myself back to a time when America was known as the "wooden country" and the most perfect member of its vast timber empire was the American chestnut tree.

In that moment, I felt that same affinity for the chestnut that has so long sustained efforts to restore the tree. Whether such an affinity for another species expresses itself as chestnuttiness or as a desire to swim with a dolphin or reside in a redwood tree, this is where the will to grapple with our hard and pressing environmental problems begins: in relationship to something other that you love beyond any utility, beyond all logic.

Practically speaking, of course, the tree's salvation depends on scientific answers. Yet in the end, the daunting challenge of saving the species—or any species, for that matter—requires a marriage of science and passion. The American chestnut has been lucky enough to inspire just such a marriage, though whether it proves to be enough to ultimately bring back the perfect tree remains an open question. "Everyone who works on chestnut is passionate," one veteran chestnut researcher said to me. "You have to be: the odds aren't in your favor."

Part One

The tree looks like an aging champion struggling to stay upright until the last round. It is badly bruised. A major branch is missing. But it still has a heavyweight's build and a veteran's endurance. Perhaps 150 or 200 years old, this tree is one of the few survivors of a century-long plague that has brought down nearly every mature American chestnut tree from Georgia to Maine. At sixty feet tall and nearly four feet wide, it's the largest chestnut left in the species' historic range.

The tree stands alone in a field in central Virginia. Its devoted fans have brought me here to witness the grandeur of this vanished species, which they are fervently trying to bring back. Efforts to resurrect the American chestnut rest, in part, on living relics like this tree. The tree's supporters ask me not to disclose its location, to protect both the privacy of the landowner and the well-being of the tree. People have been known to steal souvenirs from these rarities—bark, leaves, shoots, and even the trees themselves, if they're small enough to dig up.

Though it's early May, it's already hot; the air has a heavy, liquid quality. Fat bumblebees weave drunkenly from one wildflower to the next. Even the grasshoppers seem to be jumping in slow motion around me as I wade through the weedy field.

I squint at the old chestnut, trying to imagine its earlier life. I see it in sun-dappled woods, surrounded by other towering trees—chestnut, oak, and poplar. That romanticized image dissolves when my guide for the day, plant pathologist Gary Griffin, points out that this spot likely has been cleared for centuries. You can tell by the welter of low-lying branches that the tree never had to fight to reach the light, he explains. "The Indians might have planted corn right here and had their corn and chestnuts," he adds. The European settlers who followed would have done the same, as did one of the recent owners, a farmer whose family had worked the land since the late nineteenth century. The tree was already big when the man was a child in the early 1900s. As he told Griffin, his family knew the value of a good nut tree, so they carefully plowed around it. Their care was rewarded: each fall, the tree yielded bushels of shiny brown nuts.

Until recently, the tree had the company of a few other chestnuts in the nearby fence row. One succumbed to the chestnut blight; another was pushed over by a pasturing horse. Now the tree stands majestically alone, behind a horse-proof fence erected by volunteers. We step through the gate and into the tree's shrunken kingdom, a shady, chaotic patch of yarrow, blackberry bramble, and thistles.

It's soothingly green beneath the tree's magnificent canopy. The bark is deeply furrowed. All along the main stem are sunken blackish spots, healed scabs from the tree's epic battle with the chestnut blight. Patches in the crown are brown and dying. The oval, saw-toothed leaves are bumpy with bug infestation. Last winter's storms brought down a branch bigger around than a man's leg, leaving the tree with a lopsided look. "I don't know how much longer the poor fellow's going to last," says the current owner of the land.

Yet the tree hangs on, sixty-plus feet of blind hope. New shoots sprout from its roots. And the tree remains faithful to its seasonal script, even though it's a lonely solo performance. Each June, it bursts forth with bushy, cream-colored flowers, undeterred by the absence of other chestnuts to receive their pollen or reciprocate. Each October, the branches dangle dozens of burs, the prickly brown husks that are supposed to protect the tree's precious cargo of seeds. The ground around the tree is littered with the dried-out burs of last fall. I nudge a few open with the toe of my shoe. Every single one is empty.

I'm not someone who hugs trees or talks to them. Yet in such a situation, it's easy to anthropomorphize. When I press my hand flat against the weathered trunk, I could swear I feel life itself pulsing inside.

ONE

Where There Are Chestnuts

Early McAlexander looks through the window of his granddaughter's car onto a wide open hill fringed by a line of white pines. "All this land used to belong to my father," Early says in a voice that's surprisingly steady for a man of ninety-two. His Virginia accent twists and pulls the vowels like taffy. "I was raised up where that house is now," he adds, looking across the blacktop road to a large, modern, red-brick house with a quasi-colonial portico. It's a far cry from the house in which he and his six brothers and sisters grew up: a four-room log cabin built before the Civil War. In Early's day, the log exterior was covered with clapboard, a common bid by mountain families for respectability. To Early's amusement, the man who bought the cabin from the family moved it to a new lot up the road and stripped off all the clapboard siding to reveal the original rough-hewn logs, this wealthier generation of mountain dwellers' bid for authenticity. Early's family has lived in this area at the crest of the Blue Ridge Mountains, in Patrick County, Virginia, for generations; he's not sure how many. But he knows his great-great-grandfather hailed from here and fought in the Confederate Army until he died of pneumonia in a Richmond hospital. His worn grave marker is in the family cemetery, which still stands near where the cabin once stood.

Early is a dapper, spry man with a full head of snow-white hair, a hearing aid in each ear, and liver-spotted hands that are still steady enough to wield a chain saw or guide a tractor-mower (much to his protective granddaughter's horror). On this windy day in early April, he's dressed in a navy blue blazer, striped tie, and crisp white shirt—his Sunday best. We've spent the morning the same way he has spent most Sunday mornings for the past sixty years: at the Baptist church in this tiny mountain community, Meadows of Dan (population 1,934). Though the white-steepled church can hold at least two hundred congregants, there were only about fifty present on this day. Most were elderly. They came in carrying well-thumbed bibles and asking about one another's health. Many have known each other for decades, since they were schoolchildren together in another time and another world, when this land was laced with dirt roads linking family farms, the hillsides were dotted with fragrant haystacks, and children knew the woods flanking the fields as well as they knew their own home. Many date the end of that world to the late 1920s, when the American chestnut trees all began to die.

Patrick County sits on the southern edge of Virginia, snug against the North Carolina border; it is a wedge-shaped, 470-square-mile area that stretches from the rocky edge of the Blue Ridge Mountains in the north to the rolling clay lands of the Piedmont in the south. According to the official county history published in 1999, Patrick County's southern border "is about the same distance from the equator as the Rock of Gibraltar, the southern part of the Caspian Sea and Death Valley, California." In a further effort to fix the county's coordinates, the authors note that the county seat, Stuart, lies 2,530 miles north of the equator and 3,670 miles south of the North Pole. What the official history doesn't note is that Patrick County also lies in the heart of the historic chestnut belt and that it was once one of the biggest producers of chestnuts and chestnut products in the region.

Only a handful of artifacts scattered around the county testify to the chestnut's former presence. They include the split-rail chestnut fences bordering the Blue Ridge Parkway, which winds along the county's northern border; the chestnut paneling that lines the walls and ceiling of the Methodist church in the village of Woolwine; and the jar of slightly moldy nuts on display in the Patrick County Historical Society Museum.

Like much of the south, the county luxuriates in its history. Officially formed in 1791, the county was named for Patrick Henry, the firebrand orator—"Give me liberty or give me death!"—of the Revolutionary War. The county seat was named for the confederate war hero J. E. B. Stuart. Silver-colored square historical markers frequently appear along the two-lane roads that crisscross the county: here is Stuart's birthplace; here, the site of the Frontier Fort; here, the homestead of tobacco king R. J. Reynolds. Local family histories and genealogies fill a whole bookshelf in the modest county library. "You know," one woman explained, "that's a Southern hobby." Yet there's a whole other history unnoticed and unremarked on by either texts or roadside markers, a history intimately bound up with the tree that once covered the mountains of this region. "Up here there was a world of chestnuts," one elderly resident recalled. His words speak not only to the abundance of the trees in the region, but also to the role they played in the community and culture. Just as chestnut wood once served as the unseen solid backing for the veneered furniture that used to be manufactured here, so the tree itself once provided the unsung foundation of the lives of the county's poorest residents. Its story is also their story.

The American chestnut belongs to a storied clan of trees known as *Castanea*—a branch of the beech family—which flourishes in temperate zones across the northern hemisphere. Consider the genus a diaspora, its far-flung population a legacy of an ancient time, tens of millions of years ago, when the land masses of North America and Eurasia were joined in a single supercontinent known as Laurasia. Chestnuts, or rather their remote ancestors, grew all over Laurasia. Eventually the land masses pulled apart, the oceans widened, and the multitude of plants, insects, and animals on each new continent were left to pursue their own distinct paths of development. The chestnuts of China became a different species from the chestnuts of North America. Their ancestral links would later prove the American chestnut's undoing— and the potential source of its salvation.

Although botanists quibble over the precise number, most count at least seven distinct species of *Castanea*. (The name refers to the region of Kastanea in what is now Turkey, where Bronze Age humans are thought to have first started cultivating the tree.) The Caucasus Mountains of southern Russia gave rise to the European chestnut, or *Castanea sativa,* which closely resembles the American tree. Four more members of the family emerged in Asia: the Japanese chestnut (*Castanea crenata*), the Chinese chestnut (*Castanea mollissima*), the dwarf Chinese chestnut (*Castanea seguini*), and the treelike Chinese chinquapin (*Castanea henryi*). Meanwhile, a Mutt-and-Jeff pair of trees emerged in North America: the often shrublike Allegheny chinquapin (*Castanea pumila*) and its grand towering cousin, the American chestnut tree (*Castanea dentata,* so-called because the edges of the leaves look like a row of sharp teeth). Even the untrained eye can spot some of the differences distinguishing the species. The leaves of Japanese chestnuts look like a thin spearhead, for instance, while American chestnut leaves look more like a canoe. Asian species have fine hairs on the leaves (hence the Chinese chestnut's nickname, hairy chestnut); American chestnut leaves are relatively bald. Chinquapin burs contain just one nut, while Europeans usually have three fat seeds to a bur. Other distinguishing details, such as the shape of the buds or precise shade of the twigs, demand a practiced eye or even a botanist's hand lens. Even so, mistaken identities are common.

Despite the differences, all *Castanea* members share certain traits. They all bear nuts that are flavorful nuggets of nutrition (high in fiber, protein, vitamin C, and carbohydrates; low in calories and fat), and they can be cultivated with relatively little care—so little that some nineteenth-century critics complained that raising chestnuts induced peasants "to laziness." The trees are fast growing, and if you cut down a chestnut, dozens of stems will sprout as abundantly as weeds from its roots—a system of regeneration known as coppicing. Such qualities have endeared the trees to people across time and place. The Romans considered the chestnut one of the pillars of civilization, along with the olive, the grape, and grain. Wherever imperial legions planted the empire's flag, they also planted chestnuts. Thus the chestnut trees that shade old Roman roads in England and the orchards that flank the craggy mountainsides of the southern Mediterranean. Visiting Corsica in the early 1900s, American geographer J. Russell Smith asked one villager how long the local chestnut orchards had been going. "Oh a hundred years, five hundred years, a thousand years—always!" the man replied. Likewise, in the hilly regions of Japan and China, farmers have cultivated the trees for millennia.

In most parts of the world, the prized chestnut was a cultivated tree, raised in areas where cereals would not easily grow by peasants who recognized that a family with a chestnut orchard would never go hungry. But in North America, devotion centered on a tree that was never tamed, a wild forest king whose dominion sprawled over more than two hundred million acres. American chestnuts spread along the length of the eastern seaboard and west to Ohio, Kentucky, and Tennessee.* Legend has it that a squirrel could travel the chestnut canopy from Georgia to Maine without ever touching the ground. Along the way it would pass over at least 1,094 places with *chestnut* in their names. The chestnut was in many ways the quintessential American tree: adaptable,

---

*Ironically, the best-known chestnut reference—Longfellow's famous poem "The Village Blacksmith," which begins, "Under a spreading chestnut tree/the village smithy stands"—does not refer to a chestnut at all. The tree to which Longfellow paid tribute was a horse chestnut—a wholly different genus (*Aesculus*) from the American chestnut (*Castanea*). Longfellow was well aware of that fact, but decided to sacrifice botanical precision—"under the spreading *horse* chestnut tree"—for poetic meter.

resilient, and fiercely competitive. Given the right conditions, no other hardwood could beat out the American chestnut in the race to the forest canopy.

Despite, or because of, the trees' abundance, they were rarely corralled into formal cultivation. One reason may be that the nuts, while sweeter than other types of chestnut, were also far smaller: little acorn-size kernels that were difficult to peel. When colonial Americans began planting chestnut orchards, they ignored the native trees, turning instead to the Old World trees that produced bigger, plumper nuts. Thomas Jefferson, for instance, imported European cultivars for his orchards at Monticello. When another wave of interest in chestnut cultivation hit in the late nineteenth century, breeders such as Luther Burbank again disregarded American chestnuts in favor of imports from Japan. It was a development that would have dire consequences for the native trees.

Although untamed, American chestnuts were a boon to all who dwelled in their vicinity. Unlike other nut-bearing trees, chestnuts are perennial and prodigious producers. (It's said that this predictability is the source of the expression "a chestnut" to mean an often-told tale.) Oaks, which shared the chestnut's forest niche, might offer a huge crop of acorns one year, then nothing the next. Because chestnuts are late bloomers, flowering beyond the reach of even the latest frost, the trees could be counted on for nuts every year, and lots of them: a single tree might bear as many as six thousand nuts. Such bounty supported an abundance of wildlife: bears, elk, deer, squirrels, raccoons, mice. The huge drives of wild turkeys that thrived in pre-Columbian Appalachia—estimated to be as many as ten million birds—feasted on the nuts, as did the enormous flocks of passenger pigeons that once blackened the skies in mass migrations.

The Native American tribes that shared the forests with American chestnuts were equally reliant on the trees. Here was a source of food that, unlike acorns, didn't need to be boiled for hours to be palatable; these nuts were sweet right off the tree. It is small wonder the Cherokees developed rough chestnut orchards in the woods by burning competing trees. The trees also were a rich source of remedies. One account advised: "Tea of year old trees for heart trouble; leaves from young sprouts [to] cure old sores, cold bark tea with buckeye to stop bleeding after birth; apply warmed galls to make infant's navel recede; boil leaves with mullein and brown sugar for cough syrup; dip leaves in hot water and put on sores."

The Iroquois celebrated the sustaining gifts of the tree in the story "Hodadenon and the Chestnut Tree." Hodadenon lived alone with his uncle; the rest of their family had been killed by a group of seven evil witches. Their only food was a cache of dried chestnuts that was magically replenished at every meal. One day, Hodadenon foolishly destroyed the last of the magical nuts. His uncle cried that they would starve, so Hodadenon resolved to steal more chestnuts from a grove of trees jealously guarded by the seven witches. After many tries, he managed to get into the grove and take the nuts he needed, an act that broke the witches' curse and restored his family to life. Hodadenon gave each of his relatives a chestnut and told them to plant the seeds everywhere. The nuts, he declared, were a sacred food, to be shared forevermore with all who wanted them. In that spirit, perhaps, the Iroquois, as well as other Native Americans, sold chestnuts to the European settlers who arrived and surely showed them how to take advantage of this most useful tree.

But it was in Appalachia, in places like Patrick County, Virginia, where the ties between the chestnut and people were most tightly bound. "If ever there was a place defined by a tree, it was Appalachia," says folk historian Charlotte Ross, of Appalachian State University. The American chestnut "was our icon. We loved that tree."

On the steep slopes and in the cool, moist hollows of the southern Appalachian mountains, chestnuts grew so abundantly that they accounted for as many as one in four forest trees, and in some places, even more. Chestnuts were big trees everywhere, but this land gave rise to giants—trees a dozen feet wide and ten times as tall. One Goliath in

Francis Cove, North Carolina, measured seventeen feet across. In spring, the trees bloomed long bushy catkins of cream-colored flowers that filled the woods with a pungent perfume and made the forests look, from a distance, "like a sea with white combers plowing across its surface," as the naturalist Donald Culross Peattie wrote.

Until the early eighteenth century, few whites had ever laid eyes on the Appalachian region's oceanic forests. The first European settlers had hugged the coasts, reluctant to venture too deep into the rough unknown mountains to the west. But by the mid-1700s, population pressures and rising land prices in the coastal communities forced many residents across the Appalachian divide in search of new homelands. Scots-Irish, English, Germans, and Scandinavians began migrating south from Pennsylvania, across the Alleghenys, through the gently rolling hills of the Virginia Valley, and into areas such as present-day Patrick County. The lucky first arrivals got to claim the rich bottom-lands; their children and new arrivals staked farms higher up the hills, with each succeeding generation climbing farther up the ridges to where "the bare bones" of the mountains poked through the thin skin of soil. To clear the land, residents burned the brush, girdled the trees, and planted their crops—corn, wheat, barley, rye, and oats—among the remaining stumps. The Scots-Irish in particular were skilled high-land farmers. They brought with them farming customs well-suited to the mountains, such as the use of common grazing lands. They also brought a taste for corn whiskey and a stringent brand of Presby-terianism that gradually morphed into the fundamentalist "hard-shell" Baptist sects whose tiny chapels are still scattered throughout Patrick County.

Farm conditions along the Blue Ridge were hard. But in the abun-dant chestnut trees settlers found a singular source of wealth. Those tough enough or desperate enough to brave the hardships of carving out a homestead in the middle of the wilderness were rewarded by a com-panionable ally: a tree of seemingly limitless largesse. Here, they found chestnut trees so enormous that just a few supplied all the logs a man needed to build a cabin for his family. The wood was light, strong, and so easy to split that to make a rail fence, one man marveled, one could just cut the length needed, "stick a wedge in it an' it'd just pop open." However much was cut down, the tree would quickly replace, the stumps resprouting with a speed and vigor unmatched by any other hardwood. "By the time the white oak acorn makes a baseball bat the chestnut stump has made a railroad tie," wrote J. Russell Smith. A family could gather enough nuts in a single autumn month to help stave off hunger all winter long. "There was one time of year when we had food," recalled one man who grew up on Buffalo Mountain in Patrick County. "That was in the late fall after the gusty winds of a chestnut storm left the ground strewed with nuts. Pa and Ma would take us out by lantern light to beat the hogs to them, for the hogs knew every tree as well as the humans did. [My brother] Hasten said that the chestnut were like the manna that God sent to feed the Israelites." Chestnut leaves, farm women soon learned, could be brewed into a broth to loosen a deep cough; they could be packed into a poultice that soothed burns; they could even be stuffed into mattresses, though the bedding rustled so loudly folks called them "talking beds."

No one needed to buy land to pasture cattle or hogs when the forests supplied such a wealth of forage. Farmers would simply notch their mark in the ears of their livestock and turn the animals loose to roam the woods until they were to be butchered or sold. A pig could grow stout as a barrel on chestnuts, acorns, and hickory nuts. That ample carpet of nuts, sometimes inches thick, allowed drovers to move huge herds of hogs, cattle, and even turkeys across the slopes of the southern mountains to supply food for laborers on the plantations to the Southeast. The wildlife that also feasted on the nuts ensured a steady supply of game for the dinner table. "There wasn't no kind of game that roamed these mountains that didn't eat the chestnuts," Georgia native Jake Waldroop recalled. "The chestnut supported everything."

Folklorist Ross believes the chestnut not only supported settlement in the Appalachians but invited it. The early Scots-Irish settlers wrote letters home describing the riches the woods offered. "The chestnut mast is knee-deep," one man boasted, referring to the heavy accumulation of nuts. "C'mon over cousin," another wrote to his family in Ulster, Ireland. "This is the best poor man's country." And their countrymen followed. Over time the mountains filled with enclaves of tough, independent-minded people who were used to wrestling a living out of the poorest farmland.

Few ever bothered to actually cultivate the trees—who needed to when the trees grew so plentifully? In general, mountain families treated the chestnuts as a community resource, a bounty to be shared by all, like the abundant wild game, valuable ginseng, or juicy summer blackberries. But many also had their own chestnut "orchard"—a grove of trees they had saved from the plow or discovered deep in the woods. They'd tend the trees as if they'd grown them themselves, carefully clearing away underbrush to make it easier to collect the nuts when they began to fall. Such a grove, one Patrick County farmwoman declared, "is a better provider than any man—easier to have around, too."

Chestnuts, like other edibles foraged from the forest, were critical to the subsistence farmers who dominated southern Appalachia until the early twentieth century. Yet, as valuable as the trees were to the region, they "had little or no cash value until it was possible to ship them to areas outside the chestnut's range," as Goddard College historian Ralph Lutts points out. By the mid-nineteenth century, the nation's expanding transportation networks had reached Appalachia: steamships were plowing down the region's riverways, and roads and railroad lines were being laid across and through the Blue Ridge. The growing web of transportation lines gradually reached the isolated mountain communities, connecting them not only with the towns in their vicinity but with the national economy as well. Chestnuts were one of the few items of currency that the mountain farmers had to offer—along with hogs, moonshine, dried apples, and, most important of all, lumber. The region's vast untouched timber riches were what brought the railroads and roads in the first place. Having exhausted the pine and hardwood forests of the East and upper Midwest, lumber barons were now casting their eyes on the billions of board feet to be found in Appalachia.

In Patrick County, it was the arrival of a railroad line in 1884 that opened up what Lutts calls "the chestnut trade." The Dick and Willie, as residents affectionately called the Danville and Western Line, was just a short stretch of narrow gauge track that ran between Stuart and Danville, two counties to the east. But it supplied the tobacco farmers in the south of the county with a reliable and relatively fast way to get their crops to larger cities and gave the mountain farmers in the north of the county a reason to start treating chestnuts as a viable cash crop. By the beginning of the twentieth century, chestnuts had become one of the most important crops in Patrick County and neighboring counties, according to Lutts, who has painstakingly reconstructed this micro-economy from oral histories and the old account books of the county's now-gone general stores. Indeed, nut collection had become a major industry throughout the southern Appalachian forests.

For children of the Blue Ridge, chestnut harvest was a magical time. Early McAlexander remembers eagerly awaiting that day in late September or early October when the first hard frost pried open the spiky burs that encased the precious nuts. His mother would grab him and his younger siblings, and with tin buckets in hand they'd set out for their "orchard," a dozen or so towering trees in the woods bordering the cornfield up the hill from their home. They'd have to get there early to beat the squirrels. They would step carefully over the grassy ground beneath the trees, thick with the glossy brown nuts and half-cracked sharp burs. Sometimes Early would pop a few nuts in his mouth right then and there, savoring the sweet carroty taste. But most went straight into his bucket.

Back home, his mother would set aside some nuts to be roasted on the hot coals in the wood stove. The rest would be used to acquire the things the family couldn't make on their own—school supplies and sugar, shoes and long underwear. Typically, farm families either bartered the nuts for merchandise or were paid in "due bills"—scrip issued by the little stores that dotted the mountainside and served as each community's economic center. Stores like Akins', DeHart's, Hopkins', Pike's each issued their own due bills—small circles of cardboard, tin, or brass that were marked in varying denominations, stamped with the store's name, and redeemable only at that store. Early's family would haul their sacks of nuts to Pike's store in Meadows of Dan. There was a closer store just over the ridge to the west in Mayberry, but Early's grandmother considered that neighborhood godless country because of all the moonshiners operating there. "The crust over hell is just a half-inch thick over there," she'd warn Early. (Despite her admonitions, Early courted and eventually married a Mayberry girl.)

The nuts didn't bring a lot of cash. Families like the McAlexanders might get five to ten cents a pound at the start of the season. But as the market became saturated, prices dropped; after a few weeks, they could expect only two or three cents a pound. (Retailers, on the other hand, were making at least ten times as much on the chestnuts they sold.) Still, even a few dollars made a big difference to struggling mountain families. That's why Early's mother faithfully herded her children out to the chestnut orchard during the harvest season. "Raising seven children," he explains, "it'd take all the money they could get hold of."

It was the same story all over the mountain, indeed, all over southern Appalachia. "I picked up enough in one day to buy me a pair of old rough shoes," one Patrick County resident recalled. Another remembered collecting nuts so she could buy "an eight-day clock" for her mantel. A Georgia man recalled the mountain folk who would appear each fall in his local store with chestnuts to trade. "We'd hardly ever see these people at all, except when they came out to go to the store, and in the fall we'd see them coming, maybe the parents and three or four kids coming down the trail. The old man would have a big coffee sack full of chestnuts on his back, and the little fellers would have smaller sacks, and even the mother would have a small sack of chestnuts caught up on her hip. They'd all trek to the store, and they'd swap that for coffee and sugar and flour and things that they had to buy to live on through the winter. That's the way they made their living."

At the height of the season in Patrick County, families delivered so many thousands of bushels of chestnuts that the storerooms of the local stores were knee-deep in nuts. The stores were the first link in a chain that led back to cities like Baltimore, Philadelphia, and New York, where the nuts would be sold hot-roasted on the streets. The Patrick County storeowners bagged the nuts in cloth sacks and hauled them to the railway depot at the bottom of the mountain in Stuart. "This was not an easy trip," Lutts notes. Until the county got its first paved roads in the 1930s, it could take two days to make the thirty-five-mile round trip between Meadows of Dan and Stuart. Still, store owner James Hopkins would cart two thousand pounds of nuts at a time down the mountain. Over a single weekend in October 1915, about thirty wagonloads of chestnuts were brought to the Stuart depot from Meadows of Dan.

The trade was also a boon to Stuart's railway stationmaster, who oversaw the shipment of nuts to urban markets. During chestnut harvest, "you could hardly find a place to put the bags of chestnuts down, because everyone was a chestnut dealer, just about," recalled the son of the man who ran the station at the turn of the century. By 1903, the Dick and Willie had been upgraded to standard gauge and the train was moving thousands of pounds of chestnuts every day during the season. Because the nuts were perishable, they had to be shipped express, and the stationmaster made a commission on each shipment. Those shipments, his son recalled, were the best money the stationmaster ever made.

By the early 1900s, chestnuts had become an even more important source of income than cattle for Patrick County farmers. According to the U.S Agricultural Census of 1910, Patrick County produced more nuts than any other county in the state: nearly 160,000 pounds, almost all of it chestnuts. The 360,000 pounds of nuts harvested in Patrick

County and its four neighboring counties represented nearly half of Virginia's entire nut crop that year.

While Appalachia's fond memories for the American chestnut tend to center on the sweet mahogany nuts, in fact, the most valuable parts of the tree were its timber and bark, at least in the unsentimental calculus of dollars and cents. When the lumber boom hit the southern Appalachians in the late nineteenth century, chestnut was one of its major targets.

The notion that their backyards were filled with an untapped resource was not entirely new to the region's mountain dwellers. With the introduction of steam-powered mills in the early 1800s and their steady proliferation throughout the region, mountain farmers had already begun treating the woodlots on their property as potential sources of cash. By the middle of the century, the mountains were filled with small-scale, one- or two-man logging operations that would cut down the best trees along a waterway and float the logs to settlements and sawmills downstream. Logging was an important seasonal income for many mountain families. "Still the forest was only dented, not broken," notes writer Chris Bolgiano. "Seventy-five percent of Appalachia remained forested in 1900."

By then, industrial-scale logging had arrived. Timber barons, who'd already made millions emptying the Great Lakes pine forests, had begun opening new operations in the South and the southern Appalachians in the 1880s. The sheer scope of their acquisitions was mindboggling in a region where mountain farmers typically held fewer than two hundred acres. One of the first businessmen on the scene was Alexander A. Arthur, creator of the Scottish Carolina Land Company. Arthur bought up sixty thousand acres—ten square miles—in eastern Tennessee alone. By 1895, the mountains echoed with the clang of locomotives and the buzz of sawyers and steam-powered sawmills. The industrial loggers cleared the forests with "unparalleled speed and efficiency," observes environmental historian Donald Davis. "Virtually no stand of timber was off-limits, including trees old enough to have witnessed the passing of Hernando de Soto in 1540."

No other species saw the axe as frequently as chestnut. What made it so desirable? It wasn't its looks. Though the wood had a pleasant sandy color and even grain, it couldn't hold a candle to the lustrous surfaces produced from black walnut or cherry wood. Nor was it the strongest hardwood; oak won hands down when it came to tests of strength. Black locust was harder and more durable. Chestnut oak (an unrelated species) was more acidic, a trait valued for tanning leather.

But in a pinch, chestnut could fill in for any of those other woods. It had a utilitarian versatility no other tree could match. It was, in that sense, the perfect tree, or as close to it as you could ever hope to find. The wood was lighter than most other hardwoods, making it cheaper to ship. It contained a high amount of tannins, acidic chemicals that allowed chestnut to defy rot and warping better than almost any other wood. And it was wildly abundant. Such a winning combination of traits, *American Forestry* magazine reported in 1915, "has given chestnut a greater variety of uses than almost any other American hardwood."

The mammoth chestnuts felled in Appalachia wound up touching nearly every aspect of early twentieth-century American life. Straight chestnut poles held up the lengthening miles of telegraph and telephone wire unspooling across the nation. Sturdy chestnut ties supported the ever-expanding railroad lines. Chestnut beams shored up mine shafts. Builders used chestnut to frame and shingle houses and occasionally for interior trim. Furniture makers employed chestnut nearly as much as oak, using it as a core stock for tables, bureaus, or desks that were then finished with veneers made of pricier woods. Chestnut was also a favorite of casket makers who could again disguise its virtues: the grieving widow might want an impressive mahogany coffin for her dearly beloved, but that was only affordable if the core were made of humble chestnut. Chestnut found its way into nearly anything made of wood, from pianos to packing crates. It served literally cradle to grave.

The tannins in chestnut wood and bark were used to turn rough hides into leather. Europeans had employed chestnut to tan leather for centuries, and in the late 1800s, Americans began adopting the methods. By 1915, tannin extraction had become a thriving industry in the South and over two-thirds of the tannic acid produced in the United States came from chestnut wood and bark.

Like so many wood-related industries, tannin extraction was a wasteful process in which enormous quantities of pulverized wood were discarded once the valuable acids were leached out. But in 1912, a chemical engineer at the Champion Paper and Fibre Company in North Carolina figured out a way to extract tannins from thinly shaved wood chips, which could be then used for paper production. The innovation revolutionized the industry. Companies were able to sell the same wood twice and make twice the profit. Soon chestnut pulp was being used for all sorts of low-grade paper products, from newsprint to government postcards.

As the raw material for such an array of products, chestnut accounted for one-fourth of all the hardwood lumber cut out of the southern Appalachians. By 1909, about six hundred million board feet of chestnut were being cut each year, not including the thousands of trees felled annually for utility poles, fencing posts, or cordwood. Count those in, and one observer of the time estimated that "chestnut has the largest cut of any single species of hardwood in America." At the peak of its production, between 1907 and 1910, chestnut wood contributed more than ten million dollars annually to the economy of Appalachia. Nevertheless, the people of the region did not gain much from the intensive logging. True, the timber boom brought mill jobs to the region, but most of the profits flowed out of Appalachia to investors in the North and overseas.

Of course, chestnut wasn't the only tree disappearing into the maw of the Appalachian timber boom. The appetite for all of the region's trees was enormous, peaking in 1909 when four billion board feet of hardwood lumber—enough foot-wide boards to circle the equator thirty times—were cut from the mountain forests from Maryland to Georgia. By then, it was beginning to dawn on Americans that the country's vast seas of timber could not be tapped forever. Just as the American frontier had been pushed to the ends of the continent, conservationists were now warning, the country's foremost natural resource was in danger of being exhausted.

At the turn of the twentieth century, citizen and forestry groups pushing for a national park to preserve the Great Smokies and the Black Mountains persuaded Congress to appoint a team of surveyors to examine the southern Appalachian forests. The surveyors were alarmed by how quickly the magnificent virgin stands of chestnut, oak, poplar, maple, gum, cypress, and pine were vanishing. In a report submitted to President Theodore Roosevelt in 1902, the U.S. Geological Survey described the serious damage the industrial loggers had inflicted on the forests through their "inexcusable slovenliness." The loggers had lumbered through the mountains as clumsily and carelessly as evil fairy-tale giants, leaving in their wake swaths of crushed trees, acres of torn-up earth, and destructive fires. Even worse was the loggers' rapaciousness. If the lumbering operations continued at their present breakneck pace, the surveyors concluded, "within less than a decade every mountain cove will have been invaded and robbed of its finest timber, and the last remnants of these grand Appalachian forests will have been destroyed."

Little did the survey team know that sawmill's whine was not the only danger facing the Appalachian forests. The forests would soon confront an equally grave threat that even then was wending its way toward the mountains. This peril would be even harder to control than the human hunger for profits.

TWO

A New Scourge

Here's one way it might have begun:

A tiny yellow speck drifts weightlessly on a warm spring breeze, floating in a neither-here-nor-there state, that "hungerless sleep" of a spore. The wind pushes the spore this way and that. It lights onto an oak leaf and is shaken free, comes to rest on a twig of poplar, then tumbles loose and resumes its aimless flight. A sharp gust propels it against the branch of an American chestnut tree. As chance would have it, the bark is cracked from the slight scratch of a squirrel's sharp claw. The spore slips into the crevice. With awful randomness, all the elements have conspired to deliver the spore just where it needs to be. Now, like a spark dropped onto a pile of dry brush, it flares to life.

On a hot summer day in 1904, Hermann Merkel, chief forester for the New York Zoological Park (now known as the Bronx Zoo), stood puzzling over one of the park's American chestnut trees. The other trees nearby wore healthy crowns of green, but this tree did not. Several branches were dangling withered brown leaves, as if autumn had arrived a few months too early. And it wasn't the only ailing chestnut.

In recent months, several in the park had suddenly and mysteriously begun to die.

Merkel was bewildered and concerned. The chestnuts were prized trees in the native forest that was the pride of the newly established Zoological Park. The woods were dense with chestnuts, oaks, birch, dogwoods, locusts, pines, poplars, and other trees and shrubs that had been carefully protected and preserved for more than eighty years by the former owners, a prominent New York family. In building the park five years earlier, the Zoological Society had been determined to give as much attention to landscaping as to the animal collection. There would be a formal concourse to mark the entryway, but the rest of the park was "as far as possible [to] be kept in its natural condition." Only native flora were to be planted on the grounds; those seeking exotica would have to head across the road to the city's other newly created natural attraction, the New York Botanical Garden. Merkel, a German native who probably had learned his trade from the famed foresters in his homeland, was well suited to the task of maintaining the landscaping. He and his crew worked hard clearing dead brush from the woods, planting thousands of new trees and shrubs, sowing flower beds with perennials, and placing fast-growing maples and poplars in unshaded spots. By 1904, more than a million visitors a year were making their way by carriage, train, or the recently completed subway to the city's latest must-see destination. There they could spend a day wandering the verdant grounds and touring an assortment of rare and wondrous beasts and birds. The collection included chimpanzees, two snow leopards, an Indian elephant named Gunda, a Malayan sun bear, and a small herd of American bison, whose beleaguered species the zoo's director was determined to save from obliteration. On sweltering summer weekends, the park drew residents of Manhattan's crowded Lower East Side tenements; they'd camp out in the cool shade of the hemlock grove "where lines of laundry could often be seen hung out to dry."

But now something was undoing Merkel's hard work. Could insects be responsible? That didn't appear to be the case. On close inspection of the ailing chestnuts, Merkel noticed unusual marks on their trunks and branches: a ring of dry bark around the affected branch and a peppering of minute orange dots. It looked like some kind of fungus, though not one he had ever seen before. He decided to treat the trees with a fungicide and keep his eyes on them.

By the following spring, Merkel knew he had a serious problem on his hands. Nearly every chestnut tree in the park was infected, from stately elders to twiggy young sprouts. Merkel sent off samples of diseased bark and a plea for help to the U.S. Department of Agriculture (USDA) in Washington, D.C. The agency had no experts in forest diseases on staff; it would be another two years before it established a formal lab to deal with such problems. So the sample was given to Flora Patterson, an expert on mushrooms and fungi. She was blasé. There was nothing mysterious here, she declared: the culprit was a common canker-causing fungus called *Cytospora*. True, *Cytospora* had never been known to harm chestnut trees, but she saw no cause for concern. Cut off the affected branches and burn them, she advised. Then spray the trees with "Bordeaux mixture," a powerful concoction of lime, salt, and copper sulfate that the French had used to successfully combat a fungal disease afflicting their grapevines.

With an emergency appropriation of two thousand dollars, Merkel set about trying to treat his sickened trees. The task was immense, and his crew of foresters and tree surgeons worked late into the summer nights to get the job done. They cut away diseased branches from 438 chestnuts. Sometimes the infection was so widespread they had to amputate every limb off a tree, leaving only a woeful-looking bare trunk. So many trees needed to be sprayed that Merkel brought in a power-spraying machine: a horse-drawn wagon mounted with a 150-gallon tank and an eight-foot scaffold. It looked unwieldy, but it was actually the least convoluted rig he could find that would allow him to maneuver his way through the thick woods. Using ladders and the scaffold, the men clambered up the trees, their spray nozzles pointed aloft. From a distance, they looked like humongous long-nosed insects. The spray's pale-blue residue gave the trees a ghostly cast.

Even as he was spraying the trees, Merkel was skeptical that the treatment would work, given how fast this mystery disease was sweeping through the park. He decided to get another opinion and sent word across the road to the New York Botanical Garden's resident expert on fungi, an ambitious young Virginian named William Alphonso Murrill.

Tall and robust, with a fastidiously groomed beard and an affable manner, Murrill, age thirty-four, had only recently begun working at the botanical garden. But he would rise rapidly through the ranks. In just a few years, he would be appointed assistant director, and the garden's staff would become accustomed to seeing his imposing, immaculately dressed figure touring the expansive grounds at least twice a day. Often, he would return at night to make sure all was well.

Murrill came from a long line of Virginia gentry, though by the time he was born in 1869, the family was richer in learning than in money. His parents, former schoolteachers, raised him and his six siblings on a series of farms. He spent a happy childhood roaming the countryside catching frogs and moles and collecting wild pawpaws, walnuts, and chestnuts. He recalled those years in one of his three self-published memoirs, all written—bizarrely—in the third person: "The sights and sounds of the fields and woods made a deep impression on his childish heart and a love for nature was planted deep in his breast." For the rest of Murrill's life, the natural world was a source of wonder and solace; in later years, he would insist that nature study was "the great uplifter of the race." Nothing made him happier than an afternoon spent tramping around the countryside, butterfly net in hand, tin collecting case for plants slung over one broad shoulder and backpack crammed with lunch, specimen bottles, twine, paper, and other gear over the other. He'd gather whatever caught his avidly curious eye: flowers, insects, plants, fossils, rocks, and small animals. He was a born collector whose treasures included butterflies and bibles, stamps and shells. That

acquisitive passion drove his professional life: over his career he collected a staggering seventy-five-thousand-plus botanical specimens,
including seventeen hundred that were new to science.

Propelled by ambition and a scholarly bent, the young Murrill pursued studies in agriculture, mechanics, literature, and Greek, earning
two bachelor's degrees and a master's. At each step of the way he
excelled. At the age of twenty-three, he took a job teaching at Wesleyan
Female Institute in Staunton, Virginia. He knew, however, that he
didn't want to spend his life as a teacher, and in between a busy schedule of classes, hikes, Sunday school lessons, and trips to the nearby
University of Virginia to hear lectures, Murrill gave serious thought to
his future life work. As he recalled—with a typical lack of modesty—
in his autobiography: "With a splendid heritage of health, brains, character and determination, he was anxious to labor in the field best suited
to his particular qualifications, thus assuring an easier and more certain
success." Eventually, he decided to pursue a career as a scientist, a calling which he thought belonged to those dedicated to "beauty, justice
and truth." He initially planned to study zoology, but a friend convinced him there were more job opportunities to be had in botany. He
earned a PhD at Cornell University, cultivating a specialty in the study
of fungi.

Murrill's wife, Edna Lee Lutrell, whom he'd married while at Cornell, often accompanied him on his mushroom-hunting excursions,
painting illustrations of the fungi he collected. But when he began traveling abroad, she refused to follow, for she was deathly afraid of water.
Murrill believed that rearing children—ideally, one boy and one girl—
was "one of the main objects of matrimony." Yet this was one ideal he
could not realize: a son born to the couple died in infancy, and they
never had another child. In later years, the marriage deteriorated, and
eventually Edna moved out and filed for divorce. It must have remained
a bitter memory; when he published his autobiography decades later, at
the age of seventy-six, he never mentioned her.

Murrill was a man with many interests: he loved poetry, wrote hundreds of songs, read Greek and Latin, had a fine singing voice, and could entertain a parlorful of guests on the piano. He was a prolific writer, penning a number of children's books, five hundred scientific articles, and hundreds more for popular magazines. He had been raised in a religious household and as an adult read Bible verses—in different languages—to himself every night. Yet he considered science his true religion. "I am wedded to science," he fervently declared at the age of twenty-six. Unlike his marriage to Edna Lee, this one never faltered. One way or another, almost any issue could be resolved through careful study and the application of scientific principles. Like many of the era, he was a believer in physiognomy and was convinced that the same close observation that yielded so much information about a botanical specimen could be used to reveal human character. The shape of one's figure, the depth of a man's chest, the width of a woman's hips, the coloring of his hair, the flush of her cheeks—all of these characteristics might illuminate an individual's history and character. This led to some strange conclusions, such as his insistence that a snub nose was a sign of ignorance and laziness, while a straight nose indicated "mentality and culture." (His own nose, naturally, was long and straight.)

When it came to the plant world, Murrill held strong and precise convictions. In botanical circles, his interest and skill in discerning subtle differences earned him a reputation as a "splitter," who classified specimens into ever more discrete species and genera. For years he was criticized and attacked by "lumpers," who accepted a higher level of individual variation among organisms than he did. But Murrill refused to budge in his classifications, and decades later, experts conceded that, in many cases, he had been correct.

In his self-published memoirs, Murrill comes across as a strange mix of dreamy romantic and calculating pragmatist. He is also often pompous and didactic. He refers to himself as "The Naturalist" and offers maxims, often clunky, of his own devising, such as, "To be strong and independent, a man doesn't have to drive his lawn-roller over his neighbor's chicken coop." Yet though he seems a blowhard in print, his effect in person must have been different, for he had a reputation as "a charming Southern gentleman" who socialized easily with some of the most powerful and prominent people of his time, from European royalty, to the DuPonts, to the great naturalist John Burroughs.

After graduating from Cornell, Murrill moved to New York City to take another teaching job at DeWitt Clinton High School. But he had his sights set on bigger things. He joined the city's influential Torrey Botanical Club, where he made valuable contacts with leading botanists of the day, including the powerful director of the New York Botanical Garden, Nathaniel Lord Britton. Murrill used his vacations to travel in Europe conducting research for a series of articles that he published in the club's bulletin. His break came in 1904, when the staff mycologist at the botanical garden resigned. Britton tapped Murrill to fill the post. It was the moment Murrill had been waiting for, his chance to prove his mettle as a professional naturalist. Not long after came Merkel's worried message about the zoo's dying chestnuts. It would lead him into the greatest challenge of his career.

Murrill hurried over to take a look at the trees in the park. He agreed with Merkel—this looked like a fungus, but not a *Cytospora*. So what was it? Murrill cut out specimens of diseased bark from infected trees and then returned to the botanical garden, where he carefully examined the chestnuts there on the grounds. Many of the trees, he found, were under assault by the same unidentified enemy. It had even reached chestnuts in the garden's vaunted hemlock forest, a gorgeous forty-acre wood of virgin timber. In one tree, the deadly parasite had taken root around a heart and set of initials some lovesick lad had carved into the trunk.

The infection was too widespread to conduct reliable experiments outdoors. Instead, Murrill set to work in his lab in the garden's Museum building, starting the steps that German pathologist Robert Koch had established twenty-five years before to isolate and identify a pathogen. He grew specimens of the fungus until he had satisfied himself that he had a pure culture. He then transferred the cultures onto various media—agar, bean stems, and sterilized chestnut twigs—and placed them in glass test tubes sealed with wads of cotton wool. Sure enough, the fungus grew, the fungal filaments fanning out in a pure-white mat of mold that later sprouted a lush bloom of what Murrill described as "beautiful yellow" pustules. Then he infected living chestnut twigs and watched again as the mycelium took hold and blossomed with the same sunshine-colored, spore-producing spots. The next step was seeing if the infection could be induced in living trees, but for that he had to wait out the winter, during which deciduous trees like chestnuts hibernate in a dormant phase. Once spring arrived and the trees' growth systems were back up and running, he inoculated a number of potted young chestnuts in the garden's greenhouses. As expected, he reported, "the actively growing fungus, when transferred from bean stems to the branches of the young trees, attacked them with vigor and soon caused their death."

By spring, he had worked out the essential life cycle of what would come to be known as the chestnut blight. Succeeding generations of scientists equipped with more powerful technology would fill in the details of its precise mechanisms, but Murrill firmly established the basics with his glass test tubes, bell jars, microscope, and careful field observations. He outlined his findings in June 1906 in an article in the *Journal of the New York Botanical Garden.* He had determined that the fungus works beneath the cortex, the tough outer skin of the tree. It begins when spores gain entry into the vital space between the inner bark and the cambium, the thin layer of life-sustaining cells that carry water and nourishment from the roots to the branch tips of a tree. As the spores germinate, they extend tiny threadlike filaments that eventually weave together to form a mat, the mycelium or body of the fungus. The mycelium pushes, wedgelike, through the living tissue of the tree, and as those inner cells die, the bark above also dies, leaving a sunken, pale-brown depression. Later, fiery-colored fruiting pustules push up through the bark, minuscule volcanoes filled with millions of spores.

Murrill found that this fungus, like many, produces two types of spores. The first type, produced asexually, is extruded in sticky masses of reddish-brown threads that spread through rain or on the feet of insects, birds, and animals. After the fungus has cycled through several asexually produced generations, it starts to generate sexually produced spores, which typically erupt in late summer or early fall in an explosion of powdery yellow specks that are carried far and wide by the wind. When the fungus was most active, usually in the spring, the whole process unfolded with devastating speed. As Murrill reported: "Mycelium inserted beneath the bark of living chestnut twigs on December 13 developed a prominent spore mass by December 27."

The fungus was an efficient executioner. Once it penetrated a point on a tree—a branch, for instance—the mycelium would quickly encircle the limb until the limb was girdled and the food and water supply was completely cut off.* If the attack commenced on the tips of branches, the disease could only progress slowly, since the affected area was small and nourishment scanty. If, on the other hand, it hit at the base of a young tree where it could tap into a treasure trove of moisture and food, the fungus grew fast and the tree's life was quickly in danger. The fungus could kill a mature tree in just two to three years.

"There is no mistaking the blight when it appears," Murrill reported. First, a flush of orange-red spots would appear on the bark and the area beneath would sound hollow if tapped. If the tree was young, a round, sunken, discolored patch on the bark would appear, with cracks running up and down. Infected sprouts would swell at the base and could be easily snapped off. Finally, the leaves would turn a distinctive dark brown, "as though scorched by fire."

As much as Murrill had learned about the new disease, there were still many unanswered questions. For instance, he wasn't sure how the fungus gained entry to a tree in the first place. His experiments suggested it wasn't able to muscle its way through the outer skin unless

---

*In fact, the tree's own defensive effort to seal off the invading mycelium also blocks the transport of water and nutrients, ultimately leading to its death. In essence, the tree commits suicide.

there was some break in the bark, however tiny. He presumed infection took place through wounds, be they caused by weather, the scramble of squirrels, the nesting of birds, the chewing of insects, the lumberman's axe, or what he called "the savage hordes of small boys" who every fall pelted the trees with sticks and stones to dislodge the nuts. Then, too, he suggested, the chestnut's legendary powers of regeneration might make it more vulnerable to this new scourge. Most of the chestnuts in the region were incarnations of previous chestnuts, sprouted from the original stumps. Such repeated resprouting, he suggested, sapped a tree's strength, undermining its ability to fight off infections.

Nor did he know the identity of this new lethal predator. Murrill searched the reference books and consulted other mycologists, but as far as he could tell, the disease had never before been described. He finally decided it was a new rogue member of a large genus of fungi known as *Diaporthe*. Members of the clan generally do not prey on living tissue; their appetites are limited to dead wood. This pest, on the other hand, was definitely a parasite with far more destructive habits, a point he tried to underscore in the name he chose for it: *Diaporthe parasitica* Murrill. (The classification would prove controversial; within just a few years taxonomists would reassign the wily fungus to a different genus of molds, *Endothia*. It would be reassigned yet one more time in 1978, when scientists decided that its true lineage was with the genus *Cryphonectria*. Today it is known as *Cryphonectria parasitica*.) Murrill had no clue where the fungus originated. He suspected—wrongly as it turned out—that it was native to the East Coast and that it was the product of a slow and quiet mutation in the normally harmless *Diaporthe*.

Because the disease did its dirty work under the bark, Murrill was dubious that any amount of spraying of the tree's surface, even with as strong a brew as Bordeaux mixture, could have an effect. Still, he tried to be hopeful, suggesting that older trees might be rescued by cutting out the affected areas, burning the cut limbs, and dressing the wounds with creosote or tar. He thought young trees had more of a fighting chance and that "vigilance and care should largely control the disease" among them. But even as he was writing the words, it was becoming clear those hopes were in vain.

Like many New Yorkers eager to escape the suffocating heat, Murrill left town for the summer of 1906. On his return in August, he was shocked by how rapidly the plague had spread, fueled by weeks of warm, moist weather. "I now know of very few chestnuts in this portion of the city that appear to be worth trying to save and I do not consider any immune," he reported in the *Journal of the New York Botanical Garden* that September. "The natural result must be the death of practically all the chestnut trees in the infected area, unless some exceedingly active enemy speedily appears; which is extremely unlikely." The disease was not only ravaging all the parks in the Bronx, but it had leapfrogged south across the thirteen-mile-long island of Manhattan to infect chestnuts in the green swards of Brooklyn. Even more worrisome were unconfirmed reports that the disease was present in New Jersey and as far south as Maryland and Virginia. This was clearly an epidemic, and as with all epidemics, Murrill believed, there seemed little to do except let it run its course.

Even as Murrill was sounding the alarm, he failed to grasp the magnitude of the threat. He still assumed that the epidemic would burn itself out and that the dead and dying trees could then be cleared away so that new chestnuts could be planted to take their place. The word *blight,* with its implications of pestilence and permanence, had not yet entered his vocabulary. He called the disease the "chestnut canker" for the lesions it produced, but the phrase also suggested something that might eventually be managed. This disease would not be contained or controlled, however; the very existence of the American chestnut was in peril.

"Chestnut Trees Face Destruction," the *New York Times* headline announced on May 21, 1908. Four years after Merkel's discovery, the epidemic had become so widespread that even the most casual gardener could not help but be aware of it. "The wail of the chestnut lover is heard from all parts of New York, Long Island and adjacent country," the *Times* reported. Dying chestnuts were now major news, though not quite important enough to join such stories on the front page as the new speed record set by the steamship Lusitania, the story of a woman who developed an unseemly "mania" for football, or the first birth of a Rocky Mountain goat at the zoo in the Bronx.

Chestnuts may not have been as significant for city dwellers as they were for residents of rural Appalachia, but they were nevertheless cherished trees. "The chestnut trees are our special friends of the forest," one fan wrote in *American Forestry* in 1912, "and around them are particularly pleasant memories of the time, when in our youth, we gathered their fruit." Nutting parties were an annual autumn ritual in the cities and budding suburbs throughout the chestnut belt. "Not only country boys—all New York goes a-nutting," Henry David Thoreau observed. People flocked to chestnut groves in the great parks of the Bronx—van Cortlandt Park, Crotona Park, Bronx Park—or rode the train just a little bit farther north to the wooded outreaches of Westchester County. Once they might have hunted squirrel or rabbit in those hills, but by the turn of the century, the main quarry left was chestnuts.

Dried brown leaves would cling to the woolen hems of women's long skirts as they looped ropes around the branches of chestnut trees and yanked hard to shake the nuts free. Waiting children scrambled on their knees to gather them up. If a tree's branches hung low enough, adventurous boys or men clambered up to stand on the limbs and stamp a few times to rattle the nuts loose. (Females were strictly discouraged from this mode of chestnut-hunting.) It could be a perilous venture: every season brought reports of casualties, like the New York lawyer who died of a broken back after falling twenty feet while trying to shake some nuts down for his children.

In the outskirts of Philadelphia, the writer Clarence Weygandt reported, boys prowled the thick stands of chestnut armed with the requisite weapons for the hunt: clubs fashioned from broomsticks or hickory wheel spokes that were weighted at one end with metal clock weights, pieces of lead piping, or best still, the iron nuts used to fasten railroad tracks in place. So many iron nuts were stripped off one suburban Philadelphia railroad line that the track walker took to carrying an extra supply of nuts during chestnut season. Weygandt wrote appreciatively of the pleasures of chestnut clubbing: "It requires strength and dexterity and long practice to send even a skillfully weighted club to the top of an eighty-foot tree. . . . Who is there who does not recall the joy of a strike. Talk of a three pound trout or a six pound bass in the same breath with this rapture!" Young boys were not the only ones drawn to the woods in the dim October dawn; Weygandt regularly spotted grown men "in whom the country heart is still alive" scouring the area for nuts.

Other nuts could be found in the woods on a crisp fall day. There were walnuts, butternuts, beechnuts, and hickory nuts, too. But the chestnut seemed to spark a special devotion. Was it the beauty of the nuts, shiny and smooth as polished rosewood? Their sweet, delicate flavor, which could be savored raw, as well as boiled or roasted? The casual prodigiousness with which the trees carpeted the ground with their seeds? "The very fact that we have, besides the general term nutting, only the one specific term chestnutting, tells the story," Weygandt wrote. "Who has heard of walnutting, or butternutting or shellbarking?"

Perhaps the love of chestnutting stemmed in part from the pleasure of foraging, that most ancient mode of sustenance. "I love to gather them," Thoreau wrote, "if only for the sense of the bountifulness of Nature they give me." That awareness, honed through foraging, was hardly necessary to survival in a city. Yet chestnutting helped sustain a connection to the natural world that was fast disappearing under ribbons of asphalt and walls of concrete.

Now New Yorkers were facing a disease that threatened to eradicate every last one of their chestnut trees. The blight had accelerated rapidly in just a few years. In Brooklyn's Prospect Park, alone, fourteen hundred trees had died by the summer of 1908. At the New York Botanical Garden, workers had cut down at least three hundred dead or dying chestnuts, including grand old giants as wide across as a man is tall. Murrill had watched helplessly as dozens of chestnuts around his home in nearby Bronxwood Park died. All told, he estimated, five to ten million dollars' worth of chestnut trees had been lost in the greater New York area. And the outbreak had continued to broaden, threatening pandemic proportions: there were now reports of the disease in Connecticut, Massachusetts, and Washington, D.C. Appalachia was still blissfully ignorant of the spreading plague. The chestnut trade in places like Patrick County, Virginia, was still booming—though not for long.

With his new job as the assistant director of the botanical garden, Murrill's duties had grown. An engaging speaker, he was becoming a fixture on the garden club lecture circuit. He continued to expand the garden's collection of fungi and was getting ready to launch a new journal devoted to mushrooms called *Mycologia*. Still, the chestnut disease was consuming a good part of his time. In ongoing experiments, he was learning new and unsettling things about this pathogen. He found the fungus had unparalleled strength: when other fungi had accidentally gotten into cultures of blight fungus, the blight mycelium rolled right over them, diminishing Murrill's hopes that the disease might be brought to a halt by some equally powerful pathogen.

More disturbing, though, was his discovery that the fungus did not confine its predations to the American chestnut. It also attacked at least three other species of *Castanea*. He'd found it on native chinquapins in the botanical garden, as well as on one of the garden's Japanese chestnut trees. When he inoculated a number of those trees with the fungus, all had succumbed, though later it would become clear that the Japanese trees were generally resistant to the fungus. Worst of all, a Long Island man with an estate full of European chestnuts had informed him that those trees were also susceptible. That last revelation was deeply alarming, for Murrill knew how valuable chestnuts were in Europe, especially in the mountains of Italy, where the nuts were a staple of the diet. He took it upon himself to notify the Italian consulate in New York of this concern and spent a day sharing his data with a member of the Italian legation. "He was a man who had been in the chestnut business," Murrill told the *Times,* "so he recognized at once what the spread of the disease would mean to the people there." Murrill began urging the U.S. government to act to prevent the disease from being introduced to Europe or to other parts of the country. "There should be a law to prevent the shipping of our chestnut trees to other states," he insisted, on learning that some trees were recently shipped to California. Though Canada would soon pass an import quarantine, the U.S government was slow to heed his call.

As the leading expert on the new disease, Murrill enjoyed the spotlight, but he grew weary with the more tedious aspects of that position. There seemed to be a never-ending stream of what he termed "piteous pleas" from homeowners anxious to save their beloved trees. Each tree was worth about one hundred dollars, and Murrill knew a well-placed mature tree could add as much as a thousand dollars to a property's value. Unfortunately, he had little advice to offer aside from four succinct words: cut the trees down. The city's rich and famous beseeched him for help, yet not even Teddy Roosevelt or John D. Rockefeller could do anything to save the chestnuts on their estates. Murrill had little patience for pseudoscience, and now he fumed over the multitudes of quacks traveling the countryside trying to cash in on people's desperation with bogus remedies. It was said a tree could be saved by pouring poisonous solutions on the roots or filling in holes with sulphur. Murrill scoffed at the suggestion: "It would do as much good to fill the hole with gravel as to use sulphur in that way," he told the *Times.*

He was equally irritated by the continuing barrage of speculations about the causes of the disease. There was no shortage of theories, scientific and otherwise. Murrill got letters from people who saw the blight in apocalyptic terms, blaming "sinfulness and extravagance [and] the general wickedness of the people of the United States" and suggesting that "perhaps prayer or a grand religious revival might stay it."

One scientist attributed the outbreak to the demise of woodpeckers that might have killed off spore-carrying bugs. Another suggested the disease highlighted the dangers of permitting people to hunt native birds: "It is very likely that some of the birds that have been reduced almost to extinction had the all important duty of keeping this particular enemy of the chestnut in subjection. . . . Now we pay for our carelessness by losing the trees." Amateur entomologists linked it with a variety of unnamed bugs. One man described a tiny black insect he'd seen on his trees before they succumbed to blight. A Philadelphia florist insisted that it was caused by a small black beetle that looked like a ladybug. That was "simply out of the question," Murrill snapped in response, clearly annoyed that years into the epidemic he was still having to defend his most basic findings. "The chestnut canker is caused by a definite parasitic fungus. . . . There is absolutely no doubt about it."

But perhaps most frustrating of all was the official response of the USDA. The agency had finally become interested in the chestnut problem, but as Murrill saw it, the government scientists were feeding false hopes. In 1907 the agency established a Laboratory of Forest Pathology to deal with the growing roll call of tree diseases: peckiness, pine rot, ink disease, plum black knot, and of course, chestnut blight. Forest pathology itself was a relatively new discipline, a latecomer to a science that traditionally had been concentrated on diseases affecting food crops and orchard trees. That focus began to change at the turn of the century with the rise of the conservation movement and growing interest in the nation's forests as a splendid but endangered resource to be enjoyed and exploited. In 1905 the U.S. Forest Service was established with the goal of preserving timberlands for continued use through scientific management. Suddenly, there was an interest in promoting healthy forests. As Secretary of Agriculture James Wilson declared, "the rapidly growing interest in forestry problems has created a widespread demand for information as to diseases affecting trees."

Chestnut disease was certainly not the only problem on the new pathology lab's agenda. The lab had its hands full battling what the *New York Times* called an "appallingly vast army of parasites." The incomparably valuable white pines of the Northeast were under attack by a new lethal pathogen that sapped the life from their sprays of delicate green needles, turning them a scorched-looking, rusty brown. The graceful vase-shaped elms were being stripped of their leaves by a vicious beetle that had entered the United States from Europe. That tough forest stalwart, the hickory, was under siege from another bark beetle. But destructive as each problem was, none compared to that of the chestnut blight. "It is no exaggeration to say that it is at present the most threatening forest-tree disease in America," wrote Haven Metcalf, the first chief of the Forest Pathology Lab and another young up-and-comer.

Metcalf was a thick-cheeked New Englander with a prominent bulbous nose and round tortoiseshell glasses. Raised in rural Maine, he got his undergraduate degree at Colby College and then left his home state to pursue graduate degrees, hopscotching among various of the leading universities of the day to study botany, bacteriology, and mycology. He earned a PhD at the University of Nebraska, where he studied with Charles Bessey, one of the pioneers of American plant pathology. (Bessey had been among the first botanists to advocate the use of laboratory techniques and equipment; in 1873 he startled colleagues at Harvard by outfitting his office with a microscope, jars of preserved material, reagents, scalpels, needles, razors, and other equipment and hanging a hand-lettered sign on the door that read "Botanical Laboratory." Soon lab work was a requirement for botany students.) After a brief series of teaching stints, Metcalf joined the USDA's Bureau of Plant Industry in 1904. Though his prior experience was in agricultural diseases, in 1907, at the age of thirty-two, he was picked to head up the newly created Forest Pathology Lab. He quickly surrounded himself with a staff of impeccably credentialed young scientists and set them to work on the chestnut crisis.

Unlike Murrill, Metcalf was not yet persuaded that the chestnuts were beyond salvation. He insisted that individual trees might be saved by cutting off the affected branches and spraying them. Murrill disputed the suggestion, noting such methods had been tried and failed. Treating a large tree would cost at least a hundred dollars, "and it's a waste of money," he bluntly told the *New York Times*. "A tree sometimes takes the disease in twenty places at once, and they may be in the highest branches of the tree where a squirrel could barely reach them." After grappling with this chestnut killer for several years, Murrill had become firmly convinced that "there are absolutely no remedies against it, in spite of what Secretary Metcalf says."

For a man who waxed rhapsodically about the transcendent glories of nature and who wrote that the trees one knows "will never be forgotten, but will be recognized and loved as the faces of one's friends," Murrill was remarkably unsentimental about the plight of the chestnut. His autobiography suggests that he coolly regarded the chestnut's bad luck as his good fortune: "The chestnut canker was just another timely round in the ladder of luck he was climbing to fame and influence. When the opportunity appeared he was ready."

Perhaps Murrill remained unaffected because he was at heart a collector, a taxonomist, driven by a passion for identifying and classifying new species. Once he'd catalogued the chestnut's foe, stamped his name on its identity, and established its workings, his interest in the fungus seemed to wane. Then, too, Murrill was a scientist first and foremost, clear-eyed and strictly tethered to the facts on the ground. And the facts, as he now saw them, left no room for hope. "If this disease continues as it has begun, there is, theoretically, no reason apparent why it should not sweep from the country practically every tree, both native and cultivated, of the genus *Castanea,*" he told members of the Torrey Botanical Club in 1908. If he felt grief or pain over the potential loss of this particular friend, he never expressed it. When a reporter asked him about the decimation of favorite shade trees like elms and maples by various pests, he replied that the solution was to simply stop planting such vulnerable trees. "Certain trees, like the chestnut—which is doomed—the sugar maple and the elm are too sensitive to ordinary cultivation, especially in cities." Better to plant hardier varieties like oak or sycamore, he advised. "Otherwise, it is tempting fate."

But Metcalf and others were not yet willing to consign the chestnuts to fate. Though Metcalf eventually came to agree with Murrill that individual trees were beyond rescue, he was still hopeful that the epidemic could be staunched before it reached the valuable chestnut stands of Appalachia. He, like other federal scientists, thought the answer was a quarantine. The use of quarantines had helped wrestle such agricultural pests as pear blight and peach yellows to the ground, as well as human scourges from the Black Death to yellow fever. As then–Secretary of Agriculture James Wilson observed, "There is no contagious disease known that does not yield to sanitation and quarantine." In the fall of 1908, Metcalf decided to test the efficacy of quarantine in the area around Washington, D.C. Scouts from his lab scoured the woods within a thirty-five-mile radius for signs of infected trees. They found 1,014 "points of infection," ranging from a group of nursery trees imported from New Jersey to a single lesion on a wild chestnut in a forest. Every affected tree was cut down and destroyed, and Metcalf directed that the site be monitored for the next several years.

Metcalf knew what was riding on the outcome of the experiment. Failure ensured the loss of one of the country's most important trees, a resource worth at least three to four hundred million dollars, or about nine billion dollars in today's currency. "The stake for which we are fighting is nothing less than the present stand of chestnut timber in America," he told a reporter. "Unless the disease is controlled by human agency or unless some natural enemy appears to check the disease— and there is no hope of this—the chestnut tree will become extinct within the next ten or fifteen years."

THREE

Let Us Not Talk
about Impossibilities

Pennsylvania governor John Tener looked out over the glittering chamber of his state's House of Representatives. Every leather seat was filled, but not by the familiar crowd of legislators. On this late February day in 1912, the hall was packed with scientists and bureaucrats, foresters and businessmen from across the eastern seaboard who had all journeyed to Harrisburg to talk about just one subject: a new, fantastically ambitious plan to stop the spreading chestnut blight. The visitors' gallery was packed with reporters, Harrisburg residents, even detouring tourists drawn by what was sure to be a day of dramatic debate. The air was thick with a sense of urgency and simmering conflict.

Tener, the official host of the conference, stepped up to the podium to speak. At six feet, four inches, he cut an imposing figure as he outlined the dire situation facing the delegates: "It seems unthinkable that a disease of this character should have invaded so large an area and that no means of preventing its spread is yet at hand. Unless this disease be stopped by concerted action among the States, it is certain that within a few years very few living wild chestnut trees will be found in America. It is, therefore, entirely in accord with the American spirit that we make every effort to destroy or check the advance of this blight."

Tener's rousing words were intended to launch the biggest offensive

48

yet in the fight to defeat the blight. So far, it had been a mostly one-sided war. For six years, the fungus had been sweeping down the East Coast, mowing down chestnuts in its path. Efforts to halt it had been mostly fruitless, though valuable information about the new enemy had been gained along the way. By 1911, the fungus appeared to have established redoubts in at least ten states, making it clear that the disease had now reached pandemic proportions. At this point, Pennsylvania stepped into the fray. In June 1911, Tener signed a bill establishing a special commission dedicated to the eradication of this new foe and committing the grand sum of $275,000—the equivalent of about $5.6 million today— to the war chest. Pennsylvania's plan was audacious—and heartbreakingly naïve. There was no question that the chestnut population in the southeast part of the state was doomed; the blight was too well-established in the area around Philadelphia to subdue. But the pathogen had yet to make inroads in the west, where there was fifty to seventy million dollars' worth of chestnut trees, including mammoth stands of wild trees and a flourishing orchard industry of hybrid European trees. The plan? To halt the blight in its tracks. The state would cut out every single infected chestnut tree—and if need be, healthy ones as well—in the western half of the state. And it would establish and maintain a blight-free "immune zone" between east and west, a several-hundred-mile-long fire line to contain this biological wildfire.

The hubris of the plan was breathtaking. With the humble tools of ax and saw, Pennsylvania was proposing to vanquish a microscopic enemy that reproduced itself by the millions every year and that had already dispersed itself across thousands of square miles. The effort was propelled less by rational calculation than by a blind desire to act. And so the Pennsylvania Chestnut Tree Blight Commission was inaugurated in a burst of patriotic fanfare and flag-waving, as though, forest pathologist George Hepting noted, the state was "single-handedly going out to fight an army to preserve the Union, instead of a scientific battle against an insidious parasite, requiring weapons that simply were not in man's arsenal." Before the summer was even out, five commissioners—mainly business leaders—were appointed, a staff was hired, and work got under way. Field agents started scouting the central part of the state to map the advance line of the epidemic. They had started none too soon, for while it had been predicted the blight was confined to the counties east of the Susquehanna River, the scouts soon discovered it had already hopped that watery barrier and set up shop in several counties on the river's western edge. By year's end, the commission was still working out the details of its campaign. It was hoped that the upcoming exchange of information and ideas at the conference in Harrisburg would help flesh out the plan.

The Pennsylvania program enjoyed public support and was backed by USDA scientists, but a handful of experts, including William Murrill, considered it pure folly. Murrill told the *New York Times* before heading to the meeting in Harrisburg, "There is not an instance where an individual tree or a grove has been saved by the methods they propose for forests. When public funds are requested there should be reasonable hope of success. It is as if a doctor called to a bad case wrote a prescription knowing at the time that would be absolutely useless." Murrill knew he would have few allies in Harrisburg. Still, he felt it his duty to appear and speak out, if not to dissuade Pennsylvanians from the effort, then at least to deter other states from following down the same misguided path.

Ironically, he was the one who had originated the so-called "cutting-out method" to thwart the blight. In one of his first bulletins on the chestnut bark disease, Murrill had advised chestnut owners "to cut and use all trees, both old and young, that stand within half a mile of diseased trees. . . . This may not prevent the spread of the disease, but it will at least retard its progress." But those words had been penned back in 1908 and were aimed at owners of small woodlots, not the guardians of the country's forests.

Now, nearly four years later, his pessimism had only deepened. No matter how diligently he had pruned and removed infected trees in the botanical garden, the fungus had continued to hunt out new victims;

only two chestnuts remained of the park's original 1,500. "The effects of the disease are even more disastrous than was at first supposed," he told one reporter. "It has swept like a tidal wave over the woodlands about New York City leaving not a single native healthy tree standing." The tsunami had gathered such speed and reach, Murrill was now thoroughly convinced nothing could contain it.

Scientists from the USDA disagreed. Haven Metcalf and colleagues at the agency's Bureau of Plant Industry had high hopes for the Pennsylvania plan, based on their own small-scale experiment with eradication outside Washington, D.C. After three years of carefully monitoring the site, the quarantine line seemed to be holding. Metcalf concluded he had succeeded in containing the scourge. He announced the good news in a Farmer's Bulletin published in the fall of 1911: "The disease has not reappeared at any point where eliminated and the country within a radius of approximately 35 miles from Washington is apparently free from the bark disease, although new infections must be looked for as long as the disease remains elsewhere unchecked." This was no mere academic exercise. Metcalf was convinced he had found a strategy for containing the epidemic—one that could be employed throughout the chestnut's range: "If carried out on a large scale, [the method] will result ultimately in the control of the bark disease."

Metcalf's confidence in the scheme sprang from two beliefs. He was certain the fungus came from overseas—most likely from Asia, as scientists had repeatedly noted that Japanese and Chinese chestnuts were relatively resistant to the fungus's attack while their American cousins buckled at the first onslaught. Some experts still contended the blight was caused by a normally harmless native parasite that had suddenly become destructive. If that were true, the organism would be too entrenched in the landscape to subdue. But, if, as Metcalf suspected, it was a relatively recent émigré still feeling its way across new terrain, then it ought to be subject to control.

He was also heartened by his understanding of the way the disease spread. While Murrill likened the blight to an onrushing tidal wave, Metcalf saw it more as a smoldering wildfire that lurched forward by sending out spores in advance—"sparks, so to speak, which become in time centres of new conflagration." He thought it a fairly easy thing to locate and extinguish those early sparks, since they typically lit on only one or two trees. "We have discovered that if these advance spots of infection can be located and the diseased trees destroyed, there is no further spread of the disease in that immediate locality," Metcalf confidently told one reporter.

As far as Metcalf was concerned, the only practical question now was whether any other state could be persuaded to join Pennsylvania in battle. For as Metcalf acknowledged in the 1911 Farmer's Bulletin, the federal government had no authority to cope with this type of national emergency. All Washington could do was appropriate money for research, and not much at that. It was up to the states to muster their own defenses by each establishing their own quarantine lines. And therein lay the rub: quarantines require cooperation. "If one State elects to undertake control of the disease it will be seriously handicapped if neighboring States do not," Metcalf warned. His top priority was protecting southern Appalachia, home to what his boss Beverly Galloway called "the largest and best chestnut forests of the country." There was no time to waste: the blight had already ignited a few hot spots as far south as central Virginia. But Metcalf was confident that if the states bordering the region could be persuaded to follow Pennsylvania's example, the pandemic could be squelched. His arguments were persuasive. In December 1911, at the meeting of the American Association for the Advancement of Science, the country's premier scientific gathering, the conferees passed a resolution urging each of the twenty-two states in the chestnut's range to appropriate fifty thousand to a hundred thousand dollars to fight the blight. By early 1912, bills to that effect were pending or in preparation in four states, and a federal bill appropriating eighty thousand dollars to blight eradication was in the works. Momentum for a broad quarantine seemed to be building; it was critical that Metcalf's strategy win hearty endorsement in Harrisburg.

The skies were overcast and the air just a few degrees above freezing as the hundreds of delegates to the Pennsylvania Chestnut Tree Blight Commission conference filed up the steps of the magnificent statehouse in Harrisburg. With a gilded dome modeled on St. Peter's Basilica in Rome and a central stairway fashioned after one in the Paris Opera House, the recently completed capitol was a testament to the Keystone State's ambition and wealth. Teddy Roosevelt had called it "the handsomest building in America." The crowd streaming through the massive front doors that day included some of the most prominent plant scientists of the day. There was Murrill; George Clinton, of the Connecticut Agricultural Experiment Station; William Farlow, of Harvard, the dean of American mycology and one of the pioneers of plant pathology; and Arthur Graves, a Yale University botanist who would spend many of his later years trying to resurrect the American chestnut. Hermann Merkel, the New York Zoological Park forester who had discovered the blight, also attended, as did lumbermen, orchard-owners, conservationists, and agricultural officials from a dozen states across the chestnut range. There was even a representative from Canada's department of agriculture. The one face missing was Haven Metcalf's; he had suffered an accident two days earlier and was forced to send a deputy in his stead.

The conference was billed as a scientific meeting. To be sure, the two days were filled with reports describing the latest findings on the fungus. But the meeting's true center of gravity hovered over the growing tension between what one reporter called the "progressives," the crusaders committed to an all-out attack on the blight, and the "reactionaries," the scientists who considered it futile. The result was a classic clash of politics and science.

Though Metcalf's work provided some scientific rationale for the Pennsylvania plan, the spirit moving many of the "progressives" was a simple and basic human emotion: the desire to do something. It was unbearable to simply let this miserable microorganism have its way while the scientists plodded along with their investigations. To do nothing "is un-American," thundered R. A. Pearson, the conference chairman and former New York agricultural commissioner, in his opening remarks. "It is not the spirit of the Keystone State, nor the Empire State, nor the New England States, nor the many other great States that are represented here, to sit down and do nothing when catastrophies [*sic*] are upon us. . . . That is not the way great questions are solved. If we had waited until the application of steam should be thoroughly understood, we would be still waiting for our great trains and steamboats, which are the marvel of the age." The chamber burst into loud applause.

Pearson was soon followed by Franklin Stewart, a pathologist from the New York Agricultural Experiment Station. It could not have been easy for the mild-mannered scientist to speak, for it fell to him to articulate the antiwar line. Given the jingoistic mood in the room, he knew that what he had to say would be about as popular as if he were espousing the virtues of Bolshevism. "Mr. Chairman and ladies and gentlemen," Stewart began. "My views are so much at variance with what I conceive to be the sentiment of this conference that I hesitated somewhat to present them. I feel like one throwing water on a fire which his friends are diligently striving to kindle. But a sense of my duty to the public and, also, myself, impels me to proceed."

Stewart considered the Pennsylvania plan wholly impractical. In explaining why, he took aim squarely at its supporting rationale—the ostensible success of the USDA's experimental quarantine in Washington, D.C. His analysis pulled no punches. Contrary to Metcalf's claims, said Stewart, the federal scientists had not yet proven that an "immune zone" could work. The experiment itself was faulty, Stewart argued, because the scientists did not include a "check," a control site to compare what would happen if infected trees in the area were not removed. "There was no check, and experimenters are agreed that experiments without checks have little value." What's more, he argued, the area was not as blight-free as Metcalf had indicated. Just two months earlier, Stewart had examined chestnuts within the immune zone and found several ailing trees. It was likely "they became infected in 1910 or earlier and must have been discharging millions of spores at the very moment Dr. Metcalf was writing his statement that the country within a radius of 35 miles of Washington was apparently free from the disease."

Stewart went on to explain the scientific factors that had persuaded him this pathogen was much more difficult to control than others. Unlike plum black knot, for instance, the chestnut disease eluded detection in its early stages, yet it took only a month from when the fungus infiltrated a tree for it to start producing "multitudes" of spores. Those spores were disseminated through a variety of means, some of which couldn't be prevented. Who could waylay the wind or rain? In addition, the behavior of the parasite was still not understood, suggesting it might act in unanticipated ways. No matter how carefully scouts combed the forests, it would be impossible to locate every single diseased tree. And even one diseased tree could "start an uncontrollable epidemic," which in turn would require the establishment of a new immune zone. The Pennsylvania warriors would be chasing an ever-advancing front.

Stewart then addressed the gung-ho forces head on: "It has been asked 'What then would you have us do? Stand idle while the disease destroys our chestnut forests?'" He conceded it might be worthwhile to restrict the movement of diseased nursery stock—a measure the Pennsylvania Commission was already committed to. Beyond that, he stated, carefully emphasizing every word, *"It is better to attempt nothing than to waste a large amount of public money on a method of control which there is every reason to believe cannot succeed.* [Italics in the original.] I believe in being honest with the public and admitting frankly that we know of no way to control this disease." In place of the applause granted other speakers, there was only a cold silence as Stewart gathered his papers and returned to his seat.

Though Murrill was present, he remained quiet. Only two other scientists spoke up in support of Stewart's dark conclusion: a member of Delaware's Board of Agriculture and Connecticut's George Clinton, who agreed Pennsylvania's effort was futile, but for different reasons—he believed the fungus was a native pathogen and thus too widespread to be eliminated.

For the rest of the day and well into the night, speaker after speaker rose to challenge Stewart's bleak assessment. "One continued negation" is how one commission supporter characterized it. Few of the objections rested on scientific grounds. Most ran along the lines of the outraged declarations of Pennsylvania deputy commissioner of forestry Irvin C. Williams: "Whenever I hear a man talk about 'impossibilities' then something begins to boil. . . . Let us not talk about impossibilities until we know we are up blank against the stone wall. . . . Let us investigate and work; not investigate first and work afterwards. Let us get busy all along the line and when we have utterly tried out every method and are absolutely and abjectly defeated, then it's time to talk about impossibilities."

From today's perspective, Williams's faith in the power of human determination seems archaic and naïve. But in an era buoyed by a sense of endless possibility, before vistas had been lowered by two world wars, pandemic influenza, the atomic bomb, AIDS, the destruction of rainforests, and wide-scale extirpation of species, who could fault the Harrisburg leaders for their conviction? Past crusades had successfully vanquished some of the most deadly contagions afflicting humans, plants, or animals, including yellow fever, cholera, and hoof and mouth disease. With the determined application of "sanitation and quarantine," scientists had subdued pests such as the peach yellows and the San Jose scale. Why should this plague be any different? Not even the skeptical scientists could conjure a world without chestnuts. They may have considered the blight beyond their immediate control, but they were still certain that the pandemic would eventually burn itself out. "It is unlikely the chestnut will be exterminated," Stewart had assured the conference delegates. Nature in all her fury had never before extinguished a species through disease. Surely she wouldn't let this defiant intruder succeed.

As the delegates assembled the next morning, the mood was ugly. Pro-Pennsylvania forces were primed for a fight, as eager to cut down their opponents as they were the dreaded blight. Williams proclaimed that he would "go after" any visitor who expressed opinions similar to Stewart's. A commission member confided to a reporter that the pessimists from New York and Connecticut "are jealous of Pennsylvania and are trying to throw cold water on the work of this state. We have taken the lead in this work and these members hate to think of being outdistanced."

Stewart, surely unaccustomed to such hostility, looked weary as he took his place and sat with his head in his hands. Murrill also seemed drained of his usual vigor and held his tongue for much of the day. It wasn't until the last paper was read and the only agenda item left was a vote on resolutions calling on other states to adopt a Pennsylvania-style plan that the gentlemanly Virginian finally rose to speak. He requested a few minutes to explain "very briefly and plainly as to why the chestnut canker cannot be controlled by [the] cutting-out method proposed." He succinctly ticked off a series of reasons, echoing the same points Stewart had made.

It was the opening Williams had been waiting for. The brewing tension between the politicians and the scientists boiled over. Williams castigated the scientists for delivering "useless" conclusions: "They are simply guesses in the future, strokes in the dark; they amount to nothing. One man can guess at something as well as another. If the practical men of America are to pin their faith to guesswork . . . then I say it is pretty much time to call off the scientists and let us look to somebody else."

"The politicians," the Connecticut pathologist Clinton sarcastically suggested.

"Yes, sir, they will help," answered Williams. "You will find that when a politician sees something good, he goes for it and generally gets it. He, at least, has courage enough to try." Williams tore into Murrill's objections and then delivered the nastiest blow: he accused the New Yorkers of failing to act quickly enough in the early years of the blight to prevent the pandemic: "If instead of sitting down and nursing their hands in idleness and allowing this scourge to go on, simply because they could not originate sufficient interest in their states, they had gone out and done what they could, this thing would probably not have come upon us."

It's not hard to imagine how deeply offended Murrill must have been by Williams's accusations. His response, however, was measured: "For the last seven years I have known this fungus. Immediately when I found it, when the infected trees were shown me by Mr. Merkel, I began the most industrious investigation of it, and I venture to say that many of those present have been guided to knowledge of it through my extensive correspondence on the subject."

What's more, he added, he did have a plan for dealing with the crisis, though it wasn't one likely to satisfy the desperate urge for action: "I believe in carrying on investigations a little further and, if possible, in finding some rational method, so that we can use our funds to much better advantage." Focus on research, he entreated the delegates, starting with carefully controlled eradication tests in selected forests and orchards. "Let that be a scientific, thoroughly scientific test, under this Commission, and, after the season is over, let us have a report and decide what further must be done with this magnificent appropriation which the state of Pennsylvania has so generously made." For the first and only time, one of the "reactionaries" won a round of applause.

But his words could not cool the fervor that filled the room. In a nearly unanimous vote, the conference delegates supported the resolutions urging the states and federal government to adopt the same plan as Pennsylvania and to establish quarantine lines. There was only one recorded dissenter: Murrill.

Though he was outvoted, Murrill didn't consider his efforts a defeat. As he later wrote in his autobiography, it had been "the battle of his career." And he wasn't through. Back home, he lobbied against measures pending in both New York and Virginia to mount Pennsylvania-style campaigns. New York's bill was voted down, and Virginia committed only a paltry five thousand dollars. And while there had been talk of similar legislation in Maryland and West Virginia, none ever materialized. "Suffice it to say that because of the Naturalist's determined opposition not a single other state spent money on the scheme," Murrill congratulated himself. The Keystone State was on her own.

After his grand stand at Harrisburg, Murrill gradually removed himself from the ongoing campaign against the blight so that he could concentrate on his true professional passion, mycology. But his career soon took a tragic turn. In 1918, he journeyed to Europe on a collecting trip, but then failed to return to New York when he was due. The botanical garden contacted his various associates abroad, but no one knew where he was. Months later, he reappeared, claiming that he'd been in a hospital in a small town in France, near death from a long-standing kidney condition. But the story didn't satisfy the imperious head of the garden, Nathaniel Lord Britton. Murrill was demoted and his salary slashed. It was a crushing blow to his self-esteem; after further run-ins with Britton, he eventually quit. Depressed and debilitated, he moved back to Virginia, built himself a cabin in the woods, and severed all ties with New York and the professional world of mycology. One day in 1926, a former colleague happened by the "Tin Can Tourist Camp" in Gainesville, Florida, a dingy trailer park for tourists. There he spotted a frail and haggard-looking Murrill playing a piano concert for the camp's residents. Murrill had been drawn to Florida by the rich variety of mushrooms there, but he had no real means of supporting himself. The man who had always dressed impeccably was now shabby and unkempt. The colleague, another mycologist from the University of Florida at Gainesville, helped to get him clothed and fed, found him a house, and arranged a makeshift office for him on the third floor stairwell landing of a university building. From that modest platform, Murrill happily spent the rest of his long life—he died in 1957—identifying and classifying species of Florida fungi.

With the debate over their methods laid to rest, the Pennsylvania crusaders now got under way in earnest, in cooperation with the federal government. To command the campaign, the commission hired Mark Alfred Carleton, the USDA expert on foreign-plant introductions— "one of the big men of the department," according to Haven Metcalf, his boss. Carleton, then thirty-six, was tall and heavy-set, with a receding hairline and thick mustache. His specialty was grains, not trees, but he was used to uphill battles like this one and was well-suited to the struggle by his prodigious energy and obsessive temperament. He's a "fighter," Metcalf wrote the secretary of the Commission, assuring him that "a man that has already 'delivered the goods' as often as he has can probably do it again." Metcalf was referring to the fact that Carleton had already changed the agricultural habits of America's breadbasket, almost single-handedly.

Carleton grew up in Kansas watching farmers struggle to raise crops in country that was blistered by drought in summer, scoured by bitter winds in the winter, and regularly visited by scourges such as the wheat-withering black stem rust. That youthful experience set his life's direction; he became determined to find wheat varieties that could survive in that unforgiving land. As an adult working for the USDA, Carleton noticed that the wheat crops of Kansas Mennonite farmers were prospering while their neighbors' failed. Interviewing the Mennonites, he learned they were using grain they had brought with them from Russia. In 1898, after teaching himself rudimentary Russian, Carleton traveled to the arid steppes of Russia in search of the hardy seed. He returned with a durum wheat known as Kubanka, a variety said to be so tough that it could grow in hell. Two years later, he made another excursion to Siberia, where he collected an equally rugged variety of winter wheat called Kharkov.

But, as his biographer Paul de Kruif wrote, "it took a knock-down-and-drag-out fight to get American men to grow those Russian wheats." Farmers complained the Russian kernels were so hard-shelled that millers couldn't grind them, and that even if they could, there was no market for the flour. So Carleton created one. The Russian wheats were prized in Europe for making macaroni. Carleton became a "macaroni messiah," according to de Kruif. He denounced the "white, pasty, doughy mass of sticks, served in dilute tomato sauce" that passed as pasta in this country. Consulting cookbooks and chefs, he filled government bulletins with recipes for semolina fritters, soufflés, and puddings—all made from durum wheat. Gradually farmers began replacing their American varieties with Kubanka and Kharkov, especially after it became clear the Russian grains were less disease-prone than the native grains and delivered far bigger yields. By 1914, half of the nation's yield of hard red winter wheat was Kharkov.

Now Carleton faced an equally monumental mission. He was eager for the challenge; what attracted him to the job was "the prospect of a good scrap." Pennsylvania's battle plan divided the state in half: the eastern zone where the blight was raging, and the western zone, where it had yet to gain a foothold. The dividing line, the advance front of the pandemic, ran in a rough diagonal across the middle of the state, more or less along the ridge of the Allegheny Mountains. Carleton's job was to keep the blight from breaching that line by bringing it under control in the east and eradicating any early outbreaks that erupted in the west. The sheer magnitude of the task was daunting. The western zone contained some 6.5 million acres of woodland, and every square inch had to be surveyed for the disease, step by tedious step. In the east, there were tens of thousands of dying trees scattered across more than three million acres of woods to be dealt with.

To bolster the mission, the law establishing the commission granted Carleton and his men "the power to use all practical means to destroy the chestnut tree blight." They had the authority to enter any property—regardless of who owned it—in the search for diseased and threatened trees. Though the law encouraged cooperation with timber owners, the commission could punish individuals who refused to comply with its orders with fines or even jail time. Nursery inspections were authorized, and no stock could be shipped from blighted to blight-free areas without the approval of the commission's inspectors.

By the spring of 1912, Carleton had two hundred field agents under his command, most of whom he dispatched to the western counties to start scouting the woods. It was arduous work: eight to ten hours a day tramping through dense forest, constantly on the alert for the enemy's tracks, which might be found anywhere from the base of a tree to its crown eighty feet above. The scouts had to keep their eyes peeled for the slightest of signs: a peppering of sun-colored spots, a sunken patch of bark high overhead, a handful of pale or withered leaves, or a dying branch. As Carleton explained it, his field agents had to be agile enough to climb trees, diplomatic enough to negotiate with all classes of timber-owners, and articulate enough to communicate their mission, since a good part of their work was holding meetings to teach landowners how to spot the disease and deal with it. The thin-skinned need not apply, for when an agent "meets opposition he must be able to withstand criticism and see that the requirements of the law are carried out." All this earned only dismally low wages. Not surprisingly, most of the agents were young high school and college graduates.

In Pennsylvania's more populous eastern half, the blight's chief targets were the grand ornamental chestnuts shading parks and yards. There, the commission allowed homeowners to try to save their beloved trees. It had an able squad of tree surgeons who advised homeowners on ways they could prune and treat their trees to hold the blight in check. Early in 1913, the commission announced it had found a possible cure for individual chestnut trees that involved cutting out the diseased parts, slathering creosote over the wounds and then repeatedly dousing the trees with Bordeaux solution. (The ever-skeptical Murrill questioned the value of the cure: "Speaking *practically*," he commented archly, "trees covered continuously with copper sulfate and lime do not fit very well into a gorgeous landscape scheme, especially if they are liable to drop a limb or two every few months or to drop out entirely some time while the owner is asleep.")

The commission offered no such mercy for any diseased tree found in the western part of the state or along the quarantine line. There, the goal was to destroy every vestige of the blight. Whenever a scout found an infected tree, he would mark it with the commission's official stamp and tack on a yellow tag. The owner then had twenty days to remove the tree. Agents tried to be on hand to help with the removal, for effective eradication called for more than simply chopping a blighted tree down. The tree had to be cut close to the ground, and the lumber, as well as the stump, stripped clean of its bark, where the fungus resided. At that point, the wood could be salvaged for use, for by now, research had shown that the bare wood was neither infected nor infectious. Any part of the tree that wasn't slated for use—diseased sections, branches, leaves, bark—had to be piled on top of the stump and burned. Not a single particle of bark or the smallest of twigs could be left on the ground, lest they spark a new infection. For all their diligence, the field agents never considered that they might be spreading the deadly spores on the soles of their boots or the blades of their axes. And it's likely that they did.

Finding outlets for the mounting stockpile of chestnut wood was another of the commission's major tasks. For if owners couldn't make a profit off their cut-down trees or at least recoup expenses, they'd be less willing to comply when their trees were tagged. There were more than thirty commercial uses of chestnut, one commission staff member noted, "and it seems likely that all the chestnut wood which will be produced can be utilized, provided that it can be delivered to factories and other consumers at a price which will allow it to compete with other woods." To that end, the commission persuaded the railroads to offer reduced freight rates for the blighted lumber. It also set up an Office of Utilization to help together bring timber sellers and buyers.

By early 1913, Carleton was delighted with the progress of the campaign. His search-and-destroy forces had disposed of more than thirty thousand blighted chestnuts in the western part of the state. Carleton and his supporters were optimistically predicting that "the blight will practically be wiped out by the close of the year."

Among the many pressing questions that puzzled the scientists studying the chestnut bark fungus, one stood out: Where had it come from? Was it, as George Clinton maintained, a native species, a black sheep from a benign family of fungi that had suddenly and dramatically turned bad? Was it able to destroy chestnuts because the trees had been weakened by seasons of drought? Or, as Metcalf suspected, was it a new arrival from overseas that held the power to annihilate chestnuts simply because the native trees had not evolved any defenses against it? As Charles Darwin observed in 1835, "What havoc the introduction of any new beast of prey must cause in a country . . . before the instincts of the indigenous inhabitants have become adapted to the stranger's craft or power."

If the fungus was an import, it would hardly have been the first. Since the Pilgrims and earlier, settlers on American shores have brought with them the flora and fauna, insects and microbes of their homeland. Indeed, from time immemorial, farmers, ranchers, foresters, and gardeners have sought out exotic additions to improve upon or enliven the local resources—often, as writer Yvonne Baskin points out, "with ludicrously little knowledge or forethought." Three thousand years before Columbus's travels to the Americas triggered the global shuffling of crops known as the Columbian Exchange—New World potatoes, corn, chocolate, and tomatoes in exchange for Old World wheat, wine grapes, sugar cane, and onions—the queen of Egypt was sending ships down the African coast in search of incense trees for her garden at Karnak. But even deliberate introductions had "the stranger's craft or power" to wreak havoc in a new locale. Some of today's most notoriously destructive plants—such as Johnson grass, Japanese honeysuckle, Brazilian pepper trees, water hyacinth, barberry, and kudzu— were intentionally introduced in the nineteenth century through seed catalogues.

The native landscape has been equally affected by the arrival of unbidden stowaways—pathogens, seeds, insects, and animals that hitched rides on imported goods, the vessels carrying them, or even the stones and soil used as ballast, which was routinely offloaded to shore to make room for cargo. "Ballast lots sprouted in the major cities of the U.S. East Coast" from the tons of earth and rocks dumped ashore throughout the nineteenth century, according to writer Alan Burdick. Botanical clubs flocked to the lots to see exotic new arrivals such as bristly oxtongue or black bindweed. Burdick quotes one amateur botanist's excited notes from 1876: "As I review these ballast deposits and detect so many strangers . . . I feel a reawakening of that interest which a ramble about our fields and woodlands fails to create." Ah, that unslakable human thirst for something new. For the American chestnut, it would bring nothing but disaster.

The federal experts in Washington, D.C., didn't need confirmation of the chestnut blight's origin to grasp the growing danger of imported pathogens. Other recognizably exotic diseases were knocking at the door. "Within the past few years," USDA scientists warned farmers in 1912, "very serious European plant diseases have been brought to North America upon imported plant material." Of particular concern were two parasites that had ravaged Europe and now crossed the Atlantic: potato wart and white pine blister rust. The former threatened one of the country's top agricultural crops; the latter, its most valuable timber tree. Although the federal scientists understood how introduced diseases could explode into epidemics, they felt hamstrung by the lack of any meaningful way to prevent that from happening. Unlike European countries, the U.S did not have a national quarantine system. American authorities relied instead "on a loosely organized and haphazardly maintained practice of inspection after importation. Often nurserymen, in an obvious conflict of interest, held the final say over the movement of plant material." Just as Murrill had called for tougher laws, Metcalf and his D.C. colleagues began pushing for a national quarantine law to replace the leaky patchwork of state regulations then in place. Finally, in 1912, they succeeded in persuading Congress to pass the Plant Quarantine Act, which for the first time allowed the federal government to regulate the importation of nursery stock, as well as fruits and plants and vegetables, and which granted the government the power to establish and maintain quarantines for plant diseases and insect pests. Of course, by then it was too late for the American chestnut.

In early 1913, Metcalf and his colleagues at the Forest Pathology Laboratory learned that the celebrated plant explorer Frank Meyer was mounting a new expedition to northern China. Meyer was a Dutch-born, mostly self-taught botanist who seemed to draw more comfort from plants than people. He had already spent close to a decade in Asia on behalf of the USDA. His journal entries testified to the singular joys and hardships of the job. There was the sublime beauty of the untouched landscapes and the excitement of discovering uncatalogued flora. But the explorer's life also meant coping with blinding snowstorms and scorching heat, dealing with cheating interpreters, and staying at filthy inns where he was "bitten by not less than six kinds of vermin." Above all there was the intense loneliness of being a stranger in an alien land. Still, Meyer was dedicated to this mission to, as he put it, "skim the earth for things good for man." Over the years he had sent home dozens of potential crops, including new varieties of peaches, persimmon, pawpaws, apricots, almonds, and the sweet citrus we know as Meyer lemons. During one earlier trip to China, he had come across groves of chestnut foresting rocky mountain slopes and duly gathered the nuts for introduction in this country.

Now Metcalf and his colleagues wanted Meyer to revisit the chestnut groves and examine the trees closely for signs of the blight. So that he would know what to look for, they sent him specimens of diseased bark to take along. After a six-day journey by mule to the mountains north of Peking, Meyer found his quarry: chestnut trees infected with what appeared to be the same fungal disease. He immediately cabled the news to his bosses in Washington, D.C. In a letter a few days later, he elaborated on what he had seen: "This blight does not by far do as much damage to Chinese trees as to the American ones. Not a single tree could be found which had been killed entirely by this disease, although there might have been such trees which had been removed by the ever active and economic Chinese farmers." Meyer enclosed a small, two-inch-square sample of diseased bark, along with nuts from the Chinese trees. The latter, he suggested, could be crossed with American chestnut trees to give the natives "more hardiness and resistancy [*sic*] against disease." The strategy would fuel the next century of efforts to rescue the American chestnut from oblivion.

When Metcalf received the Chinese specimen, he carefully lifted the bark and methodically examined it with his hand lens. "It looks like it," he told his boss. "However, cultures will soon show." Metcalf and colleagues Cornelius Shear and Neil Stevens worked feverishly over the next several weeks, following the same steps that Murrill had used just a few years before to identify the new pathogen. They grew cultures of fungus drawn from the sample, used those to inoculate American chestnuts, and then watched the now-familiar mycelial fans creep insidiously across the native trees. It was unquestionably the same disease. The time span from when the federal experts received Meyer's first cable to when they finished the last experiment was a mere forty-two days. The chain of evidence was now complete (or nearly so—one last link would be added in 1916 when Meyer discovered that the fungus also lived on chestnut trees in Japan, where it had an equally benign effect).

No one could say where or when the first blight spores arrived in America. But how was no longer a mystery. The "miserable stowaway," as one observer had called it, gained entry on imported chestnut trees—likely on Japanese chestnut trees, which Americans began bringing into the United States in the late nineteenth century. Nurseryman S. B. Parsons of Flushing, New York, was the first to test American tastes for Japan's *Castanea crenata*. He imported a shipment in 1876 and found ready customers up and down the East Coast. (One pair of the trees still survives in Connecticut.) A New Jersey nursery brought in one thousand grafted Japanese trees a few years later. And in 1886, Luther Burbank, that influential purveyor of botanical fare, planted a box of seeds sent to him from a collector in Japan. He soon had ten thousand trees growing in his California nursery, which undoubtedly were dispersed hither and yon. As chestnut researcher Sandra Anagnostakis notes, "Any or all of those early Japanese imports could have carried blight." From there, the blight spread by mail order, carried far and wide by Americans' hunger for novel additions to their gardens.

The plant explorer's discovery helped explain the astonishing rapidity with which the pandemic had engulfed the eastern seaboard. It was not that blight had emanated from a single outbreak in New York. The East Coast was dotted with outbreaks—Long Island, New York; Trenton, New Jersey; Fairfield, Connecticut; Cape Cod, Massachusetts; Lancaster County, Pennsylvania; Bedford County, Virginia—wherever someone had planted an Asian chestnut tree. New York City just happened to be the first place anyone had noticed the stealthy microorganism at work. By 1911, when Pennsylvania set out to contain the unruly invader, it was already too late.

Yet in the end, political machinations, not scientific revelations, were what brought the Pennsylvania Chestnut Blight Commission's grandiose effort to a close. In the summer of 1913, the commission requested that the state appropriate another $275,000 to continue its campaign. This time, the legislature balked and would commit only $100,000. The commission's leaders considered the sum inadequate to sustain the all-out war. Perhaps in an effort to force the legislature's hand, the commissioners refused to accept anything less than the full amount they had requested and urged Governor Tener to veto the lesser appropriation. The brinksmanship failed; the legislators refused to grant more money. In early August, at the height of the season in which the fungus was most active and sure to be spewing millions of spores, the commission called it quits.

The commission's final report in 1913 was a sober document, showing none of the boisterous optimism of its earlier pronouncements. In his last missive from the front, Carleton tried to put the best gloss he could on the commission's accomplishments. The blight had been eradicated from most of the western half of the state, where some fifty thousand trees had been cut down. The effort, he insisted, had delayed the fungus from gaining headway in Ohio, as well as nearby parts of New York and West Virginia. Quarantine and treatment measures had bought time for Pennsylvania's orchards. All told, he believed the campaign had slowed the blight's progress in the state by a good five years. But he had no illusions about what the future held for the American chestnut: "It is not a pleasant prospect to consider the serious results likely to follow after this method of eradicating the disease, conducted by the Commission, is obliged to cease."

Commission chairman Winthrop Sargent was more blunt in assessing the impact of the commission's end: "The complete loss of the present commercial stand of chestnut in Pennsylvania . . . seems absolutely certain." He continued to defend the cutting-out method, insisting that it ultimately might have held the blight in check. But even if it hadn't, he argued, the work was not in vain. "This is not the last tree disease that will sweep over this State. All efforts to control this disease would be justified even if we only learned how to control the next one." And therein, he concluded, lay the real lesson of the blight: "the necessity of more scientific research upon problems of this character" so that the next marauding invader could be contained before it got out of control. But if that lesson was clear to him, he wasn't so sure it was understood by other state or federal authorities. Indeed, he feared that the same lack of attention that allowed the blight to take hold continued to define the official response to the disease, as well as to new worrisome outbreaks, including white pine blister rust, which was starting to gain ground in East Coast forests. Once again, Sargent warned, skeptics were underplaying the potential threat posed by a forest disease. In both cases, the pathogens were traced to overseas homes: China, in the case of chestnut blight, and Europe, in the case of the blister rust. Yet so far neither federal nor state government had been willing to spend the money to dispatch scientists to study the diseases on their home turfs. "In this connection," he wrote, "it may not be amiss to call attention to the fact that in Pennsylvania there is, aside from the employees of the Commission, only one professional plant pathologist! Yet the preventable damage which one plant disease—chestnut blight—has done, would pay for the work of more plant pathologists than there are now at work in the entire world."

A Whole World Dying

The male flowers of chestnut trees develop on long pendulous spikes called catkins. A single catkin holds dozens of tiny pollen-producing anthers. Catkins are fuzzy and floppy, so that when a tree is in full bloom it looks as if it is sporting cream-colored dreadlocks. A blossoming chestnut is beautiful, but the smell is not. In their most fertile season, chestnuts give off a pungent odor that is alluring to insects only. One diehard friend of the tree described the scent as having a "saving tang of acrid," but most would consider the description overly generous. I've heard it compared to old shoes, semen, or "a whorehouse on a hot summer's day." "It's skanky," declared one arborist as he offered me a catkin to sniff. I was reminded of a high school locker room.

Despite the strong odor—or because of it—the flower of the European chestnut, close cousin of the American tree, is reputed to have powerful healing properties, at least according to Edward Bach, the late English homeopathic physician. In the 1930s, Bach used extracts from thirty-eight flowers and plants to develop remedial tinctures for various malaises of mood. Chestnut extract, he determined, was the antidote for despair, "for those moments which happen to some people when the anguish is so great as to seem to be unbearable . . . when it seems there is nothing but destruction and annihilation left to face."

Would Bach's theory work in reverse? Would a people accustomed to regular exposure to these bracing flowers suffer from their absence? Would the disappearance of that sour scent from the summer breeze affect the psyche? I wonder if it is possible, though I know it's a fanciful idea. In any case, as the blight reached Appalachia and the beloved trees began to topple, the region filled with despair, an ecological grief that has dimmed with time but still lingers, vaporlike, in the air.

It's not hard to catch whiffs of that sorrow in places such as Patrick County, Virginia, where chestnut trees once made up as much as 25 to 30 percent of the forest. Even now, the long-gone trees remain a steady presence in family stories, as I learn during a visit to the county. A retired schoolteacher shows a fuzzy black-and-white photo of the dying chestnut that stood on her family's farm, the sentinel she relied on to let her know that she was nearing home. "That was the emblem of my childhood," she says. A former truck driver fondly describes the trips he and his grandfather took to the forests to try to "doctor" ailing chestnut trees.

The most poignant story comes from Coy Lee Yeatts, longtime proprietor of the Mayberry Trading Post, the last of the county's traditional country stores. At eighty-two years old, he still spends his days perched on a stool behind the counter with genealogy books, a television, and a cardboard box labeled "Coy's whittling" close at hand. With his stooped back and great bald head, he looks a bit like Yoda. The store, built in 1892, once was a thriving center for the mountain community of Mayberry, housing the post office as well as a general store. Now it has the feel of a place that has slipped out of time. The store's hours are painted in shaky writing on the front door. Inside, the shelves are sparse and dusty, and the main trade seems to be what Coy Lee and his wife, Dora, sell to the tourists who wander in off the nearby Blue Ridge Parkway: maps, regional histories, homemade jams and relishes, arrowheads, soft drinks, and cigarettes. The couple never was "blessed with children," says Dora, so they can only hope the store will continue when they are gone.

"Did you collect chestnuts when you were young?" I ask Coy Lee, after we've chatted awhile and I've settled into one of the stools on the customer side of the counter.

"Yeah," he says, adding with surprising precision, "the last like that was about the seventh of June, nineteen hundred and twenty-eight." That day he and his younger sister went looking for nuts by the chestnut near his family's house. "I knew that you could dig the chestnuts out from under the leaves in June, peel and eat 'em. That's what we did." That last taste of chestnut is seared in his memory because that night his sister developed appendicitis. The doctors could do nothing for her. The next day she died.

By then, the blight had been present in Virginia for at least fifteen years. Spot infections had been reported in the state earlier, but by 1912, it was clear to USDA scientists that the legions of spores had breached the botanic Maginot line—the Potomac River—and were now swarming across northern Virginia.

Unlike Pennsylvanians, Virginia lawmakers weren't willing to mount an all-out assault on the blight, perhaps in deference to lobbying by one of their native sons, mycologist William Murrill. But neither were they willing to let one of the state's most important trees go without at least a token fight. Chestnut products brought in some $2.5 million a year (about fifty million dollars today), and chestnuts were the most common forest tree in many parts of the state. In 1912, the legislature voted to set aside funds for investigating and preventing the blight, but then appropriated only a meager five thousand dollars. Still, the appropriation was enough to establish a Chestnut Blight Laboratory at Virginia Polytechnic Institute and State University (VPI) in Blacksburg and keep it going for a couple of years. A newly minted VPI plant pathologist named Flippo Gravatt was placed in charge. He would find in the plight of the chestnut a mission that would occupy much of his professional life. He soon joined the USDA, where for the next thirty-plus years he served as one of the chief chroniclers of the tree's slow, sad demise, as well as one of the pioneers in efforts to resuscitate it. (Indeed, from his vantage point with the agency's Bureau of Forest Pathology, Gravatt bore witness over the years to a steady march of destructive invaders, including pine blister rust, gypsy moths, Dutch elm disease, and sweet gum disease.)

Gravatt and four other inspectors traveled the state to determine how widespread the disease had become. The situation didn't look good, he reported in 1914. The disease "had a firm foothold" in the northern part of Virginia, where there were several large outbreaks affecting thousands of trees. Spot infections peppered locations as far south as Richmond and Roanoke. All told, the blight was present in eighteen of the state's ninety-five counties. Countless multitudes of spores now filled the air, an invisible deadly cloud spreading southward fast. The disease was helped along in its progress by an outbreak of cicadas in 1911; the insects' nibbling left chestnut trees in the afflicted areas covered with minute wounds. Each tiny puncture was a doorway for the ravenous spores, a direct corridor to the vital cells under the bark. The infection rate skyrocketed, increasing by an average of 600 percent a year.

Under Gravatt's direction, the state made halfhearted efforts to cut out infected trees in the comparatively narrow chestnut zone in northern Virginia. His goal was much less ambitious than those of the Pennsylvania warriors, who by now had abandoned their campaign. He had no illusions that the pandemic could be staunched. His only objective was to delay it, holding back the main line of infection long enough for landowners in Virginia, as well as the other Appalachian states, to profit from their timber. As he explained, "Every year's delay in the southward progress of the blight also means a year longer to market chestnut products, a year longer for the [tannin] extract plants to operate." When even that effort ended in 1915, Gravatt understood the implication. As he later wrote, "the chestnut stand of the southern

Appalachians was doomed." The rescue mission was over; all that was left was a salvage operation.

This was not the first time the chestnut trees of the southeast faced trouble. Since the middle of the nineteenth century, observers had noted that across the Piedmont region—the low rolling hills that lie between the rocky Appalachians and the sandy coastal tidelands—chestnut trees were dying. So were the trees' shrubby kin, the chinquapins. This "death wave," as one scientist called it, had gradually encompassed the lowlands of Maryland, the Carolinas, Tennessee, Alabama, and Georgia. In the years after the Civil War, some southerners thought the disease killing the trees was one that returning soldiers had picked up in the Yankee prisons up north.

In fact, the culprit was another destructive fungus—a water mold identified decades later as *Phytophthora cinnamomi,* a vexsome member of a large family of parasites. A closely related *Phytophthora* had long afflicted European chestnuts. Europeans called the pestilence "ink disease," after the midnight-blue ooze that stained the soil close to the roots of an affected tree. Like the blight, *Phytophthora cinnamomi* was not native to the American landscape. It likely arrived in the United States in the 1840s or earlier, possibly via trading ships operating between America's southern ports and the East Indies or Asia. It may well have been carried on exotic plants imported for the gardens of antebellum estates. If ever a tree suffered for the whims of botanical taste, it is the American chestnut.

Phytophthora is, in some ways, even more destructive than the blight. While the blight fungus kills the trunk and branches of a chestnut, it does not destroy the tree's remarkably resilient root systems. A blight-stricken tree can continue to resprout from its root collar for years, though as the sprouts near maturity, the fungus reasserts itself and strikes them down again. The root system will eventually wear out, but it takes repeated cycles of struggle. *Phytophthora cinnamomi,* however, goes straight for that regenerative root tissue, knocking out the species' ace in the hole for ensuring survival. When the root rot attacks, the tree's death is swift and final.

Over the course of the nineteenth century, *Phytophthora cinnamomi* significantly shrank the southern range of the American chestnut. But because *Phytophthora* prefers low elevations, it never reached the heart of chestnut country, the rugged, thin-skinned slopes of the southern Appalachians. By the early twentieth century, the tree was mostly gone from the lowlands, but in the highlands, where dense stands of chestnut still flourished, the tree was gaining in importance. The trade in chestnut timber and nuts was booming. Even as the people of the Piedmont were growing accustomed to a landscape without chestnuts, people of the mountains were lashing their livelihoods ever more tightly to their perfect tree.

It's impossible to pinpoint exactly when the blight reached the Blue Ridge. It was surely present there by the late teens, when every man between the ages of eighteen and forty-five was being inducted to fight in World War I. By that time, however, the general public had begun to lose interest in the chestnut's epic struggle. The tree's battle disappeared from the headlines as the front pages filled with news of more pressing battles in Ypres, Verdun, and Somme. The significance of a pandemic pathogen killing millions of trees also paled in comparison to a pandemic influenza killing millions of people around the world. Gravatt's work on the chestnut was interrupted by the war; he joined the navy and served in a naval hospital in France. When he returned to the region, he found that the blight had made significant progress during his absence; by 1925, the front line of the blight was deep in North Carolina and sweeping south and west at the rate of about twenty-four miles a year—light speed for a microorganism.

Even then, it was hard for the people of Appalachia to appreciate what was happening to their forests. Gravatt wrote, "When from a mountain top one looks over thousands of acres of vigorous chestnut, it is indeed hard to believe that within a few years the view will be changed to one of dead and dying trees." Anyone curious for a glimpse of that mournful future needed only to look at the impact of the blight in the tree's northern range. In New Jersey, government experts seeking chestnuts turned up only about twenty living trees, and all those were infected. In Connecticut, once known as "the Chestnut State," the trees had become so scarce that when scientists at the Agricultural Experiment Station in Hamden needed a peck of nuts, they had to get them from North Carolina. Pennsylvania was forced to bid farewell to the nation's oldest and largest chestnut—a tree seventy feet tall and thirty-four-and-a-half feet around—which had become so ill it was beyond salvage. It took 330 sticks of dynamite to demolish the three-hundred-year-old colossus. The explosion left a crater ten feet deep and twenty-five feet wide.

Newspapers and magazines were now publishing elegies to the vanished trees. "Good Bye, Chestnuts," grieved one 1923 article in *American Forests*. "What was formerly a majestic, soul-inspiring landmark is now but a rotting stump. No more are they seen on Main Street; no longer do they stand in battalions in the forests. They are as few as the veterans of the Civil War and just as decrepit." An editorial in the *Los Angeles Times* wistfully asked, "Will eating chestnuts by crackling log fires become one of the lost arts preserved by a devoted people only in poetry and romance?"

The blight reached Patrick County in the mid-1920s. Early McAlexander was about thirteen years old when it hit his family's "chestnut orchard," a grove of a dozen or so wild chestnut trees bordering his father's land near the crest of the Blue Ridge Mountains. The trees were heavier with nuts than anyone had ever seen. They must have been sick already; like the dying movie hero who rallies to choke out a few last vital words, blight-stricken chestnuts often have a last burst of productive energy before succumbing to the disease. "I remember Mama even took us into the woods to pick up chestnuts that year," Early recalls. It was the last time the trees put out a good crop of nuts.

The Appalachian chestnuts seemed to sicken and die more rapidly than the ones in the Northeast. Gravatt noticed the difference, though he had no explanation for it. Certainly the disease was spreading faster, a fact likely due to the dynamics of disease development. Infectious diseases spread exponentially. By now, there were so many spores swirling around the forests and so many infected trees that the blight had reached the point of explosive growth. Whole ridgelines died in a single season. As one Georgia man put it, "You could just almost see [the trees] a'dyin' they died so fast."

Within a few years, the hillsides of Patrick County were filled with the silvery skeletons of dead trees—"gray ghosts," people called the standing snags. It could be years before a carcass finally toppled. And when the trees fell, their mourners heard it. "Quite often as we sat on our porch in the cool of the evening, we could hear a heart rendering [*sic*] 'thud' and know that another giant had severed its final root connection to Mother Earth," one North Carolina man recalled. In the wake of the blight, some areas looked as if a hurricane had swept through. One man passing through the Blue Ridge Mountains in central Virginia in 1926 came across what he described as a two-mile "graveyard of giant trees": "All the trees had been uprooted and lay on the ground. The rains and the snow had washed away the dead bark and bleached the trunks a grayish white. No underbrush of any sort grew there. The area was as free from tree growth as are some of the western plains."

It took about twenty-five years for the fungus to complete its rout of the southern Appalachians, an area covering thirty-three million acres. The protracted crisis was the biggest the fledgling U.S. Forest Service had faced to date. The unprecedented death of so many trees prompted worries about the increased risk of forest fires in the region, as well as concerns about the future health of the forests. But the top question occupying forestry experts was a practical one: how to minimize the financial impact of the loss of millions of trees. A good portion of the timber was inaccessible, beyond the reach of existing rail lines or roads. But there was still an estimated fifteen billion board feet available for salvage. Professional forestry journals filled with detailed analyses of such issues as the rate of sapwood decay and heartwood shrinkage as lumbermen tried to determine what kind of value they could get from the ever-diminishing stands of chestnut.*

Now working for the USDA, Gravatt wrote bulletin after bulletin throughout the 1920s and 1930s urging owners to cut their chestnut trees before they became too deteriorated to use. If cut within a year or so of death, blighted trees could be harvested for utility poles, which brought the best price. It was also possible to produce lumber from standing chestnuts for up to ten years after the tree died. The trees could be used for their tannins even longer. Though tannin extraction was the least profitable use, it proved the most long-lasting, ensuring that chestnuts remained nearly as valuable in death as they had been in life. Extract plants like the Champion Fibre Company were still cutting chestnuts for pulp and tannin twenty years after the blight had blown through North Carolina. An old photograph of the company's plant in Canton, North Carolina, shows a vast field filled with stacks of chestnut cordwood stretching as far as the eye can see.

The extract companies had by now found ways to glean tannin from

---

*One of the problems was that trees smitten by the blight were avidly consumed by the larvae of the chestnut timber borer beetle. The larvae gnawed tunnels through the wood of standing trees, leaving the timber riddled with tiny holes. In the era before World War II, that wood, known as "wormy chestnut," was considered defective and nearly worthless. These days it's highly prized and pricy, valued by antique wood aficionados as a handsome wood for interior trim, flooring, furniture, and picture frames.

every part of the tree, not just the bark. That innovation, coupled with the deluge of raw material, invigorated the region's tanning industry: by 1930 there were twenty-one plants in the southern Appalachians producing half of America's supply of vegetable-based tannins. Most of it was shipped north, where it was used for the production of heavy leathers for shoe soles, belts, and harnesses. Champion's operation hummed along until 1951, when the company finally announced it was closing its extract department "due to the depletion of the supply of chestnut wood." By that time, synthetic materials had largely replaced organic tannins and the industry as a whole was on the wane.

Throughout the blight's lengthy killing spree, forestry experts debated the best way to stretch out the supply of chestnut for as long as possible. Some urged the chestnut-using industries to adopt systematic logging plans and take wood only from blighted areas, refraining from cutting uninfected trees until it was absolutely necessary. Others saw no reason for such restraint. In 1926, the director of the U.S. Forest Service's Appalachian Forest Experiment Station told the region's loggers, "The best thing to be done is to chop down the good remaining chestnut trees, worth millions of dollars, use them up and permit nature to grow other kinds of trees in their places."

Unfortunately, his was the advice generally followed. It helped seal the species' fate.

In any outbreak of an infectious disease, some individuals are less susceptible than others. Not everyone exposed to the Black Death in fifteenth-century Europe died. About half of the Aztecs survived the smallpox outbreak that devastated their nation (only to be done in afterward by Cortez). Something in the genetic constitution of such survivors enabled them to fight off the deadly microbes. Likewise, the population of American chestnuts was not uniformly susceptible to the blight. Some trees had no defenses against *Cryphonectria parasitica* and crumpled at the first attack. Others were able to muster a partial defense and struggle on as invalids for a number of years before finally surrendering. And there were others, some unknown small percentage, that had the innate capacity to fight the fungus to a draw. Some whisper of moxie in their DNA that allowed these trees to mount the kinds of defenses their Asian cousins successfully deployed. They could form tough callus tissue at the edges of a canker to block the invading mycelial wedge.

Perhaps such extraordinary native trees could have been used to seed a new population of American chestnuts that would be able to withstand the blight. A handful of scientists at the time hoped as much and issued public appeals for reports of blight-resistant trees. The leader of a New Jersey Boy Scout troop responded with the report that his scouts had found one such tree in the Ramapo Plateau, the *New York Times* reported in September 1926: "His Scouts, with admirable self denial, obeyed orders not to eat one of the nuts, but saved every one, and some were planted nearby . . . and the others turned over to the Brooklyn Botanic Garden for distribution to experiment stations."

Yet today there are only a few hundred "survivors"—mature trees that have endured the blight—in the entire chestnut range. How many more might there have been? There's no way of knowing. At the height of the pandemic, the prevailing attitude was that any chestnut was a dead chestnut—or soon would be. The U.S. Forest Service urged lumbermen to cut, and they did—indiscriminately.

By mid-century, the blight had reached the southern limit of the chestnut's natural range. Chestnuts in Alabama, Mississippi, and northern Georgia were under attack. The microscopic Sherman's March had gone about as far as it could go, at least on the East Coast. (With the aid of migrating birds, traveling humans, and careless nursery shipments and importations, the fungus found a way to leapfrog beyond the chestnut's native range and hunt out plantings of the tree as far west as California and British Columbia.) A map produced by Gravatt in 1943 showed the scope of the pandemic: a long ellipse stretching nearly the full length of the Atlantic seaboard. Within that ellipse, 50 to 99 percent of the chestnuts were dead. The casualties included young second- and third-growth trees, as well as ancients that had witnessed the first Europeans' arrival on this continent.

All told, it is estimated the blight killed between three and four billion trees. Three to four billion. Enough trees to fill nine million acres. Enough trees to cover Yellowstone National Park eighteen hundred times over. Enough trees to give two to every person on the planet at that time.

"You just can't imagine how much it changed the looks of the mountains when the chestnut timber all died," one Georgia man later recalled. "It left great patches that just looked bare." Foresters worried about whether those patches would fill in, and if so, whether the replacement trees would be as valuable as the chestnut had been. In one sense, they needn't have worried. Chestnut had always shared its dominion with oaks, and when the chestnut trees tumbled, various members of the oak family rushed in to fill the void, accompanied by a variety of other trees depending on the location. New England forests repopulated with red maple, northern red oak, and chestnut oak. In Pennsylvania, black cherry and hickory trees spread their branches as well. In the southern Appalachian forests, the main successors were oaks and hickories, which until then had been a bit player in most of the region's forests. (Oak's ascension to dominance was not an entirely beneficial change in the eastern forests. Now, decades later, large swaths of woods contain an unnatural concentration of same-aged oak trees. Coupled with various other factors, this phenomenon has contributed to a widespread affliction known as oak decline that now plagues the trees.)

The loss changed not only the look of the mountains but also the quality of life on them. The dependable downpour of sweet nuts each fall had sustained all manner of wildlife, from chipmunks to bears.

Oaks and hickories also produce mast—the scientific term for the accumulation of nuts and seeds on the forest floor—but not anywhere near as prolifically or reliably as did chestnuts. Researchers who compared the amount of mast in western North Carolina forests in the 1930s and the 1960s found it had dropped, on average, by about 34 percent. The mountain residents who for generations hunted those forests didn't need studies to tell them how things had changed. "W'y y'know the worst thing ever happened to this country's when the chestnut trees died. Turkeys got scarce, an' the squirrels are not there one-tenth as many as they was before," said Walter Cole, who spent his life in the Great Smoky Mountains community of Sugarlands. Others complained that raccoons, black bear, and white-tailed deer were increasingly hard to find. "We've never had a honey crop like we did since the chestnuts died," one Georgia native recalled in a 1980 interview. "There's not that much nectar in the wild now."

Though the blight gets blamed for the loss of wildlife in the mountains, in fact it's hard to separate out its effect from the impact of habitat lost to logging, development, or pollution. Some experts believe the dearth of chestnuts has hindered efforts to restore various animals to the Appalachians, including goshawks, Cooper's hawks, cougars and bobcats. The creatures thought to have been most severely threatened by the chestnut's demise are seven species of moths, all of which fed exclusively on *Castanea dentata*. But whether the moths are actually extinct has never been documented. Just as the population of forest trees adjusted to the absence of chestnut, so, it appears, have some wildlife. White-tailed deer have rebounded to the point of becoming a common pest. Wild turkeys have flourished after being reintroduced to many parts of the region.

Perhaps the beings most profoundly affected by the American chestnut's demise were the people who shared the mountains with the tree: the self-sufficient farmers who counted chestnuts as an essential ally in their struggle to scrape together a living. Chestnuts had been one of the most important sources of cash for mountain farmers. The blight not only brought an end to the nut trade, but also diminished the farmers' ability to raise and sell hogs, another vital source of income. Few could afford to grow or purchase feed, which is why for generations they'd depended on forest forage to fatten their livestock. "We didn't have no other way of bringing in nothing when the blight hit," one Patrick County man recalled. The collapse of the chestnut economy was "a right smart little jolt to a lot of people," said Walter Thomas Dudley Hopkins, another county resident. It was more than that to Joe Tribble, who grew up in eastern Kentucky: "Man, I had the awfulest feeling about that as a child to look back yonder and see those trees dying. I thought the whole world was going to die."

In many ways, his whole world did die, though it wasn't the chestnut blight that extinguished it. The blight coincided with a number of developments that together spelled the end of the independent subsistence farms that once defined the mountain communities—waves of change that were no more stoppable than the terrible chestnut pandemic. World War I. The Great Depression. Urbanization. The arrival of textile and furniture plants. The expansion of coal mines.

The tides of change pulled the youth from the highland communities. Patrick County's population dropped during the 1920s as sons and daughters of mountain families left to make their way in the towns and cities below. The years following World War II saw another wave of out-migration. Early McAlexander, for instance, left Meadows of Dan in the 1940s to work at the DuPont plant in Richmond, though it never really felt like home. During the mandatory physical exam, the company doctor wrote across his file "Mountain Man." That kind of prejudice was common. The migrants from the mountains were often scorned as hillbillies—and worse. A popular theory at the time held that shortcomings such as alcoholism, criminal behavior, mental illness, and mental retardation were inherited, leading Virginia to establish a eugenics program to do away with such problems. Not surprisingly, many of its targets were poor. Between 1924 and 1979, the state forcibly sterilized about 7,450 people, many of them impoverished mountain dwellers.

Though Early remained in Richmond for more than thirty years, as soon as he retired, he and his wife returned to Patrick County. There he built a home not far from the log cabin where he was raised. "You can get the boy out of the mountain, but you couldn't get the mountain out of the boy," Early explains. But the mountain of his boyhood was a much-changed place. By the time he returned, most of the family farm had already been sold; Early and his siblings eventually sold what was left. In the years since, the county has become even less like the place where he grew up.

Though Patrick County is still a rural area, the land now serves more as a scenic backdrop than as a vital part of people's lives. Cornfields and pastures still cover the rolling hills, but a mere 2 percent of residents now make their living from farming. The dairy farm that sits right next to the Meadows of Dan Elementary School is one of only two left in the county. Cell phone towers spike the high elevations, two-lane paved roads connect every corner of the county, and even the most remote hollows carry street signs. The old country stores are mostly shuttered or torn down; the old barter economy is long gone. "You can't even sell a egg out here at these stores now," grumbled an elderly county resident in a 1981 oral history. The county's small stores and businesses fear they are headed the same way as the old general stores now that a Wal-Mart superstore has opened in Stuart.

It is like any rural corner of America, full of distinctive vestiges of its regional past as well as the homogenizing influences of the present-day national and global economies. Past and present sandwiched in layers, like the furniture veneers the county once produced. In Stuart's compact downtown, there's the old-style country diner, The Coffee Break, "home of the Country Boy Specials," whose walls are decorated with NASCAR photos; two doors down, a café selling organically grown Honduran coffee was established a few years ago by a couple from the Midwest. "Every now and then," says the owner, "we get a convert." The big chain grocery store in Stuart sells traditional staples like pinto beans and fatback, but also stocks tofu and California chardonnays.

Folks think nothing of driving fifty miles to see a movie or to shop at the mall in Martinsville. Many Patrick County residents—"more than we'd like," admits county administrator Regena Handy—leave the county each day for their jobs.

Flip through the phone book and you'll find the same family names that have been linked with Patrick County for more than a century, though often as not, the only members of the clan left here are elderly. And the directory is filling with new names—wealthy retirees or city dwellers who want a rustic vacation home. The log cabins that once were an embarrassment to aspiring mountain families now fetch high prices. And new log cabins have risen on the hills, slightly garish, with their buttery-yellow, unweathered walls. The rising property values and scarcity of jobs make it hard for the children of longtime locals to remain in the area. "Everybody wants to stay here, but if they stay here, there aren't many ways of making a living," says Ruth Jean Bolt, a retired schoolteacher who still lives in the house in Meadows of Dan where she was raised. "So they have to leave. But in the back of their mind, [they think,] 'I'm coming back.'"

One of the best views in Patrick County is from a place called Lover's Leap, a spot more than three thousand feet above sea level where, local lore has it, a young Indian maiden jumped to her death after being forbidden to marry the man she loved. Now it's a designated scenic vista. Standing there, I look out over a panoramic view of farm fields and woods stretching for miles over a series of ridges. There are more forests now than farms, as the trees creep out to reclaim abandoned cornfields. Looking at that thick, rich blanket of green, you'd be hard-pressed to say that the land misses the chestnut.

And yet the people of that land have never stopped missing the tree. Even now, decades after the blight completed its rampage, folks are faithful in their love. "I know where there's a chestnut," retired trucker

Barry Price tells me when we meet for coffee at the Hardee's in Stuart. He speaks in an accent so thick that the words sound like marbles rolling around in his mouth. Even his siblings, he admits, have trouble understanding him. He's a tall, heavy-set chain smoker, and on this day he wears a T-shirt that reads on the back, "There's a place for all God's creatures—right next to the potatoes and gravy." He's fifty-three but looks years older, thanks to the heart attack that derailed his career as a tombstone carver and the stroke that cut short his second career as a long-distance trucker. He no longer works. Though he now lives in southern Patrick County, he was raised up the mountain on a farm in the small hamlet of Woolwine. One of the most pleasurable memories of his childhood was traipsing through the forests with his grandfather in search of the occasional surviving chestnut tree: "We'd find a tree in the woods and go out and doctor them. It didn't do much." They tried crossing American and Chinese chestnut trees "to make 'em blight-proof. It wouldn't never work. They'd grow pretty big and then get a size and start busting and cracking open."

When he drove trucks, and even now just tooling around the county, he always keeps his eyes peeled for American chestnuts. That's how he spotted the tree he wants to show me. We head south out of town and then pull over by the back fence of a huge lumber yard, stacked high with planks of the poplar, white pine, and oak that now are harvested from the area's forests. Price points out the chestnut tree. It's a sad-looking thing, little more than an upright mass of dried and withered sticks. There are a few burs on the branches, remnants of the previous fall, but Price has checked and found that they are invariably empty. Even if the tree can't "barr" nuts, as he puts it, he likes knowing that it is still there.

It's certainly not the only chestnut tree left in Patrick County. The forests here—and across the tree's old range—are full of puny sprouts tenaciously rising from the remains of fallen trees. There are tens of millions across the species' native range. Such a plethora of sprouts means the American chestnut can't be listed as an endangered species. Yet in a functional sense, it is, for few sprouts are any more productive than Price's dying tree. The blight is as tenacious as its host, destroying most of the saplings before they become mature enough to blossom and reproduce. As long as the duel continues, *Castanea dentata* remains stuck in biological limbo—unable to advance itself, unwilling to die out, a species that is vanquished but refuses to disappear.

The scrappy sprouts are a vastly diminished version of the tree's former self, but that former self is not wholly gone. It persists in the stories and memories of the people who loved the chestnut tree, and like any dearly departed, it grows more magnificent and mythic with every passing year. "The American chestnut is still a living memory around here," says Kathy Newfont, a historian at Mars Hill College in North Carolina who is compiling oral histories about the chestnut tree. After she ran an ad in the local paper requesting people's reminiscences, she says, "my phone rang off the hook."

Newfont is a handsome, thirty-something woman with light brown hair and blue eyes who grew up in the region. "Why do people still care about the chestnut so much?" I ask her over breakfast at the Wagon Wheel diner in Mars Hill. "Some people say they're conflating the chestnut with the preindustrial way of life—that it's an easy symbol," Newfont says as she piles her fork with fried egg and biscuits. "I think elements of that are true. People miss their youth, their way of life, their parents and brothers and sisters. They miss their communities." But she believes that only partly explains the deep well of nostalgia that Appalachia harbors for its iconic tree. There's something else, she says, something powerfully simple at work. "I think for people who had the direct experience of eating the nuts, picking them up, seeing the trees bloom, toasting the nuts—they literally miss that. . . . They literally wish they could taste a chestnut."

The only consolation may be a common belief that began circulating when the chestnuts started to die—something Coy Lee Yeatts repeated when I visited his store. "You know," he told me, "the old-timers used to say that after a hundred years the chestnuts will come back."

Part Two

Out in the forest a chestnut sapling grows . . .

I could be talking here about woods in upstate New York, in western Pennsylvania, near the Chesapeake Bay, or in the Great Smoky Mountains, but the sapling I have in mind lives in the Jefferson National Forest in Virginia, a place with a primeval, magical feel. The woods here are full of towering tulip poplars, birches, and sassafras, as well as thickets of mountain laurel with polished leaves. On this June day, the air is still damp from the rain a few hours before and the foliage is wet and dripping. A thick scrim of green above dims the afternoon light. A thick layer of duff makes the ground springy under my feet.

I veer off the established trail and push into the understory in search of chestnuts. There's a sapling. It's a reedy little thing, maybe fifteen feet tall, three fingers wide, and joyously alive. The stem is a glossy red-brown, the long lance-shaped leaves a vivid deep green. Were there no such thing as chestnut blight, a sapling like this might remain a tough little punk for decades, biding its time until a break in the canopy blesses it with the sunlight it needs to shoot for the sky. Chestnuts can wait in the understory for decades for the right opportunity. This stem, however, like nearly all the American chestnut trees to be found today, is probably the second or third incarnation of a tree, a growth from roots that surely spawned previous generations of chestnut. Such resilience makes the chestnut supremely equipped for long-term survival.

Yet its foe, *Cryphonectria parasitica*, is also tooled for the long haul. In the absence of chestnut trees to wage war on, the fungus pulls back to a quiet state of readiness. The spores attach themselves to the bark of scarlet oak, post oak, maples, hickory, sumac, and perhaps other trees— no one is quite sure of all their refuges—and retreat for years, even decades, into dormancy, as spectators to other forest dramas. When the chestnut root marshals the resources to send another sapling skyward, the spores attack again.

In the 1920s, when the first wave of saplings began sprouting from the root collars of blight-destroyed trees, there was a brief round of hurrahs. A writer in the *New York Times* cheered to see how "the intelligence of the chestnut tree . . . struggles hard against obliteration." But optimistic predictions that the tree had found a way to outwit the blight soon faded as the sprouts succumbed. It was clear, then, that the only way the chestnut could ever win its long-running duel was through human intervention.

Love for the tree has gone a long way toward keeping its prospects alive. For decades, a succession of dedicated scientists have pursued the quixotic goal of saving the American chestnut, a dream sustained by the millions of sprouts that keep rising to life and the few hundred mature trees that keep hanging on to life. In these aspiring saplings and venerable patriarchs, chestnut devotees see a glimpse of the forests that once were, and once again may be.

Scientists' efforts have followed, more or less, two broad strategies: trying to fix the tree so it can withstand the fungus, or trying to fix the fungus so it can't hurt the tree. Since the earliest days of the blight, breeders have struggled to develop a blight-resistant chestnut tree. In the mid-twentieth century, a new avenue opened when scientists discovered that the blight might be undone by its own naturally occurring enemy. More recently, researchers have pinned their hopes on the promise of biotechnology.

Despite repeated setbacks, would-be rescuers of the tree say they are closer to their goal than ever before. Yet with every passing year, fewer sprouts rebound and more old veterans succumb. The fight to save the chestnut has drawn strength from the tree's tenacious grip on a landscape that may already have passed it by. The drama is being played out in real time and seems to be nearing the final act. Can the species hang in long enough for deliverance?

FIVE

Rolling the Dice

I've got a handful of chestnuts scattered on the desk in front of me. They come from well beyond the American chestnut's native range. I scooped them up while walking through an orchard of various chestnut varieties in southeastern Minnesota. These nuts are a pack of mutts, their lineage a jumble of Asian, European, and American chestnut species. Looking them over, I am struck, as always, by the beauty of *Castanea* seeds. I love the rich mahogany hue, the glossy surface that begs to be touched, the pleasingly roundish shape that tapers at one end in a pucker as dainty as a baby's kiss. I like picking each up and holding it in the crook of my index finger so I can rub my thumb across the shell, working it like a worry stone.

In a Platonic sense, each is a fine representative of the essence of a chestnut. Yet looking closer, I also see how different each nut is. One is darker brown than the rest, with black meridians running its length. Another's shell is a rich palette of red-browns that glow like strands of hair caught in the sunlight. Yet another is dull, with patches of gray-green fuzz. This one is plump all the way around; that one has an underside as flat as a supermodel's belly. I know that were I to crack each open they would likely taste different. The most American of the bunch would have a sweet carroty taste if eaten raw, while those heavy on European or Japanese ancestry would be bland or even bitter. The variety in this group of nuts isn't simply due to the fact that they are mongrels. I've seen the same subtle differences when sorting through the pound or two of Italian chestnuts I buy each year at Thanksgiving to stuff my turkey, or when I sift through a precious pocketful of American chestnuts I picked up in a rare grove of trees in Wisconsin.

Truly, each chestnut is its own nut, utterly individual, as the progeny of any sexual union must be. Each is the product of a unique genetic combination, as well as a repository of countless other possibilities. Buried within the tight coils of each nut's DNA are not only the instructions for this one tree to be, but a warehouse of blueprints for past generations, as well as potential generations to come. Therein lies the breeder's dilemma, whether the goal is a beefier cow, a blue-ribbon poodle, or a blight-resistant chestnut tree. How do you coax forth just the right mix of desirable genes while sending unwanted ones to the back of the closet?

If you're after a trait determined by a single gene, that's not so problematic, as Gregor Mendel famously showed with his sweet pea experiments. When Mendel crossed plants that bore yellow peas with those that bore green peas, the first generation of offspring, the so-called F1s, were all yellow, since yellow is what he called a "dominating" trait. But in the next generation, the F2s, green peas reappeared, making up a quarter of the group. Over thousands of crosses, Mendel discovered a distinct and reliable inheritance pattern: a three-to-one ratio of yellow to green, or what we would now call dominant to recessive traits.

Mendel was lucky. He happened to test traits with simple genetics, traits that are controlled by a single gene which takes either a dominant or recessive form, or allele, and which are transmitted independently of one another. How much more difficult it would have been to distill rules of inheritance had he happened to focus on traits like hair color or blood type, which are controlled by multiple genes or by genes that are linked to one another. Consider a trait determined by two genes, such as the color of wheat kernels. Now the possibilities multiply, and for every cross, every roll of the genetic dice, there is, on average, a one-in-sixteen chance of getting a given outcome at the F_2 generation. If three genes determine the expression of the trait, the probabilities stack up even higher: one in sixty-four. And the ratios rise by a factor of four with every additional gene: for four genes, one in 256; for five, one in 1,024, and so forth.

Given those odds, trying to breed for a specific trait that's controlled by several genes would seem to be as much a long shot as trying to get rich through a game of craps.

"Is plant breeding really so . . . dicey?" I ask Greg Miller, a veteran chestnut breeder and owner of the Empire Chestnut Company in Carrollton, Ohio.

"To some extent," he says. "But we try to load the dice as much as we can." When it comes to plant or animal breeding, he explains, loading the dice depends on three things. The first is choosing the "base population," the groups you want to combine. "It's really important to pick a good base population," one that strongly expresses the trait you are seeking. Next, you arrange your matches, choosing which two individuals you want to join in marriage. And last is "selection," picking out which progeny of the arranged match come closest to embodying the traits you are seeking. The success of any breeding program, Miller says, depends on making the right choices at each of those steps. There are many ways to improve the rightness of those choices and boost the odds of getting what you want. That's where the science, and art, of breeding come in.

Over the centuries, farmers and agricultural experts have perfected breeding of flowers and grains like corn. But breeding trees, especially forest trees, is a newer science, and in many ways, a much more complicated one. A corn grower will know in a season or two how a given cross may work. A tree breeder has to wait years, even decades, for the results to become clear. As a result, says Miller, "the rule of thumb in tree breeding is you never know the best way of doing it until it is done."

Fans of the American chestnut lost decades of precious time learning that lesson the hard way.

Arthur Graves was one of the earliest and most dogged of the scientists who became caught up in the crusade to save the chestnut tree. Born in 1880, Graves was a tall and courtly Yale University–trained botanist who began his professional career just about the time the chestnut blight was making headlines. Graves spent months in 1911 touring Massachusetts by motorcycle to survey the extent of blight damage there and then made his way to the Pennsylvania Chestnut Tree Blight Commission conference in Harrisburg in 1912 to eagerly back Pennsylvania's effort to thwart the fungus's spread. By 1914, when it had become clear that neither axes nor chemicals nor any other weapons would suffice to stop the canny parasite, Graves began arguing that the only solution was to "outwit" it by "producing a kind of chestnut tree that the parasite didn't like."

How? Graves had an idea. He knew that both Japanese and Chinese chestnuts were relatively unaffected by the blight. He also knew that an enterprising breeder in Washington, D.C., named Walter Van Fleet had been crossing American chestnuts with other members of the *Castanea* clan until the blight brought a "summary termination," as Van Fleet put it, to his experiments. In theory, different species should resist interbreeding, but Van Fleet had established that, in fact, the various species of chestnut were quite amenable to pairing up.

Van Fleet's goals had been horticultural—he was seeking new and improved orchard trees that would yield better varieties of nuts. But now in the wake of the blight, Graves was convinced the same strategy of crossing blight-resistant Asian species with the vulnerable American chestnuts could be used to create a new and improved forest tree. "The most hopeful indications for chestnut in North America in the future lie along the lines of breeding experiments," Graves wrote in 1914.

Although the work may be "slow in yielding results, [it] may eventually prove to be the only means of continuing the existence in our land of a greatly esteemed tree."

Strong as his convictions were, it was another fifteen years before Graves got around to acting on them. By that time, he was working as curator for public instruction at the Brooklyn Botanic Garden and living in New York. But he had a summer home sitting in the middle of an expansive woods in Hamden, Connecticut—land that he had bought with a fellow graduate student while both were still at Yale. The land was situated on the south side of a hilly formation known as Sleeping Giant because of its shape. It was a perfect place to start breeding hybrid trees. Over time, Graves filled the site with the biggest and most diverse collection of chestnuts in the country, if not the world.

Graves made his first controlled cross in 1931, employing much the same methods that are in use today. Like many trees, chestnuts bear both male and female flowers. Yet nature has guarded against inbreeding by seeing to it they are self-sterile; a chestnut does not readily self-pollinate (nor can a clone or graft be successfully mated with its parent tree). To play matchmaker, therefore, a person must mimic the delicate choreography by which the wind or insects carry the minute yellow grains of pollen from one tree to another. After choosing a mother and father tree, Graves would carefully wrap a paper bag ("common grocer's bags, size 10 or 12") around the female flowers from the selected mother tree before they were fertile to guard against pollination from other sources. Once the flowers were ready, he'd unbag them, take a long bushy catkin of male flowers from the father tree—which, thanks to the blessing of airmail, could be located anywhere—and gently draw it several times across the mother tree's tiny, pineapple-shaped female blossoms in a motion like a violinist playing adagio. Then he would rebag the flowers for a few weeks to safeguard the sanctity of the union. The budding nuts would be bagged again in September to protect them from "squirrel marauders."

For those first crosses, Graves picked an American chestnut near Washington, D.C., as the father tree and Japanese chestnuts growing on Long Island, New York, as the mother trees. He planted the resulting nuts that autumn on his land at Sleeping Giant. The trees that sprouted seemed promising at first, growing fast and erect like their American parent. But it soon became clear they lacked their Japanese parent's blight-fighting mettle. Graves would become all too familiar with such disappointments.

Over the next thirty-plus years, he crossed American, Japanese, and Chinese chestnuts, as well as native and Asian chinquapins, in scores of different combinations—more than 250 in all. He even tried crossing native chestnuts with a species outside the immediate family, a chestnut oak. "He knew as well as anybody that success would mean a shrieking genetic miracle," one reporter wrote. "But oak and chestnut are related, and why not tempt a miracle with the chance to happen." The miracle never arrived. Graves wasn't the most meticulous of breeders: if he ran out of pollen from one tree, he'd simply apply some from another. By 1960, he had thousands of trees growing at Sleeping Giant and other test plots and had harvested more than twenty thousand hybrid nuts.

The woods around Sleeping Giant were scattered with stumps of American chestnuts that sprouted saplings that were then over and over consumed in the fiery tracks of *Cryphonectria parasitica*. The blight's persistent presence in the area provided an ongoing test of the success of Graves's crosses and, perhaps, a continuing reminder of the urgency of his mission. With the blight pandemic still unchecked, the number of surviving mature trees or flowering sprouts was diminishing with every passing year.

Graves kept throwing the dice, confident that eventually they'd land in that righteous combination needed for the ideal tree: a soaring, hardy forest king that would brook no challenge from a lowly parasite. It wouldn't be the same old American chestnut tree, he admitted, but it could be a close facsimile. An American-ish chestnut tree. All he needed was one perfect roll of the dice. With one perfect tree he could propagate a forest of perfect trees, using grafts in the same way apple growers clone a desirable tree.

Yet, decade after decade, the dice tumbled every which way except the way that Graves wanted. This tree was too short. This one couldn't hack the cold Connecticut winters. This tree grew fast, but succumbed to the blight. His efforts were stymied by a basic problem: Japanese and Chinese chestnuts not only look different from their American cousins, they also grow very differently. They tend to be shorter and shrubbier and less tolerant of the cold than American chestnuts. Blight resistance required Asian genes, yet Asian genes also led to a chestnut that was far removed from the tough, tall classic timber tree that people wanted to bring back. To get the former meant losing the latter, as Graves kept finding over and over again.

In retrospect, Graves's quest seems almost absurdly far-fetched. Yet genetics was still an infant science; Mendel's laws had only been redis-covered in 1905. (Though the Austrian monk had presented his findings in 1865, they languished in obscurity until scientists rediscovered them forty years later.) Breeding chestnuts, or any kind of forest tree for that matter, was a new proposition. No one yet had any way of knowing just what the genetics of a trait like blight resistance entailed—whether it was a single- or multiple-gene trait or one linked to other characteristics such as the tree's height or form. It would take decades of breeding expe-rience for scientists to discern that blight-resistant trees owed their good fortune to at least two genes, and more likely, three or more. The more genes involved, the more trees a breeder has to create to hit the jackpot; certainly, it would take many, many thousands more than Graves had the time or space to grow. Graves himself was aware of the need to plant more trees, and in 1940 he began seeking "cooperators"—other people or institutions who shared his passion for the tree and who would be willing to plant hybrids on their land.

Despite the repeated setbacks, Graves's enthusiasm for the project never faltered. Year after year, he filed dispatches from the field report-ing on another hybrid "new to science." He'd describe each in lovingly rich language that reflected his appreciation for nature's stupendously varied palette. The Essate-Jap was "reddish to Kaiser brown." The Kelsey had "burnt sienna bark" and twigs of "light mineral grey." The young Hamden's bark was a tint "somewhere between buckthorn brown and Dresden brown."

"He never had a shadow of a doubt about the fact that he was going to bring back the chestnut," recalls Richard Jaynes, a botanist who from 1961 to 1984 worked on chestnut breeding at the Connecticut Agricultural Experiment Station, where Graves became an advisor after he retired from the Brooklyn Botanic Garden. By then Graves was an old man, yet his step was still firm, his posture straight. Each day until his death in 1962, he'd don jacket and hat and make his way to the chestnut plantation. "He was still climbing ladders and making crosses into his eighties," says Jaynes. By that time his wife, Helen—his third; he'd outlived the other two—insisted on accompanying him. She wouldn't let him climb ladders unless she was there. She'd drive the couple's Buick from their home in nearby Wallingford to the plantation and sit in the car reading while the elderly botanist worked amongst his trees.

Graves was not alone in his efforts. A parallel effort was also under way at the USDA. In 1927, the department sent plant explorer R. Kent Beattie to scour Japan, Korea, China, and Formosa (as Taiwan was then called) for promising chestnut trees. Beattie sent back 250 bushels of nuts—a wealth of genetic material with which USDA scientists hoped to either "replace our vanishing chestnut" or restore it through crossbreeding. The department distributed tens of thousands of the Chinese and Japanese seedlings to federal and state agencies and private cooperators in an effort to determine which, if any, of the Asian species would do best in their new home. Initially, few survived, falling victim to rabbits, deer, drought, fire, farm animals, or simply poor location. Still, the experiments showed that at least a few varieties of Chinese chestnut might provide a good replacement tree, having strong resistance to the blight as well as fat, tasty nuts that would feed both wildlife and people. (Chinese chestnuts assumed even greater importance during World War II, when hostilities brought an end to the importation of Italian nuts, which until then had amounted to sixteen million pounds a year.) The USDA vigorously campaigned for foresters, woodlot owners, tannery companies, county extension agents, rod and gun clubs, nurseries, and homeowners—truly anyone who might be remotely interested— to plant Chinese chestnuts. Even now you can drive through the southern Appalachians and find vestiges of that campaign in overgrown groves of Chinese chestnuts in the forest or a stately Chinese chestnut on someone's front lawn.

Even as the USDA was promoting Chinese chestnuts as a replacement for the native trees, its scientists were trying to create new Asian-American hybrids, often in collaboration with Graves. The agency's breeding program was run by a succession of dedicated optimists—Van Fleet, Flippo Gravatt, Russell Clapper, Fred Berry, and Jesse Diller. Each was convinced that with enough perseverance the genetic dice would fall just right. Over thirty-five years, the USDA breeders joined chestnuts in every direction, ultimately hitting 40 percent of all the possible combinations of *Castanea* species. They produced some ten thousand hybrids at the agency's experimental farm in Glendale, Maryland. Starting in 1947, Diller began planting promising trees on fifteen different cleared forest plots in thirteen states in an effort to determine which had the right stuff to succeed the American chestnut.

At first, many of the hybrids grew like gangbusters—as hybrids of any type inevitably do. One lot grew so fast, a journalist noted in 1948, that after twelve years they were already big enough for farm poles. "In about twenty-five years," she predicted, "if they maintain resistance, they will be tall enough for telephone poles."

But tree science is a long-term proposition; the evidence takes years, even decades, to accrue. As one chestnut researcher recently explained to me, "How tall is a tree going to grow? Well, you don't know the answer until it stops growing." After a few decades, the hybrids stopped growing. Unfortunately, most were only fifty to sixty feet tall—far short of the height needed to beat out oaks or poplars or other forest trees in the fierce competition for sunlight. And though many showed signs of blight resistance, they were rarely tough enough, prompting Clapper to begin crossing first-generation Chinese-American hybrids with Chinese trees in the hope that their progeny would be better able to withstand the blight. Unfortunately, these offspring were even less likely to have the vigorous growth and shoot-for-the-sky form of the American tree.

By the time Clapper and Diller tallied the final results of the program in 1969, it was hard to escape the conclusion that it was largely a bust. They found that although some of the hybrids grew as fast as native chestnuts, and some had demonstrated the desired arrow-straight timber form, and some showed blight resistance, few achieved the breeders' trifecta. About 3 percent expressed the trio of desired traits to "some degree," but almost none embodied all three traits perfectly. The government breeders had run into the same catch-22 as Graves: to gain Asian blight resistance seemed to require sacrificing the very American traits they were hoping to save.

By then, both Clapper and Diller had retired. If they felt any disappointment about the results of their life's work, it never made its way into the dry language of their final report. But perhaps they also drew comfort from the fact that amid the tens of thousands of luckless rolls of the dice, one time the die had landed exquisitely right.

In 1946, Clapper paired a Chinese-American hybrid with its American parent. One of the resulting nuts was planted in the agency's orchard in nearby Beltsville. Three years later, Diller moved the hardy young seedling, along with one hundred other chestnut hybrids, to a test plot in a wildlife refuge in southern Illinois. The reserve manager logged it in as B26, a reference to its precise spot in the rows of transplanted hybrids, but among devotees of chestnut restoration, it soon became known as the Clapper tree.

The Clapper tree flourished, pushing straight up like a fist punching the sky. By 1952, Diller had taken note of the fast-growing, comely young tree. When he revisited the refuge in 1959, he was even more excited: the tree was now a thirty-foot-tall column of health and vigor. By 1963, it was unquestionably the best tree at the site: it soared up straight for forty-five feet, with a broad leafy crown and nary a sign of infection, though the baneful blight spores drifted all over the research plot. The U.S. Forest Service issued a press release announcing the news of the wondrous tree to the world. Perhaps here at last was the perfect combination of American and Asian genes. News reports started taking notice. One magazine dubbed the tree the "hopeful forerunner of a great new crop." A local paper offered a poetic tribute, parodying Longfellow's classic poem "Under the Spreading Chestnut Tree": "Under the Clapper's chestnut tree/the refuge turkey stands/A strong and husky bird is he/With hybrids in his glands."

Even though there was no guarantee the Clapper's fine qualities would resurface in its offspring, chestnut lovers around the country began seeking some of its nuts to plant. Roy Owen, an eighty-four-year-old man from Terre Haute, Indiana, wrote the refuge manager in 1973 asking if he could visit the famous tree and if he could have some of its seed so that he might "see some trees growing again on my premises before I leave this world." The refuge manager gladly sent Owen a few dozen nuts. "Today I planted them," Owen wrote back in a letter of thanks. "My friends are mostly gone, and I feel sure that we will never meet in this life, but who knows, maybe there will be a place for people like you and me, who love to work with and see growing things."

"P.S.," he added at the end. "I will write you in the spring about how they went through the winter. If anything should happen to me, my grandson, who is familiar with this, will take over."

At the time, the tree was approaching seventy feet tall and was more than a foot wide. But it had also been struggling with the blight for some five years, and over the next few years it began to lose ground. Its foliage grew thin and it started dropping limbs. By the spring of 1976, the tree was barely able to muster more than a smattering of new leaves. The refuge manager clipped scion wood (buds and stems) from the Clapper's branches and root sprouts so that later breeders could draw from this one-in-a-million gene pool. Sadly, by the fall, the main stem of the mighty tree was dead.

A refuge technician sent news of the death to Russell Clapper's son—apparently the only person he could think of to inform, because by that time, there was no longer anyone at the USDA chasing the chestnut dream. The agency had long since shut down its breeding program—a decision due more to administrative logic than science. When Jesse Diller retired in 1964, there was no one at the USDA who wanted to take his place. The breeding stock and hybrids at the experimental farm in Maryland were all destroyed and the program's records were packed away.

The federal government may have been officially out of the chestnut restoration business, but there were still a handful of scientists willing to gamble on the beloved tree.

One of the oddest efforts was undertaken by Ralph Singleton, a retired University of Virginia plant geneticist who had pioneered the field of seed irradiation, exposing corn kernels to high doses of radiation to induce desirable genetic mutations. In 1955, the organizers of a conference devoted to atomic energy and agriculture invited Singleton to talk about crop irradiation and to "dream a bit." He did. His vision entailed a wholly new strategy for endowing the American chestnut with blight resistance: he proposed irradiating chestnut seeds to accelerate genetic mutations that could correct the species' fatal flaw. He was confident this new technology would restore the old icon. It was the quintessential response to Eisenhower's call for "Atoms for Peace."

Singleton's vision caught the fancy of an Ohio chestnut enthusiast, a chemist named Albert Dietz, who had a hobby of searching out surviving American chestnut trees. After reading about Singleton's idea, Dietz sent him two quarts of American chestnut seeds that he had collected along the Blue Ridge Parkway. Singleton irradiated the seeds in the reactor at the Brookhaven National Laboratory, exposing them to three thousand to five thousand rads (three to five times the whole-body dose that would be fatal for a person). The seeds were planted that spring at a farm in northern Virginia. It was the start of a long collaboration. Dietz energetically combed the country far and wide for surviving chestnuts—his best source was a Wisconsin grove that reportedly got its start from a pocketful of nuts carried home by a Civil War soldier—and collecting nuts which Singleton arranged to have irradiated. To be sure, after exposure to such a high dose of radiation, many of the nuts failed to germinate and many of those that did germinate grew into odd-looking plants. Still, by 1977, Dietz and Singleton had about eighteen thousand viable seedlings planted at a variety of sites, including Dietz's backyard in Wordsworth, Ohio.

In a field devoted to long shots, this was the longest shot of all. There was only a slim chance that high doses of cobalt-60 would randomly induce just the right genetic mutations to secure blight resistance. And even if irradiation did trigger the needed mutations, traits induced in this way were almost invariably recessive. That's not a problem in self-pollinating crops like corn, but chestnuts need a mate. It would take two similarly mutated trees to produce an offspring that was capable of mustering adequate defenses against the blight. "It was just a shot in a million," says Tom Dierauf, former chief of forest research at the Virginia Department of Forestry, who was familiar with the project. He remembers one scientist likening the effort to trying to fix a stalled car by whacking on the engine block with a sledgehammer: "It wasn't impossible. But the odds of it working were just tremendous."

Meanwhile, at the Connecticut Agricultural Experiment Station, botanist Richard Jaynes was continuing Graves's breeding program and working with the hybrids at the Sleeping Giant plantation, which Graves had deeded to the station before his death. Jaynes is an energetic, plainspoken man who looks a bit like Donald Sutherland and, even in his seventies, retains the trim, straight bearing of someone who has spent his life working outdoors. Jaynes grew up in the area and worked as a hand at the station's farm during school vacations. After getting his PhD from Yale, he joined the station's staff in 1961. Fighting forest pests was in his blood: his father was an entomologist with the USDA Bureau of Plant Quarantine. Though Jaynes shared Graves's interest in chestnut, it was never the same all-consuming passion for him; his heart belonged to the ornamental plant kalmia (also known as mountain laurel). Officially Jaynes's job was split between chestnut and kalmia breeding—though the station administration's support for the former kept shrinking as the years went by with no measurable signs of success.

Jaynes followed Graves's basic approach, but it was by then clear to him that achieving adequate blight resistance while preserving the American tree's form would require several generations of crosses and selections. He also quickly realized that he needed far more land than was available at the station's farm or Graves's plantation if he was going to grow enough trees to find the few with the desired combination of genes. In 1966, his phone rang with an answer to his prayers. The caller was a doctor who had a deep interest in chestnut restoration and, better still, a wife who was a DuPont. Her family owned 420 acres of woodland east of the Blue Ridge in Virginia known as the Lesesne Forest. The couple had decided to turn over the land to Virginia's department of forestry so that it could be used for research in breeding blight-resistant chestnuts. The result of that call was what Jaynes described as "the largest experimental planting of chestnut since the blight swept through the stands" sixty years earlier. Jaynes dubbed the effort "Project Village Smithy" in reference to Longfellow's poem.

Approximately half the acreage was turned over to Singleton and Dietz to plant their irradiated seedlings, few of which proved able to survive the blight. The rest of the land was given over to Jaynes to plant promising hybrids and seeds, including some from the Clapper tree. As was so often the case, the hybrids initially showed great potential. But as time went on, most began to lose that valued straight-up form, succumb to blight, or suffer die-backs in their crowns, a sign that they lacked adequate cold tolerance.

Much as Jaynes admired Graves, he found he didn't have the old man's endless reservoir of enthusiasm and faith. Over the years, he says, the realization slowly dawned on him that "this is one tough nut to crack, if I may say that." The right roll of the dice hadn't occurred during the lifetimes of Graves or the USDA breeders and, Jaynes began to recognize, "it might not happen in mine either."

In 1984, he decided to retire from the station and open a nursery business raising kalmia and Christmas trees. "It was almost a relief to walk away from the chestnut work and not have the responsibility for moving ahead and optimistically presenting, 'Oh yeah, we're going to accomplish this in the next year,'" Jaynes recalls. "I enjoyed the work. But after twenty-five years of banging my head against that stone wall, I was happy to devote my time to working with kalmia." Compared to chestnut, the beautiful ornamental shrub "was a piece of cake."

By the time Jaynes bowed out, most experts in the field had come to share his pessimistic view that breeding for blight resistance was probably a dead end. But they weren't ready to abandon the dream of saving the tree. A new front had opened up in the long-running battle against the blight. Instead of trying to fix the tree, scientists now saw a way to put the fix on its intransigent enemy.

SIX

Evil Tendencies Cancel

In 1936 Robert Frost wrote the poem "Evil Tendencies Cancel." The poem concerns the chestnut blight, though as the title suggests, it is also about much more:

> Will the blight end the chestnut?
> The farmers rather guess not.
> It keeps smouldering at the roots
> And sending up new shoots
> Till another parasite
> Shall come to end the blight.

Frost scholars don't pay a lot of attention to the poem—it's not considered one of his major works. But scientists like Dennis Fulbright do. In six brief lines, the poet not only succinctly captured the chestnut's plight, but also accurately predicted a discovery that would fuel a whole new round of efforts to rescue the American chestnut. "It's pretty amazing, isn't it?" says Fulbright, a plant pathologist at Michigan State University. "It tells the whole story."

Fulbright is tall and has an athletic build. With his tousled dark hair and boyish grin, he looks a good bit younger than his fifty-three years. He grew up in Southern California, far beyond the chestnut's native home, so he wasn't weaned on the kinds of fond reminiscences that inspire many would-be saviors of the tree. He was twenty-nine years old before he even saw his first American chestnut tree. But after decades of chestnut research, he's developed a deep sense of kinship with the tree. "I'm not someone who gets into these kinds of things," he says. "But when it comes to chestnut, I really feel like I have an intimate understanding of what the trees are going through and that I can help to solve it." He's worked on wheat and tomatoes, oaks and Christmas trees, but none have sparked the kind of emotional attachment he feels for chestnut trees. His wife jokingly calls herself a "chestnut widow."

Like any love-struck admirer, he can't help looking for chestnuts wherever he goes, and he invariably finds them, even in unlikely places, such as when he stumbled across a chestnut in Mexico, or when a chestnut sapling was spotlighted by his headlights as he pulled into a campground in Massachusetts. Even after twenty-five years, the romance is still growing as he branches out from disease-oriented research into new chestnut ventures, working with growers to develop a Michigan chestnut industry and innovating new, weird chestnut products, like chestnut chips and chestnut beer.

But Fulbright has also developed an appreciation for the tree's foe, the *Cryphonectria parasitica* fungus: "You have to give it its due. . . . It's the perfect killer, like a shark." (Another veteran researcher confesses similar admiration for the fungus, though he admits "it's like admiring the Boston Strangler.") The more Fulbright has studied the organism, the more he's become enthralled: "If you're going to be wowed by a fungus, it's one to be wowed by. It's a beautiful color, it grows in culture in the laboratory, it's easy to isolate. Sometimes I think I'm more in love with the fungus than the tree. I call it the Stockholm syndrome, like when a hostage starts pulling for his kidnappers."

It's not surprising Fulbright has fallen for both the tree and its enemy. Plant pathologists don't tend to think about just one or the other. Rather, they approach the diseases they study as a triangle, with one point the host, one point the parasite, and one point the environment. Change any of those points and you can potentially change the course of the disease. In afflictions of food crops, the first line of attack is often the environment—improving the soil, adding irrigation, spacing plantings so the plant gains an edge over its pathogen. But there's no environmental fix for a pandemic like the chestnut blight, which sprawls over millions of acres of wild forest land. That leaves just two points of the triangle to deal with. You can work on the host, the tree, so that it can put up a better fight, as generations of breeders have tried. Or you can tackle the parasite, the fungus, to render it less lethal. That's where Fulbright has focused his work.

It's an approach made possible thanks to a serendipitous discovery in Europe, where the blight touched down in the 1930s. (Some say it arrived on chestnut mine timbers imported from America to Genoa; others think it sneaked in on chestnut trees planted in botanical gardens.) At first it appeared that the European chestnuts were destined for the same tragic fate as their American cousins. But twenty years into the epidemic, an Italian scientist noticed that sprouts growing from the remains of dying chestnuts had begun showing signs of spontaneous recovery. They developed cankers, but then the cankers stopped growing and actually appeared to be closing. He speculated that the trees had somehow acquired an immunity to the fungus—an idea other scientists dismissed as a biological impossibility, because it would take centuries for the trees to evolve that kind of protection.

The observation intrigued Jean Grente, a French agronomist who had made his name in domesticating the production of truffles. Grente worked for the French equivalent of the USDA, in a lab he called "Le Laboratoire de Lutte Biologique," the Laboratory of Biological Struggle. In 1965, after studying samples of fungus taken from the healing trees, Grente discovered the real reason for their recovery: the trees hadn't changed, but the fungus had. These strains of the fungus were a sickly white, instead of their normal vibrant orange. They also grew far more slowly than usual. He speculated that the blight was afflicted by a blight of its own that dramatically retarded the fungus's ability to grow and spread. Here was Frost's other parasite.

Or actually, as later research established, a virus. Incredibly enough, *Cryphonectria parasitica* had come down with the fungal equivalent of a bad cold. And the fungus responded in just the same way humans respond to a rotten case of the flu: it became sluggish and listless, and lost its appetite.

Like the flu, this virus could be passed around, as Grente found when he placed a culture of healthy fungus in the same petri dish with a sickly strain. Filaments from the two grew together and formed a new mycelial fan. But instead of the normal sunshine hue, this was the pale-orange color of sherbet. When Grente injected strains of ailing fungus into blight cankers on trees, the parasite infiltrated the uninfected fungus and the overall infection on the trees slowed down.

Grente termed the phenomenon "hypovirulence," for the way that the virus saps the blight's normal virulence. It's not a cure for the blight, but slowing the fungus's assault buys time for an infected tree. The tree has the chance to rally its natural defenses, growing a thick wall of callus tissue around the deadly canker to block the further spread of the advancing mycelial wedge. It's the same kind of scab trees form in response to any wound, whether the cause is a swipe from a car or the cut of a saw. You can see when a tree is winning its fight—healing cankers often have a gruesome, swollen appearance, like arthritic joints. One researcher calls them "big uglies." Instead of the usual flat or sunken patches on the bark that signify dead tissue underneath, healing cankers are bulging and distended by the tree's struggle for life beneath.

Grente began treating French chestnut orchards with strains of hypovirulent fungus. The strains steadily spread, and within ten years the blight epidemic there had ground to a halt. Proud as he was of his discovery, Grente also acknowledged that the credit was not his alone: "The blight has been defeated by nature, not me," he explained. "I just found the way to do in 10 years what nature does in 50 or 60." Grente's discovery pointed to a wholly new strategy for defeating the chestnut blight—the use of a biological control, much like ladybugs can be deployed to rid a garden of pesky aphids.

The discovery had come none too soon. By this time, forestry experts had all but given up on the American chestnut. The USDA had abandoned its breeding program. Plant pathology departments ruefully taught that the blight marked the field's greatest failure. There were probably fewer than a dozen American scientists doing anything remotely related to the American chestnut. One of the few places where chestnut research was still proceeding was at the Connecticut Agricultural Experiment Station, Arthur Graves's old stomping grounds. There, Richard Jaynes was still pressing ahead with Graves's breeding program, pulling in occasional help from Sandra Anagnostakis, a young mycologist.

A Kansas native, Anagnostakis had begun working on her doctorate at the University of Texas in the early 1960s, but cut her studies short when her husband landed a job at Yale University. Despite having only a master's degree, she was hired by the Connecticut Agricultural Experiment Station in 1966. "In those days it didn't really matter what sort of degree you had," she says. "Now you would have to have a PhD." (In fact, she adds, she got so tired of people mistakenly calling her "doctor" that she spent a year in Germany writing up her research to acquire a doctorate degree. She returned with the added credential in hand only to discover that "nobody cared.")

Anagnostakis spent her first two years at the station working on fungal diseases of tomatoes and corn, until one day Jaynes placed a blight-ridden chestnut branch on her desk and told her, "Here—you're a mycologist, why don't you do something about this?" She was soon hooked. Other colleagues like Jaynes have since moved on to other jobs or other fields of research, but forty years later, Anagnostakis is still passionately trying to do something about the chestnut. She hit retirement age in 2004, but cheerfully insists she has no intentions of ever retiring; she recently told her boss, "I intend to drop dead in the woods someday."

Anagnostakis is a small, sturdy woman with a round face, short salt-and-pepper hair, and the brisk air of a schoolmarm. She quickly warms up, though, when the subject is chestnuts. Her cluttered office is filled with chestnut memorabilia—photos, a painting of children gathering chestnuts, slices of wood. The license plate on her car reads "CHSNUT." She is, she says, one of three "chestnut ladies": the other two are researchers in Italy and China. Anagnostakis describes herself as a "terminal introvert," but she actually has a pretty forceful personality—and that, as much as her scholarship and longevity, maintains her authority in the field. As one colleague observed, even when she's saying something that you suspect is wrong, she says it with such assurance you begin to be persuaded.

Like many chestnut researchers, she has a strong affinity for the tree and a sense of its having a distinct personality. "It's vital, with a strong life force," she says, adding with a laugh, "and I'm not one of the sentimental ones."

"Have you read *A Feeling for the Organism?*" she asks, referring to Evelyn Fox Keller's biography of Nobel Prize–winning plant geneticist Barbara McClintock. McClintock maintained that years of standing in the fields, carefully studying individual corn plants, gave her the intimate knowledge and understanding—the feeling for the organism—that allowed her landmark insights into how corn genes operate. "I know what she meant," says Anagnostakis. "If I go out and really look at the trees, I find out all kinds of things."

In addition to her scientific work on *Castanea dentata,* Anagnostakis has become something of a historian of the species and its nemesis. She has immersed herself in the old literature in an effort to trace the entry of chestnut blight in the United States and to gain as precise a picture as possible of what the tree was once like. She has acquired, for instance, all the USDA records documenting importations of Asian and European chestnuts and is able to tell, with a quick glance at the well-thumbed index cards, the precise history of a particular tree. "Someone will call me up and say they live in Washburn, Illinois, and there's a

beautiful American chestnut tree in their yard and I should be interested. So I look in my records and find out someone from Washburn,
Illinois, got fifty Chinese chestnuts in 1912 and it happens to be their
street address. I'm breaking hearts everywhere." Though she says she's
not a confrontational person, she rarely hesitates to correct someone if
she thinks they are wrong. She has contacted mail order companies to
ask them to correct misleading claims about the chestnut trees offered
in their catalogs. "They were not happy, of course," she recalls. "I do try
to keep my mouth shut, but it's very hard."

Around 1972, Jaynes showed her Grente's paper and suggested they
take a look at his approach. She agreed that it looked interesting and
wrote the Frenchman in English, asking for samples of his fungus cultures, but got no response. So she contacted a friend who taught high
school French and asked her for help in writing him again. "Within
about a week I got cultures back in the mail. He had been intending to
get my letter translated but just hadn't gotten around to it," she recalls.

Anagnostakis, Jaynes, pathologist Neal Van Alfen, and geneticist
Peter Day began a series of experiments to try to understand the phenomenon Grente had described and to see if the same miracle could be
replicated in this country. They tested the strains Grente had sent, first
in the lab; then in trees growing in greenhouses; and last, in trees
planted at the station's farm. They inserted plugs of the European
hypovirulent fungus into the edges of cankers formed by the virulent
American fungus. When they later sampled the cankers, they found
that the different strains had joined and the new growth of fungus was
now hypovirulent. The research team reported their findings in a landmark article in 1975 in the prestigious journal *Science:* "Our results in
the laboratory, greenhouse, and field . . . suggest that this fungal strain
[the hypovirulent fungus from Europe] may become a control for the
disease in the United States." The article was accompanied by a copy of
Frost's poem.

The paper ignited a new wave of interest in rescuing the American
chestnut. Forget about breeding hybrids to achieve victory against the

blight; here was a weapon that just might bring a swift end to the protracted war. It also offered an infinitely more elegant and simple resolution: spread hypovirulent fungus in a forest of chestnut sprouts and let
it take off, like a swarm of aphid-hungry ladybugs. If Europe was any
indication, the saplings would recover and the chestnut forest would
come roaring back. It is no wonder one forest researcher declared that
hypovirulence represented "the most exciting event in chestnut blight
research in recent years."

"It really was responsible for bringing chestnut back on to the playing field," says William MacDonald, a plant pathologist at West
Virginia University and one of a number of researchers who jumped
into the field in the wake of the discovery. Suddenly there was more
money for chestnut research (though never enough, the scientists would
complain). At the Connecticut Agricultural Experiment Station, Jaynes
noticed there were now four or five other scientists interested in pursuing chestnut studies. When MacDonald hosted a symposium on chestnut research at his university in 1978, about 125 scientists, foresters, and
others showed up, the largest gathering of people with an interest in the
American chestnut since the Pennsylvania Chestnut Tree Blight Commission conference more than sixty years before.

Although the promise of hypovirulence was widely recognized, it presented bedeviling mysteries and a new disease triangle to be probed and
understood. What was the biology of the blight's own blight? How
exactly did it infect and affect its host, the *Cryphonectria* fungus? Did
American chestnut trees offer the same microenvironment for this new
host-parasite relationship as the European trees?

Presumably the virus originated in Asia, like the blight fungus, and
was dispersed around the world along with the fungus. But if that was
the case, why had hypovirulence only come to the rescue of chestnuts in
Europe? Was it possible the fungal flu was also present in the United

States but had somehow gone unnoticed? The answer came from an unlikely place, hundreds of miles beyond the chestnut's home range. In 1976, an observant cross-country skier happened by a small grove of American chestnut trees in Rockford, Michigan, likely planted by settlers long ago. The trees, she noticed, had blight cankers, but these cankers looked unusual—much like the photos she had seen in a recent news story on hypovirulence. She contacted the Connecticut researchers and sent samples to Anagnostakis, who cultured them in her lab and soon determined that they were infected with a hypovirus. But it wasn't the same as the European blight-of-the-blight. This was a homegrown hypovirus, and it seemed to be aiding these Michigan chestnut trees just as the virus in Europe had done.

Dennis Fulbright was still in graduate school when the first scientific reports on hypovirulence were published. He read the *Science* paper and found it interesting. But after presenting a seminar summarizing the work, he gave it little thought. He took a job at Michigan State University and planned to work on wheat diseases. But a colleague with an interest in the American chestnut soon persuaded him to take a look at the Michigan chestnut trees. The Rockford stand was not an isolated example, the colleague explained. There were similar old groves dating from the nineteenth century scattered all over the state's Lower Peninsula, and they contained an estimated six hundred to eight hundred good-sized surviving chestnut trees. Some undoubtedly had simply escaped the blight so far, but others—no one knew how many— seemed to surviving in spite of it. The trees appeared to be undergoing a European-style recovery.

One of the most heartening sites was a small woodlot in Grand Haven, owned by a man named George Unger, who used to gather the nuts every fall and sell them in Chicago. Years before, when the blight first reached Michigan, a county extension agent had urged Unger to chop down all his chestnut trees while it was still possible to sell the wood. "Everybody agreed; they said they're going, gone," Unger later recalled. But as Unger began sawing his way through the stand, he noticed that some of the trees sported bulging cankers instead of the usual flat dead spots. Unger had never heard of hypovirulence, but he trusted what his instincts told him—that these chestnuts were fighting back against the blight and maybe even winning. He decided to stop cutting down the trees.

Fulbright visited the stand in 1981. It was the first time he'd ever seen chestnut blight at work, and these were not your typical blight cankers. "I was very confused," he recalls. "Recovering cankers tend to look very ugly. They're swollen and broken up. The bark is fractured. There's lots of thickening of the bark. It doesn't look very pleasing. I kept thinking to myself: this is the *good* aspect of chestnut blight?" He was amazed that a layman like Unger had recognized the stirrings of recovery in the dreadful-looking growths. "It even took me, as a plant pathologist, a little bit of time to get through that."

Once he got through it, however, Fulbright was convinced that the Grand Haven trees were indeed in the midst of a naturally induced recuperation. But to his frustration, he had a hard time getting other scientists fired up about the Michigan trees. "There were all these excuses why Michigan was an anomaly and maybe it shouldn't be studied and what we're trying to work on are trees in Virginia, the backbone of the chestnut population." East Coast researchers insisted that what was happening in Michigan was due to some kind of "edge factor"—the inexplicable phenomena that often occur on the edge of natural ranges. At times he even found it difficult to persuade Michiganders of the importance of the trees. When developers bought George Unger's land and proposed plowing the stand under for housing in the early 1990s, Fulbright tried to get a local conservation group to join him in battling the plans. The group's botanist was unmoved by his pleas on the chestnuts' behalf. "Why are we trying to save these trees? They're invasive species as far as Michigan's concerned," he told Fulbright.

By the time I met Fulbright in late 2005, researchers could no longer pooh-pooh the significance of the Michigan trees. Three decades of scouring the American chestnut's natural range for other signs of hypovirulence had come up empty. The chestnut groves in Michigan are among only a few places in the United States where hypovirulence has arisen naturally and are the sole examples of American chestnuts demonstrating dramatic recovery en masse.

"What happened to Unger's stand in Grand Haven?" I ask Fulbright.

"I didn't have the heart to go there until this year," he answers. "It is houses."

No more trees. No more blight. Is this evil tendencies canceling?

Frost's poem suggests a simple leveling process. But natural systems, unlike words, aren't readily herded into the elegant forms we seek. The farmer-poet was such a close observer of nature; did he really believe it would be so easy?

Sandra Anagnostakis's experience points to what American researchers have been able to achieve with Frost's other parasite. On a warm April day, we climb into her car and drive from her office in a residential neighborhood of New Haven to the station's farm in nearby Hamden. She steers the car across a bumpy, grassy field to where there are seventy American chestnut trees planted in four neat rows. The trees were inoculated with hypovirulent fungus starting in 1978. "We treated every canker we could reach for four years," Anagnostakis recalls. Then they left the trees alone. Today, the trees are still covered with blight, but hypovirulence also remains at work. As a result, most of the trees are still alive. "I think they're wonderful," she says proudly, as we walk through the rows. "They're beautiful."

Truly, beauty is in the eye of the beholder. These trees are a far cry from the thick, imposing towers of wood that fans of the tree have in mind when they talk about chestnut restoration. Many of them look more like bushes than trees; their main stems have died back and been replaced by multiple prongs of skinny sprouts. The best of the bunch are scraggly, limby specimens, averaging no more than thirty-five feet tall. As another researcher jokes, "They're apple trees." Could this really be considered success?

"It depends on what you call successful," Anagnostakis maintains. "I'm talking about trees that survive and flower." The trees blossom abundantly each summer, and every fall she collects bushels of nuts. Even now, after nearly thirty years, the cankers on the trees are still hypovirulent and the viruses are helping the trees to stay alive, allowing her to continue her efforts to breed blight-resistant trees. To her, that is proof that hypovirulence offers a viable strategy for fighting the blight. "It's a way of bringing things into balance and giving these trees a chance," she says. It's a way to preserve the species.

Yet even Anagnostakis would admit that blighting the blight in America has not been the smooth operation that it was in Europe. Try as they might, researchers generally have not been able to spark the kind of rapid tree-to-tree spread of hypovirulence that saved the European chestnut trees. And that is the essence of biological control. The achievement Anagnostakis calls success might save an orchard or a small woodlot, but it's not going to rescue millions of acres of forest.

In the years since that first paper in *Science* was published, it's become clear that the blight-of-the-blight is a far more complex system than initially supposed. Researchers have found, for instance, that there are at least four species of hypoviruses with widely varying levels of potency. An alphabet soup of names is used to identify the different varieties. CHV1, the virus Grente isolated, can shut the fungus down. A milder Italian variant known as CHV1-Euro7 slows the fungus's spread but doesn't stop it from producing virulent spores. The Michigan species, CHV3, falls somewhere in between. And then there's CHV4, a group found in the tree's home range in Appalachia, which appears to have virtually no effect.

The host point of this microscopic disease triangle—the *Crypho-nectria* fungus—poses another set of complications, for it also is not a monolithic entity. There are more than two hundred strains of blight fungus, a fact which also has a bearing on the success of hypovirulence.

The hypovirus particles live in the liquid interior of a fungal cell, its cytoplasm. One way the virus is transmitted is when fungus cells share their cytoplasmic material. That can only happen if the fungi are compatible strains. In that case, it's love at first sight: the tiny threadlike hyphae of the two intertwine and their cells fuse, allowing them to share cytoplasmic material. That embrace, called anastomosis, leads to the growth of new fungal tissue. If one strain is hypovirulent, the viral particles are transmitted during that fungal kiss and the new growth becomes hypovirulent. However, if two distantly related strains are brought together, it's the equivalent of a bad date. The meeting ends in mutual rejection. No anastomosis. No viral transmission. This lack of chemistry is known as vegetative incompatibility.

The European fungus, it turns out, operates in a much more homogeneous dating scene. The trees in Europe host no more than half a dozen strains of blight fungus; in such a compatible group, the virus is easily passed around. The American population of fungus is far more diverse. In Appalachia alone—the historic heart of chestnut country and the place where enthusiasts most hoped biological control would work—there are dozens of strains of *Cryphonectria parasitica* hanging out on chestnut trees, a fungal tower of Babel incapable of the kinds of meet-and-greets that would permit the hypovirus to readily spread. Fulbright, Anagnostakis, and other researchers began to suspect that vegetative incompatibility was the chief stumbling block to the success of the biocontrol in this country.

In light of that suspicion, some scientists have sought a way around the problem of vegetative incompatibility by creating a new avenue for the virus to spread: via its offspring, its sexually produced spores. Virologist Donald Nuss, of the University of Maryland Biotechnology Institute, has bioengineered a *Cryphonectria parasitica* fungus that is genetically programmed for hypovirulence, which means that when it mates, the virus is passed on to the resulting spores. The approach offers two benefits for the price of one. The virus gets moved into a variety of *Cryphonectria* strains, since compatibility isn't an issue in mating. And because the powdery, sexually produced spores are dispersed by the wind, they are blown far and wide, taking the hypovirus along with them.

"On paper it looked like that might increase the spread [of hypovirulence]," says Nuss. That theory is now being tested in a forest in West Virginia, where two strains of transgenic fungus have been released. Whether they succeed in spreading better than normal hypovirulent strains is still unknown. In fact, Nuss notes, chestnut experts aren't even sure whether the sexually produced spores play an important role in perpetuating the blight. Ironically, although the tools of modern science have allowed researchers to penetrate the fungus's deepest recesses and tinker with its genes, they still don't know some of the most basic things about its natural history.

When I first read the Frost poem, I read it literally. I saw it as a neatly done act of scientific prophecy. But in reading it over and over and consulting with Frost scholars, I began to see that the poem contains a certain deliberate ambiguity. "It keeps smouldering at the roots/And sending up new shoots." I at first assumed "it" referred to the chestnut. But "smouldering" is an odd word choice—not a word one would normally use to conjure the bright promise of a tree springing back to life. So what is smoldering? Something more than just the chestnut's imperative for survival? Could it be hope—for ourselves, as much as for the tree?

Despite the repeated failures of hypovirulence, Fulbright and other scientists were unwilling to give up on the possibility that the blight-of-the-blight could be harnessed to save the American chestnut. Given the dramatic recoveries he'd seen firsthand in Michigan, Fulbright remained convinced that hypoviruses could work as a biological control, if only there was a way around the problem of vegetative incompatibility. In 1991, he got a chance to test the theory when he learned about a remarkable stand of chestnut trees growing in West Salem, Wisconsin. The grove was started in the early 1900s when a farmer named Martin Hicks planted a handful of East Coast chestnut seeds on the ridge overlooking his farm. Though chestnut is not native to the area, the trees flourished and multiplied into a dense stand of some five thousand trees. It is the largest remaining chestnut forest in the United States, and until the mid-1980s, it was happily free of the blight. Ron Bockenhauer, a retired dairy farmer whose family owns the stand, didn't even realize there was anything special about the place he calls "Chestnut Hill" until he read a news article in the 1980s quoting an expert who described the chestnut as extinct. "I wrote him and said, 'Come on up,'" Bockenhauer recalls. "From then on everybody started coming." Scientists, reporters, and chestnut pilgrims visited, eager to see hale and hearty examples of their beloved tree.

The West Salem stand was a perfect location to test the power of hypovirulence to act as an effective biological control. There were none of the complications that had muddied the results of other experiments with hypovirulence. The blight was not widespread. The trees were mature. And most important, an analysis showed that only one strain of the fungus was present in the stand. (That in itself is testimony to the disease's virulence, for, according to Fulbright, it means the outbreak was probably lit by a single spore, one lonely microscopic particle dropped from a migrating bird onto a luckless tree.) Vegetative incompatibility would not be an obstacle. If hypovirulence was going to work anywhere, it ought to work on Chestnut Hill. Here was a tantalizing chance to do what no one had ever done: stop an outbreak of the blight before it got rolling.

In 1991, Fulbright, MacDonald, and Jane Cummings-Carlson, a pathologist from the Wisconsin Department of Natural Resources, quickly drew up a plan for deploying a hypovirus in the stand. Fulbright was full of optimism, certain that this strategy could save a good part of the stand. In ten years' time, he confidently told one reporter, half the trees in the stand would be alive because of hypovirulence.

Today he cringes when recalling that brash prediction. Even in West Salem, the biocontrol has proved trickier than any of the researchers expected. The first virus strain used—taken from recovering trees in Michigan—turned out to be far too debilitating to its fungal host. It left the fungus like a bedridden invalid, too sick to budge from the spot where it was placed. After three years, the researchers decided to switch to another hypovirus, one of the European strains. This strain spread more readily over the next few years, and by 1997 it had infiltrated more than a third of the cankers into which it was placed.

Still, it wasn't moving fast enough. Though the hypovirus has spread well on individual trees, there's been limited tree-to-tree spread. As a result, even in this optimal setting, the hypovirulent fungus has not been able to keep up with the explosive growth of virulent fungus. (And the site is no longer so optimal: in recent years, two more strains of the fungus have been found there, further complicating the effort at biocontrol.) By 2002, approximately six hundred trees in the stand were infected with the virulent fungus, and many had died. Parts of the forest resemble photographs from the heyday of the blight—one path is lined by a somber row of standing skeletons. Assessing the results of the experiment, Cummings-Carlson concludes that "the fungus outsmarted us."

"Eeeow," Fulbright winces when told of her assessment. But as he scrambles up and down the steep slopes of the West Salem woods on a crisp October day, he steadfastly refuses to be discouraged. Despite the raging epidemic, there is still a verdant layer of chestnut leaves overhead and the ground is littered with broken burs and tiny mahogany nuts. He insists he is only disappointed that, as he says, "other people might consider it a failure." At first I wonder if he is just trying to rationalize the twenty-five years he's devoted to hypovirulence. But following him through Chestnut Hill, listening to him excitedly expound on what he now thinks is happening to the trees, I come to see that as much as Fulbright loves the chestnut, he also loves the process of science. It's a process in which theories are always being knocked down; that is the definition of scientific progress.

True, the stand hasn't supported the theory that vegetative incompatibility is the chief deterrent to the success of hypovirulence. "If that's outsmarting me, yeah it didn't happen like that," he says. But he adds emphatically, "I don't consider this in any way a failure. . . . I think we're finding out some really significant things about chestnut blight and chestnut trees here. And that makes me so excited that I can forget the part about the fungus outwitting me."

Fulbright is seeing something unexpected unfolding on Chestnut Hill, a turn of events that gives him a whole new reason to be optimistic. To his surprise, the trees aren't responding uniformly to the hypovirus: some are taking better advantage of the treatment than others. How can that be? "OK," he says, "this is where I stop couching my language in any way with science. Some of the trees out there seem to 'get it' and some of them don't. Some of them seem to know what we're trying to do, and others don't."

As we walk through the stand, Fulbright pauses often to point to trees that "get it" and trees that don't. Finally, he comes to a stop in front of a pair of trees about fifteen feet apart. Both were inoculated with the European hypovirus seven years ago and painted with red numbers on their trunks. Number 12 is little more than an upright carcass. Number 13, on the other hand, rises sixty feet high and is exuberantly alive, flush with shiny green leaves and bunches of nut-filled, porcupiney burs. The trunk and branches are pockmarked with cankers, but these are the healing variety, swollen by layers of protective callus tissue. The trees are the same age, the same size, and in the same location. Why is 13 bouncing back while 12 is on its deathbed?

Fulbright has a theory, though it remains unproven. He suspects that the difference has to do with the genetics of the individual trees. Number 13, he speculates, has "a smidgen more" innate resistance to the blight. If the hypovirus bought the tree some time, that trace of extratough DNA helped the tree to spend the time well. The tree got a chance to start healing itself. Whether it survives over the long term is uncertain, but for now, it is the incarnation of a chestnut rescuer's dream.

He pauses by another chestnut that also seems to "get it," as evidenced by a large, swollen canker that's starting to close. "This is exactly the way it happens in Michigan," he says excitedly. With any luck, this tree should be around for a long time, he thinks. Suddenly he throws his arms around the tree and embraces it in, well, a big tree hug. Pressing his cheek against the rough bark, he calls out with a grin, "Tell Jane I'm happy to be outwitted by this tree."

Halfway across the country, Anagnostakis has come to the same conclusion. She, too, has noticed varying responses to the hypoviruses in her test plot of seventy trees. In an effort to discern a pattern, she mapped out the plot on paper, with smiley faces for the trees doing well and frowning faces for those that failed to thrive. She's spent hours studying the checkerboard of smiles and frowns. "There's no pattern," she has concluded. "I think that this proves that there's a genetic difference in American chestnut in their resistance to blight. . . . I think the ones that survive in the presence of hypovirulence have some sort of fitness genes." If she and Fulbright are right, it would help explain why hypovirulence worked so well overseas: European chestnuts are slightly more blight resistant than the American trees. Perhaps the trees in Michigan owe their recovery to similarly providential genes.

As Fulbright has begun to consider the significance of the tree's genetics, he's started to see evidence for his theory throughout West Salem as the blight moves through the stand. The woods there are peppered with chestnuts—mostly young trees—that were never treated with a hypovirus, but which are nonetheless developing healing cankers. They aren't resistant enough to defeat the blight on their own, but they're putting up a stiffer fight than the average American chestnut tree. "It's funny to me that I'm starting to find these trees," he says, as he points out some chestnut saplings with healing cankers. "Why didn't I see them before?"

The presence of such "genetically superior" trees makes him hopeful about the long-term picture for the stand: "Ten years from now, out of five thousand trees, there will be 250 really good-looking trees up in the canopy and some lower numbers that are getting hypovirulence." Most of the forest will be gone, but there may be just enough survivors to repopulate Chestnut Hill.

Not everyone shares Fulbright's and Anagnostakis's continued hopes for hypovirulence. At least one researcher, Michael Milgroom, a plant pathologist at Cornell University, has come to the conclusion that it will never be the panacea for American chestnuts that it was for their cousins in Europe. He believes that its promise as a biological control is built on "a lot of hype"—a position that he cheerfully admits hasn't made him very popular among his colleagues. In 2004, he published a highly critical article that challenged the claims of success for hypovirulence as being based "perhaps more on hope than reality."

Reviewing the research, he bluntly concluded that, "Deployment of hypovirulence in eastern North America has been an almost complete failure." He pointed out that the only places where hypovirulence has produced significant recoveries are either where it's arisen naturally, such as in Europe or Michigan, or when it's been deployed in an artificial setting where the trees are pampered, as in Anagnostakis's test plot. That makes hypovirulence an interesting therapy for individual trees, but not a biological control. Indeed, he has trouble understanding how colleagues like MacDonald, Fulbright, and Anagnostakis have hung in with hypovirulence given the poor results. "I would have gotten out in the mid-'80s," he says. Then again, he admits, though he's fascinated by the biology of hypovirulence, he doesn't feel any particular attachment to the tree.

Most other researchers in the field think Milgroom is being too pessimistic. They say too little time has elapsed to draw any firm conclusions. No one really knows how long it took for hypovirulence to take hold and start gaining the upper hand in Europe or Michigan. The fact that hypoviruses can still be found on trees that were inoculated years or even decades ago leaves room for hope, says MacDonald. "We may just be impatient."

"But doesn't this keep breaking your heart?" I ask, as we talk about the dismal results at West Salem. "No, it doesn't," he answers, echoing a point other researchers make. "If it did, we'd be out of the whole business. The thing that keeps me coming back is we see bits and pieces of it working. There's something biologically going on here, and we may just be missing some components of it that we don't understand."

If it is true that hypovirulence works best in trees that already have what Fulbright calls "the right genetics," then it may still have an important role to play in chestnut salvation. Hypoviruses can be used, as some researchers are doing, to keep alive the rare trees that show signs of innate resistance. More important, the use of the biocontrol could be coupled with the ongoing effort to breed blight-resistant American chestnut trees, as Anagnostakis is doing. Combine a weakened fungus and tougher trees and, says the ever-optimistic Fulbright, "that really might be the whammy the chestnut blight needs."

You can look at Frost's poem "Evil Tendencies Cancel" as a straightforward declaration of hope: "another parasite" will surface to save the American chestnut. That's certainly the meaning taken by chestnut scientists, most of whom know the lines by heart. But that simple message is belied by the puzzling title. Do evil tendencies cancel? Not really.

The more I think about it, the more I realize that Frost was driving at a deeper, more complicated message. For help in digging it out, I turned to Robert Faggen, a professor of English at Claremont College and author of *Robert Frost and the Challenge of Darwin*. Frost's poems, he tells me, are often portrayed as sunny paeans to nature, simple as Christmas cards. But a much darker vision lurks beneath that Norman Rockwell surface, according to Faggen. Frost, he says, saw the natural world as a Darwinian arena of warfare, chaos, and chance, as every creature, large and small, fiercely contends for life.

Humans ascribe moral values to that struggle, and in doing so, we sustain ourselves with the illusion that we can and should guide it to the outcome we desire—we'll defeat the evil to save our good. The poem invites us to adopt another view, to consider the natural world as a neutral realm in which morals have no place. The blight and the tree, the parasite and the host are simply partners thrown together by evolutionary chance in that messy, unpredictable, strife-ridden cycle of birth and death that constitutes life. Each is simply playing the role nature assigned it.

We can hope for the chestnut, Frost suggests: "Will the blight end the chestnut?/The farmers rather guess not." But the poem's title asks us to consider what that hope means. What are the consequences of imposing human values on the natural world? The blight may seem evil to us, but from the vantage point of the fungus, that other parasite we await might be considered equally evil.

Perhaps, Frost is ultimately reminding us, our tendency to view nature in terms of our notions of good and bad, desirable and undesirable, can wreak its own kind of evil. Certainly the American chestnut would never have been pushed to the brink of extinction were it not for human agency. Humans introduced the chestnut blight. The tree's plight is a direct result of our visions of what our gardens, our personal Edens, should contain. It's a lesson to bear in mind as we press forward in efforts to redress the blight and restore our perfect tree.

SEVEN

Let Us Plant

One cold December day in 1980, Charles Burnham, a retired University of Minnesota corn geneticist, came across a publication about the American chestnut. The title was a mouthful—"The Prospect for American Chestnut Plantings in Minnesota and Neighboring Upper Mississippi Valley States"—but it intrigued him. He took the pamphlet back to his quiet St. Paul home to read it over the Christmas holidays. That happenstance discovery would lead to the most promising strategy yet for saving the American chestnut tree.

Burnham was born in 1904, the same year the chestnut blight fungus was discovered. He grew up on a farm in central Wisconsin in the days of horse-drawn plows, when clearing a field was back-breaking work. Ever after, he once told a colleague, he hated being called Charlie, since that was the name of every old plow horse in the county (though, true to his unassuming nature, he never corrected anyone who called him by the nickname). Times were tough when Burnham was growing up. He knew from experience what it meant when a late frost struck or an outbreak of stalk rot appeared in the corn. Farming may have been in his blood, but it was not in his heart. Smart and intellectually driven, he left home at the age of sixteen for the university and a life in academics.

After earning a PhD in genetics at the University of Wisconsin,

Burnham moved on to postdoctoral work at Cornell University. There, he joined a legendary group of young scientists who were laying the foundations of the nascent science of genetics through their studies of maize. It had been a mere twenty-five years since Mendel's laws of inheritance had been rediscovered, and researchers were just starting to build upon and amplify the simple rules Mendel had distilled from his sweet pea experiments. The era became known as "the golden age of plant genetics," a time when many of the basic mechanisms of genetics were discovered. A photo from the time shows a young Burnham, in shirtsleeves and dusty pants, standing with a formidable group of lab-mates, including Barbara McClintock, who went on to win the Nobel Prize for demonstrating that genes could move around on a chromosome (the "jumping gene" hypothesis), and George Beadle, who won a Nobel Prize for showing that each gene is responsible for producing a single enzyme. Burnham himself helped pioneer the study of chromosomes, in particular what happens when those wavery strands break and rejoin. Eventually he landed at the University of Minnesota, where he remained for the rest of his career.

Whether dealing with farmers, graduate students, or distinguished colleagues, Burnham's demeanor was much the same: friendly, respectful, and slightly reserved. He was demanding with students, but no less so with himself. One former student recalled, "He'd be out in the field at daybreak during the summer and work till dark and then go back and read somebody's thesis."

Burnham was a voracious reader of history, politics, literature, and religion, among other subjects. But nothing held his interest like genetics. And his passion for the subject didn't end with his formal retirement in 1972. He had no interest in kicking back or taking up new hobbies, especially after his wife, Lucille, died in 1977. Occasionally he'd go fishing for crappies or work in his garden; he was particularly proud of a clump of rare lady's slippers that he'd managed to transplant from the wild. But there was truly nothing he enjoyed more than settling down with the latest issue of *Science* or *Genetics*. Years after his retirement, he still liked to putter around the university library, which is how he came across the publication that would change the direction of his life, and the American chestnut's, as well.

Burnham may have been a corn man, but he was well acquainted with the chestnut's sad story. He'd taught at West Virginia University in the mid-1930s when the blight came stampeding through that state. He'd witnessed stately old giants dying, but also had noticed that even nearly-dead trees still often produced flowers. Those blooms meant pollen was still available, which meant there was still hope for the species—a hope which he was pleased to know the USDA was harvesting with its program to breed blight-resistant hybrid trees. Over the years he'd occasionally checked in with colleagues at the USDA and been reassured that prospects for the tree looked good.

Now, as he flipped through the pages of this report on the tree's prospects, Burnham was stunned to learn that they were, in fact, "discouraging." There had been little progress on any front for ensuring the species' survival. "I could not believe what I was reading," Burnham later recalled. What had happened to the USDA program and all those promising hybrids? The ever-curious Burnham began investigating further and his readings about the government breeding program brought another stunner. Not only had the USDA abandoned ship; it apparently had missed the boat. The government breeders had pursued a strategy that was virtually guaranteed to fail. It was as if they'd stepped up to the craps table with dice loaded to roll only snake-eyes. But Burnham knew of another strategy that would produce all the sevens and elevens the chestnut needed.

It was a method called backcross breeding; an approach crop breeders used to tweak a variety that's fine except for a single trait—such as susceptibility to a particular disease. The basic idea is simple. Say you have variety A which is prone to a disease and variety B which is impervious. You cross A with B, and then take the offspring of that union and cross it back to parent A for several generations. The result is a crop that is just like A in every way except that now it also has acquired B's resistance to disease. Grain breeders had used the method since the 1920s to engineer varieties of wheat that could withstand the scourge of rust disease. The famed King ranchers of Texas had employed it even earlier to breed a race of cattle suited to the scorching dry grasslands in the southern part of the state. The resulting Santa Gertrudis cattle—the first truly American breed—were a hardy, beefy mix of Brahmins and Shorthorns whose ability to thrive in that harsh environment made the King ranchers rich. No one had ever tried to backcross trees. But if it worked in grasses and livestock, why not in chestnut trees?

In fact, Burnham had always assumed that was the strategy used by the USDA breeders; he even remembered suggesting it to a colleague at the agency. Apparently no one had heeded his advice, as he was now outraged to discover two decades too late. Burnham called his colleague Norman Borlaug, the agronomist who won a Nobel Prize for developing the high-yield wheat varieties that launched the Green revolution in India. He knew Borlaug had worked in the Forest Service in the 1930s. "I want to talk to you Norm," he said, struggling to keep his anger out of his voice. "Why in the hell didn't you guys backcross that thing?" "Hell," Borlaug told him, "I didn't know anything about genetics when I was working for the Forest Service."

Burnham became obsessed with finding a way to set the dice back in motion and start breeding chestnut trees. Promising as hypovirulence appeared to be at the time, he was not convinced it alone would be sufficient to save the chestnut tree. Rescue efforts needed to dig deeper, he believed, and transform the very DNA of the tree. Chances are, however, Burnham might not have gotten very far had an acquaintance not mentioned that there was another Minnesotan, an eccentric farmer named Philip Rutter, who also was interested in breeding blight-resistant American chestnuts. Burnham contacted Rutter, and so began a collaboration that produced the foremost effort to date to restore the beleaguered tree, the American Chestnut Foundation. Burnham's knowledge generated the dream, but it was Rutter's energy, organizational skills, and palpable passion for the tree that brought the dream to life.

Rutter, now fifty-six, is tall, bald, with a gray-white beard and sharp blue eyes behind wire-rimmed glasses. He has a pleasant deep voice, and when he speaks each word is carefully enunciated. The cadence is similar to the way he responds to e-mails: each sentence typed on a separate line, followed by an emoticon. He often makes distanced, bemused observations about human behavior, as if he were an alien anthropologist doing fieldwork on planet Earth. Says his ex-wife Mary Lewis, "He's always looking at humans and wondering why they work the way they do." He does not so much converse as expound, and his pronouncements are often prefaced with statements like "Something people do not know . . ." or "Most people do not realize . . ." What follows could be a discourse on anything from metallurgy to squirrel behavior to the winter habits of chestnut trees.

Rutter's father was a navy engineer who moved his family all over the world. Early on Rutter developed an interest in biology. By the time he was a sixth grader in Hawaii, he was crossbreeding hibiscus flowers for scent and color. He says his interests also were shaped by the knowledge that he was distantly related to Johnny Appleseed: "I knew this at a young age and it probably served to focus my eyes on plants a little more than most people and probably gave me an exaggerated sense of responsibility." Rutter has taken that sense of social obligation further than most. "I don't see any point in not living what you believe in," he says. His life is proof that he means it.

After finishing college at Oberlin University where he studied evolution and genetics, Rutter started a graduate program in zoology at the University of Minnesota. But while the world of ideas was enticing, the reality of academia was bitterly disappointing. He was studying shrews, but he found his colleagues to be more shrewish than the animals. With interests ranging across the sciences, he felt hemmed in by the disciplinary boundaries and pained by what he calls "the gunfighter mentality": "It doesn't matter how nice you are or how good you are or how smart you are, you still have to take shit for life." His wife, who was studying lake ecology, had also become weary and disillusioned with academic life. In the mid-1970s, they quit school and moved back to the land to fashion a life they hoped would be more meaningful.

They built a rough log cabin on land they owned in southeastern Minnesota and started a Christmas tree and apple farm. But Rutter was itching for more than a private utopia; he wanted to use the farm to explore and exemplify the virtues of what he calls "woody agriculture," the cultivation of tree crops. He dubbed his operation Badgersett Research Farm and began experimenting with breeding complex hybrid varieties of chestnuts and hazelnuts. He wasn't growing American chestnuts to restore the species, but to exploit their potential as a valuable future food crop. Nut tree crops, Rutter contends, can feed the world as well as corn or wheat or other grains, but with far less damage to the environment. Unlike grain crops, nut trees are perennials, so there's no need to sacrifice precious topsoil by tilling the land every year or dousing it with chemical fertilizers. As he explains in an essay titled "Why Is the Future of the World Nuts?": "ANYTHING you can do with soybeans, or corn, we can do with these new hybrid crops. Anything. Plus more. Without losing basic productivity. While making an honest living. And with genuinely enormous environmental benefits."

Three decades later, Rutter is still growing hybrids and living in the same cluttered, fifteen-by-twenty-foot one-room cabin with his second wife, Megan, an aspiring novelist thirty years his junior, and their young daughter, Eleanor. They call Eleanor their "propagule." I visited them in late 2005; after touring the farm, we sat at the rough table they use for preparing and eating meals, as a desk, and for any other task requiring a horizontal surface. As the hours went by and we talked about chestnuts and their lives, I had the feeling the family doesn't get many visitors.

Rutter and his second wife met online, he explains a little sheepishly. His first marriage had broken up, and his two older sons had moved away. "I really needed a partner here and there weren't many walking past the door. So I started looking on the Internet, and I quickly discovered that women my own age were just flat not interested in this weird situation. So I started looking a little younger and found, indeed, there are a lot of young women who are interested in an older man. And typically one of the things they have in common is they are very, very smart." He wasn't, however, seeking someone young enough to be his daughter. Megan, who is part Sioux and spent many of her childhood summers with her godfather near the reservation in Rosebud, South Dakota, says she had to convince him that the age difference was OK.

Theirs is not an easy existence, especially during the long, frigid Minnesota winters. They cook on a wood-burning stove, which also heats the cabin; keep perishables in ice chests; and haul in water from a well about three hundred feet away. They don't have running water; jokes Megan, "We have walking water." Rutter says he deliberately built the cabin a hike from both the water supply and the dirt road that leads onto their property so as to keep him in touch with "the real world." "Here you have to get out. And periodically you get cold and periodically you get wet. And," he drops his voice to a stage whisper, "it doesn't kill ya. In fact, it's enjoyable." He even takes a certain pleasure in chopping firewood in subzero temperatures. "Because it's real. It's not exactly fun in the standard American sense, but it's extremely satisfying." Still, he's less of a purist than he was twenty-five years ago, when the family didn't even have a phone. "At this point, living this way is only half philosophical," he admits. "Half of it is purely financial. There isn't any money." What little he earns is mostly plowed back into his research operation. In 2005, he netted nineteen thousand dollars.

Living off the grid gives them a strange kind of commonality with the surrounding Amish community. Yet, unlike their neighbors, who consider them "near-Amish," the Rutters don't entirely turn their back on the modern world. The outhouse down the hill contains a sophisticated composting toilet outfitted with three seats (for a change of views), and solar panels supply electricity to their greenhouse as well as to their five computers, phone, and DVD player (they have a large collection of DVDs). When I visited, they cooked me a delicious dinner of pork chops stuffed with chestnuts and Gruyère and drizzled with high-end imported hazelnut oil.

Showing me around his greenhouse, Rutter grumbles that the Amish girls who provide part-time help have once again let the solar-powered generator run down. "My Amish girls have no clue about electricity," he complains. "They turn on the switches and leave them on."

To a hammer, all the world's a nail. Rutter's hammer is evolutionary ecology—the ways in which organisms and ecosystems respond to the pressures of natural selection. He's continually measuring the phenomena around him through the long eye of evolutionary time. In a not-atypical conversation during my visit there, Megan mentions that she discovered that cattle have a habit of peeing on hazelnut trees. "Why would bovines pee on trees?" Rutter wonders. "Perhaps to deal with canids?" (It took me a moment to realize he was talking about buffaloes and wolves.) "Well," he finally concludes, "bison and hazels did evolve together. Perhaps there's something in that interaction."

Rutter's tendency to view things in evolutionary terms is what got him interested in restoring the American chestnut. He'd learned of the tree's plight as a young man from an uncle in Ohio who loved chestnut so well he paneled his living room with old logs culled from nearby woods. But Rutter was puzzled by the species' near extinction: "The whole problem stank. It didn't make sense if you understand the evolutionary process." Epidemics never wipe out entire populations; it's not in a pathogen's interest to completely destroy its host. In a species as populous and successful as the American chestnut, certainly there should have been some trees that were able to accommodate the blight without succumbing. That virtually none did baffled him. "Almost never in the history of evolution are you going to see something like that happen. It just bloody shouldn't happen." He became convinced other factors had played a hand in the species' obliteration. And if that was the case, then there should be hope for the species. That conviction, coupled with his interest in tree crops, led him to start trying to breed blight-resistant trees. Like Burnham, he'd concluded that the best way to do so was through backcross breeding.

Rutter is a font of chestnut information, his expertise fed by a seemingly bottomless interest in the species. By the time I met him, I'd become accustomed to chestnut experts' passion for their subject. But Rutter's affinity for the tree runs deeper than that of anyone else I'd met. Even now, three decades into this interspecies love affair, he seems driven to understand chestnut, to know *Castanea* top to bottom, inside and out. The Harvard entomologist Edward O. Wilson has argued that there is an instinctive bond between humans and other species, that we have an innate need to "seek connection with the rest of life." He calls it "biophilia." If anyone exemplifies what it means to be a biophile, it is Rutter. Walking with him through his orchard on a cold and gray October morning, he has something to say about every aspect of his bare-branched charges. He remarks on the prickly burs—"the only effective anti-squirrel device ever invented"; the furry lining inside the bur—"Why is that there? It doesn't protect the nut"; the nuts—"roasted, they're like the best baked potato you ever tasted"; the root collar—"the brains of the tree"; the bark—"if you scrape half a millimeter under the bark, it's green as grass. It's making sugar all winter long."

The grassy ground is littered with opened burs and a few shiny nuts that the deer missed in their early morning browse. Here and there are the long chestnut sticks that his Amish workers use to knock the nuts from the trees. Rutter talks about how the trees often know better than he does what they need. "Most people see trees as not much different from a rock. But these organisms are sophisticated beyond most human comprehension." Imagine, he continues, if you had to write a computer program that would simulate a tree. It would have to last for six hundred years and be set up to handle everything that nature could throw at it: storms, freezes, droughts, insects, disease, and changing climates. It would have to be equipped for countless contingencies and be able to deal with them all while standing in place.

"How does the chestnut's level of sophistication compare to other trees?" I ask him.

"They're *really* different," he answers. "They break so many rules, and an awful lot of people don't like that." Given Rutter's own iconoclasm, he could be talking about himself.

In early 1981, Burnham called Rutter. They'd barely begun talking before Burnham subjected the younger man to what Rutter calls "the sniff procedure." The professor tossed out names of chestnut breeders— Jaynes, Graves, Clapper—to find out how much this backwoods tree farmer really knew. Rutter not only was familiar with each, he threw back tidbits of chestnut lore Burnham had never heard. Evidently he passed the test, for Burnham invited him up to St. Paul to talk about the prospects for resurrecting the American chestnut through backcross breeding.

By that time, Burnham had already spent several months poring through the old chestnut literature to get a handle on what the earlier breeders had done. He had gotten hold of academic papers, reports from the Northern Nut Growers Association (a trade group for orchard owners and amateur tree breeders), and even the USDA scientists' yellowing notebooks detailing their plantings back to the 1920s. There were teetering piles of paper and books all over Burnham's dark living room, and the collection had begun to spill over into the tiny kitchen.

Soon Rutter was making the three-hour trip to St. Paul on a regular basis. The two would hole up in Burnham's modest ranch house for marathon brainstorming sessions. "We'd drink, think, and talk chestnuts for days," recalls Rutter. They'd spend hours methodically plowing through the haystacks of papers for the needles of evidence to support a new breeding program. It was slow going trying to decipher the spidery handwritten notes and the coded abbreviations with which the government scientists had recorded their results. Rutter's eyes ached from scrutinizing old importation records of Chinese chestnuts brought into this country in search of trees that might be useful to a new breeding program. Given the widespread skepticism about the viability of breeding a blight-resistant American chestnut, the two knew they'd have to present a strong case. "In the legal world, they call it due diligence," says Rutter. "In the science world, it's called—I don't know—doing your homework."

One day, deep in the University of Minnesota library stacks, Rutter stumbled across a 1920 U.S. Forest Service publication that urged landowners to cut down any chestnuts they owned—dead or alive. Reading the advice, he recalls, "I actually began to cry." All at once, he understood why virtually no mature chestnuts had survived the blight. They'd never been given the chance. The Forest Service, still in its youth, had little experience with forest epidemics; its deadly simple response to the blight was deadly for the species. Rutter had always been certain some other factor played a hand in the chestnut's demise. That other factor, he now realized, "turned out to be us." As far as he was concerned, that was all the more reason for humans to come to the species' aid.

As he and Burnham pieced together what the earlier breeders had done, they began to see how their predecessors had gone astray. In their long-running quest for the perfect roll of the dice, Graves and the USDA scientists had placed all their bets on the first generation of hybrids, the so-called F_1s. But graced with hindsight and modern knowledge of genetics, Burnham and Rutter now could see that the odds of getting a perfect F_1 were virtually nil.

The Chinese trees' ability to fight the blight derived from two or three genes—that much the USDA breeders themselves had eventually discerned. What they hadn't recognized from their experiments was that those genes are incompletely dominant, meaning that they gather strength in numbers. The more of those genes a tree inherits, the better its ability to battle the blight. The Chinese chestnut's genetic baggage is packed only with blight-fighting genes, thus any offspring of a Chinese-

Chinese union is fully loaded for blight resistance (though the effectiveness of those genes can and does vary). But when a Chinese chestnut is crossed with an American chestnut, the offspring gets resistance genes just from the Chinese parent. It inherits only half the equipment it needs to resist the blight, and therefore is able to mount only a modest defense.

As the earlier researchers had dutifully recorded, many of those first-generation hybrids demonstrated an intermediate degree of resistance—not as great as their Chinese parents, but more so than their American ancestors. To fully tease out the trait required intercrossing two of the moderately resistant F1s to create an F2 generation. Unfortunately, Graves and the USDA scientists rarely made any crosses beyond the F1 generation, and on the few occasions they did, they usually backcrossed the F1s to the Chinese parents in order to boost the trees' blight resistance. Any geneticist could have predicted that the resulting trees would look more like they belonged in a Beijing orchard than a Smoky Mountains forest.

It wasn't entirely surprising that the earlier breeders had gone wrong. Most were pathologists, not geneticists. They knew the ins and outs of fungi and microbes, but understood little about the twisting ladders of DNA. Had they better comprehended the genetics of blight resistance, they surely would have tried backcross breeding, suggested Burnham diplomatically in his discussions of those earlier efforts. But Graves and the men who launched the USDA program were middle-aged in the 1930s; their training predated not only the rediscovery of Mendel's simple rules of inheritance but also the later insights of quantitative genetics, the study of traits, like height, that are governed by multiple genes which are neither simply dominant nor recessive. So they'd missed all the hopeful signs buried in their own data.

But Burnham, a man who, as Rutter says, "ate, drank and breathed genetics," read those signs. He had the training to understand the significance of the breeders' observations. And he and Rutter were heartened by what they discerned. Only two or three genes appeared to be involved in conferring resistance—the maximum for backcross breeding to easily work. The genes didn't seem to be linked to ones controlling other traits. And they were at least partially expressed in the F_1 generation, which meant that by exposing the first Chinese-American hybrids to blight, you could quickly determine which ones had picked up some resistance and easily select the best trees for the next generation of crosses. All in all, the evidence suggested that the American chestnut was a perfect candidate for backcross breeding. Hang the pessimistic conventional wisdom, the two men finally decided—the tree could be saved through breeding. One day as they sat in Burnham's kitchen lunching on grilled cheese sandwiches and scrambled eggs, Burnham swallowed, looked Rutter in the eye, and said, "We're not crazy. This is real. It can be done."

Their plan was elegantly simple. The first step was to transfer the blight-resistant genes to the American species by crossing American and Chinese trees (the most resistant of the *Castanea* species). Next, they would cross those hybrids repeatedly back to American trees to gradually phase out all other Asian characteristics besides blight resistance. Burnham reckoned it would take at least three generations of such backcrosses to produce a tree that was fifteen-sixteenths American, or 93.75 percent. Yet that still wouldn't guarantee that they would pass on the necessary resistance genes. That would require a third step: crossing the third-generation, mostly American trees with each other. The offspring of that cross would inherit resistance genes from both parents. Now equipped with a full arsenal of blight-fighting genes, those trees would go on to breed true for resistance into perpetuity. They would, Burnham predicted, be virtually indistinguishable from the original American chestnut tree. These new American chestnuts would be towering and tough and undaunted by their long-standing foe. These rolls of the dice, he was confident, were loaded to produce the long-sought perfect tree.

It takes seven to eight years for a chestnut tree to mature to flowering. Burnham could do the math: it would take a good forty years to

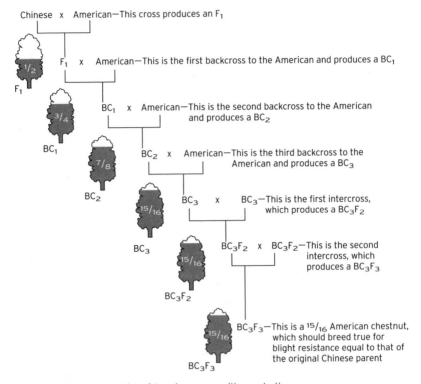

Chinese x American—This cross produces an F_1

F_1 x American—This is the first backcross to the American and produces a BC_1

F_1 — 1/2

BC_1 x American—This is the second backcross to the American and produces a BC_2

BC_1 — 3/4

BC_2 x American—This is the third backcross to the American and produces a BC_3

BC_2 — 7/8

BC_3 x BC_3—This is the first intercross, which produces a BC_3F_2

BC_3 — 15/16

BC_3F_2 x BC_3F_2—This is the second intercross, which produces a BC_3F_3

BC_3F_2 — 15/16

BC_3F_3—This is a 15/16 American chestnut, which should breed true for blight resistance equal to that of the original Chinese parent

BC_3F_3 — 15/16

Trees indicate average fraction of American genes with no selection.

The American Chestnut Foundation's backcross breeding program. With each backcross, additional American characteristics are added. It takes the first and second intercrosses to gain resistance approaching that of Chinese chestnuts. Charles Burnham and Phil Rutter thought it would take six generations to produce a tree that looks and grows like an American chestnut but can resist blight—and is capable of passing that new resistance on to its progeny. It may ultimately require additional generations to achieve that goal. (Source: The American Chestnut Foundation.)

complete the necessary series of crosses and many decades more to refill the forests with blight-resistant chestnut trees. Burnham was already seventy-five years old. He knew he'd never stand in the shade of a healthy American chestnut tree. But he urgently wanted to sow the seeds of the tree's salvation.

I've often wondered why he cared so much, but I never got a good answer from those who knew him. Other than the obligatory observation that the chestnut was a valuable timber tree, his writings express little of the emotional attachment to the tree that drove Rutter or other chestnut crusaders. Perhaps he shared Rutter's sense of social responsibility. Perhaps his interest was that of an old man who saw one final chance to make a lasting contribution, to leave behind a deeper mark than a textbook or scholarly article that would soon be out of date. As Sandra Anagnostakis has observed, "old men plant trees." Perhaps his restless intellect simply savored the challenge of solving a vexing puzzle. Or maybe he relished the chance to prove the continuing value of the science he'd spent a lifetime mastering—the mathematically driven models of classical genetics, which were being overshadowed by new advances in molecular biology. Burnham was neither an arrogant nor a flip man; still, he couldn't resist tweaking the young Turks in an article on his chestnut project written for the journal *American Scientist:* "In an era when molecular genetics and related biologies are being heralded as a solution to many intractable problems, Mendelian genetics are still a powerful tool in solving a problem that has not yielded to other approaches."

Burnham and Rutter had a theory. Now they needed material to test it. This raised a new problem: where could they find chestnuts to launch a breeding program? They knew of a few American trees here and there, including a pair that were growing at the University of Minnesota Landscape Arboretum. But they also needed Chinese chestnuts, or better still, Chinese-American hybrids. Starting with hybrids with a known pedigree would allow them to skip the first step of the breeding effort—the initial Chinese-American cross—and shave a few years off their daunting time line.

In 1981, Burnham published a letter in the journal *Plant Disease* outlining his proposal and asking for help. "I have at least one source of pollen I hope is from a first backcross. I hope to locate others. If anyone who has American chestnuts and is willing to make the crosses will send me his or her name, I will arrange to have the pollen sent." The response was . . . thundering silence.

In the chestnut world, hypovirulence was all the rage, and the forestry world considered the species beyond salvation. "You're wasting your time," scoffed one Forest Service official. "The chestnut is gone and it cannot get back into the forest."

Burnham and Rutter sought help from Richard Jaynes at the Connecticut Agricultural Experiment Station. Though Jaynes was dubious that their strategy would be any more successful than his own or prior efforts, he saw no harm in helping out. He sent Burnham a sheaf of pollen-heavy male flowers from one of the Chinese-Japanese-American hybrids in his experimental orchards. Rutter used the pollen on the American chestnuts at the University of Minnesota Arboretum to create the first generation of backcrosses. The following fall, each tree yielded two precious nuts. The new breeding program was on its way.

The program slowly expanded over the next few years as Burnham and Rutter learned about other promising parent trees, including progeny of the USDA's best hybrid, the Clapper tree. (Although the tree had died, Jaynes remembered that he had three grafts of the Clapper growing in his Connecticut test plots.) It took time to master the sheer mechanics of the breeding—learning how to ship and preserve pollen, how to best apply it to the finicky female flowers, how to orchestrate matches between southern trees that blossomed weeks before northern ones. For every success, there were many failures. But as word of the program got out, they began hearing from chestnut lovers across the native range who, undaunted by the scientific community's pessimism, had been nursing ailing trees or experimenting with breeding hybrids on their own and who now had valuable nuts or pollen to send their way. By 1983, Burnham and Rutter had backcross hybrids growing at Oberlin University, in the Great Smoky Mountains National Park, at Virginia Polytechnic Institute, at West Virginia University, and at the University of Minnesota.

The two men recognized they needed some institutional anchor to keep the effort going. This was a project that would take longer than a single lifetime, and it needed an organization that would outlast any one individual. They talked about how best to root their budding program. The fate of the USDA breeding program left both leery of handing it over to government agencies. (Rutter likes to point out that the USDA's first fruit tree breeding station now lies buried under the Pentagon.) Universities, they feared, were equally fickle; some dean could decide that plot of chestnut trees needed to be plowed under to make way for a new stadium. What was needed, Rutter told Burnham, was an independent foundation, one founded and funded strictly for restoration of the American chestnut. But it would take someone with Burnham's stature to get it off the ground. "I can call a meeting," Burnham told him.

In 1983 the two men, joined by a half-dozen University of Minnesota plant scientists gathered in a conference room at the school's plant pathology building. There they established the American Chestnut Foundation with a single mission: "the preservation and restoration of the American chestnut through funding a scientific breeding program and related research." The acting board for the new organization included Nobel laureate Norman Borlaug, former USDA breeder Fred Berry, the head of the Minnesota Nature Conservancy, University of Minnesota plant pathologists, botanists, biochemists, and geneticists, as well as chestnut veterans Richard Jaynes and William MacDonald, an expert on hypovirulence. Minneapolis lawyer Donald Willeke, a verbose lover of all things arboreal who liked to quote Churchill and St.

Augustine and who had also been involved in efforts to restore the American elm, was the board's sole nonscientist member. With the exception of Jaynes and MacDonald, not one of the sixteen founding directors actually lived in the American chestnut's native range.

The group's scientists now began trying to hammer out the mechanics of the breeding program—how many parent trees were needed, how many different hybrid lines were necessary to avoid inbreeding, how many trees had to be grown in each generation. This was all well and good, thought Rutter and Willeke, but they were becoming impatient with the relentless emphasis on scientific detail. They knew all the plans would be for naught if the foundation didn't start pushing out beyond the ivory tower to develop a grassroots base. It needed to start recruiting members. Members, the two argued, could provide not only financial support but also labor and land for growing chestnuts—ideally within the tree's native range. The issue posed the first real conflict for the new organization. The scientists chafed at the idea of turning over the group's precious genetic material to amateurs who might plant the nuts in the wrong kinds of locations, overwater the trees, contaminate pollen samples, or who knows what. Eventually, however, Rutter and Willeke prevailed, and the foundation began enrolling members and encouraging them to form state chapters.

In those first few years, the group ran mainly on "pennies and my sweat," Rutter recalls. "I wasn't getting paid anything at all." If the group was going to grow, it needed more than his free labor and Burnham's occasional small infusions of cash. Rutter now turned his attention to the difficult task of fund-raising. Starting in 1986, he began making yearly pilgrimages to the East Coast in his battered yellow Toyota Corolla in an effort to drum up money and members. Rutter knew it wouldn't be easy. How was he going to make the public care about a tree that had been gone from the landscape for decades? People had either forgotten the chestnut or considered it "an extremely dead horse," he recalls. Rutter's solution was ingenious: he began telling people that the foundation was trying to restore a tree so magnificent that it once was known as "the redwood of the east." "I made that up as a marketing tool," he says. "It was the only way to get the attention of the conservation community." Sure enough, news stories about the young organization soon began talking about its fantastic vision of restoring "the redwood of the east."

Southern Appalachia is a conservative place, and some there were shocked when "this little hippie guy," as one longtime member described Rutter, showed up in his one and only suit to speak at the local university or a garden club meeting. But Rutter was a mesmerizing speaker, able to hold a crowd like the best Baptist preacher. He'd retell the story of the chestnut's demise and talk about his hopes for the future of the species. "When the time comes," he'd say, "we can turn the blight resistant trees loose in the proper places and they will take back their old homes—all by themselves. But *we* have to give the chestnut the starting point! The tree cannot do it alone!" What the tree needed now, he'd tell people, was human help. It needed foundation members who could plant and tend various generations of hybrids and search out surviving wild American trees to help broaden the genetic base of the breeding program. His passion and excitement were infectious. Listening to Rutter, "you could not help getting involved. It came from his heart," recalls James Wilson, a longtime member of the foundation's board. Long after he'd finished speaking, audience members would still be hanging around to talk with him.

By the mid-1980s, Rutter had added to his pitch an appeal for land. Although the foundation board hadn't authorized him to make the request, Rutter was convinced the organization desperately needed a place of its own to consolidate the many plots of seedlings that were scattered up and down the East Coast. It needed a lot of land because the calculus of breeding demanded that the foundation grow a lot of trees. To get just one fully resistant tree from a Chinese-American union required tossing the dice 190 times—in other words, producing and growing 190 nuts.

Fate operates in strange ways. In 1986, Rutter was invited to speak at

Scientists' Cliffs, a summer community on the eastern shores of Chesapeake Bay. The founder of the community was Flippo Gravatt, one of the first USDA chestnut breeders, who established it as a vacation spot for federal plant scientists (and insisted that only people with PhDs could buy property there). Gravatt picked the land partly because it boasted a few surviving chestnut trees, and he built his own cabin there from chestnut logs. After his death, the chestnut cabin was turned into a community center. It was there that Rutter gave his talk.

The audience that Sunday included a pair of sisters, Jennifer and Cheri Wagner, and their ailing mother. The Wagners had spent a good part of their childhood on a farm the family owned in southwest Virginia, in the heart of historic chestnut country. As children they had often heard their father tell stories about the chestnut trees he'd seen as a child and "the shock of the blight taking 'em." Rutter's speech brought back sweet memories of their father's stories.

"It was an enthralling talk," Jennifer Wagner recalls. "You just wanted to help." Once the family talked it over, they decided they could help. They still owned the small farm in Meadowview, Virginia—twenty acres of pastureland, tobacco fields, and a rundown old farmhouse. The sisters wrote Rutter and asked if the foundation would be interested in leasing their land for its research farm.

April 15, 1989: to most Americans, the date signified Tax Day and inspired dread. But to the dozens of chestnut devotees making their way that gray, misty morning to the tiny hamlet of Meadowview, the date was cause for celebration. The day marked an exhilarating turning point in their long crusade: the American Chestnut Foundation's research farm was being formally dedicated. The American chestnut was coming home.

Rutter had driven out from Minnesota for the occasion, the back of his car filled with a few dozen precious backcross saplings ready for planting at their new home. It was still early enough in the spring that the nights threatened frost, so every evening on his trip across the country, he carefully unloaded the car and carried the potted saplings into his warm hotel room. It's not hard to imagine him stretched out on the bed while the little trees rustled happily in the heating vent's artificial breeze.

Burnham, then eighty-five years old, was too frail to make the trip. By that time he'd moved to a cramped, shared room in a nursing home and he'd grown estranged from his former protégé. Rutter attributes the estrangement to Alzheimer's disease. Burnham, he says, "started forgetting me." But others say that except for a brief period of debilitation following a stroke, Burnham was sharp as ever. He just didn't like the direction Rutter was taking the foundation; he felt Rutter's emphasis on building the organization was detracting from the scientific work demanded by the breeding program. He wasn't the only one in the group growing irritated with Rutter. "Phil is a kind of do-it-yourself person, and after a while it just starts to wear thin," says Dennis Fulbright. Whatever the reason, toward the end of his life, Burnham wanted little to do with Rutter, and his distance deeply pained the younger man.

But Burnham was still actively engaged with the breeding program. With just a thin curtain of privacy separating him from his roommate, Burnham lay in his bed, surrounded by stacks of journals and books, thinking and reading and writing about chestnuts. "He actually kept research going on from his nursing home bed," says Ronald Phillips, a former University of Minnesota colleague. When friends and colleagues gathered for his ninetieth birthday, Burnham was as optimistic as ever about the chestnut. "I'm sure it will be back," he declared. Indeed, he hung fast to the fight for the tree's life almost until the last day of his life in 1995. Albert Ellingboe, a plant geneticist whom Burnham had taught and later recruited to the board of the foundation, visited the old man thirteen days before he died. Normally, their conversations were all about the chestnut. But this time the elderly professor told Ellingboe, "Al, I can't help anymore. What goes on now is up to you."

It's a pity Burnham was unable to be in Meadowview on that April morning to see his vision come to life. A light rain began to fall as the crowd of about 150 scientists, volunteers, reporters, chestnut veterans, and those newly inspired to join the campaign marched up the muddy hill to the field where the first experimental orchards were planned. There was nothing here yet but grassy hummocks, gopher holes, and a few slender young seedlings waiting to be planted. In just a few years, it would be filled with row after row of waving chestnut trees.

Facing the crowd, Rutter felt a surge of pride. He'd quickly written out a speech for the ceremony the night before and hoped he would strike just the right tone—something momentous but also joyous, something that would speak to the marriage of love and science that had brought them all to this place. "Dearly beloved!" he declared, and then paused dramatically while the audience laughed. "We are gathered here today, in the sight of the rain and the wind, the mountains and the trees, to join with each other and with this land in a bond of holy determination. We are determined that the trees we plant shall survive, and grow, and flower. . . . Today we place our feet firmly on the trail that will lead to the restoration of the American chestnut tree.

"Let us plant!"

EIGHT

Chestnut 2.0

Many of the chestnut people I've talked to are optimistic, go-get-'em types. But even in that can-do crowd, Herb Darling stands out. A compact, outdoorsy septuagenarian with a shock of white hair and an expressive face, Darling spent his career as a construction engineer in Buffalo, New York. He built the foundations of some of Buffalo's biggest buildings, burrowed beneath Lake Ontario, and tunneled under the Niagara River—"Twice!" he notes—to bring water to his thirsty hometown. He's not the kind of person who gets hung up when knotty problems arise.

In the mid-1980s, a hunter informed Darling that there was an American chestnut growing on his property in central New York. Darling hadn't realized any chestnuts were still alive, and now that he had one—an eighty-foot giant, no less—he sure wasn't going to sit around and watch it die. Immediately he was on the phone, calling everyone he could think of to learn what he could do to safeguard the rarity. Eventually he found his way to Phil Rutter, who offered to come out to New York and take a look at the tree, because in those early days of the American Chestnut Foundation, that was the sort of thing he did. After examining the tree, Rutter delivered the bad news. "Your tree's not going to last more than three to five years," he said, pointing out all the spots where the blight had set up shop.

"I want to try to save it," Darling told him. Rutter suggested the only therapy he knew of: applying mudpacks to every canker to suffocate the blight fungus. And so, even though the tree was as tall as a six-story building, Darling and his son erected scaffolds around it and packed mud onto every canker they could see. The tree lasted five years, instead of three. But the fact that it still died "got me so mad," Darling recalls, "I decided to do something."

The something he's doing is a controversial move in chestnut circles. Instead of joining the American Chestnut Foundation's backcross breeding program, Darling and fellow chestnut enthusiasts in the Foundation's New York state chapter have opted to pursue a different strategy for saving the species. They're counting on the ultimate can-do science: biotechnology. In particular, they're counting on Charles Maynard and William Powell, a pair of scientists at the State University of New York College of Environmental Science and Forestry (SUNY-ESF) in Syracuse who are trying to bioengineer a blight-resistant chestnut tree by taking genes from sources wholly unrelated to the *Castanea* family and inserting them into the DNA of American chestnuts.

It's easy to see why Darling is enamored with the high-tech approach. Old-fashioned breeding is a time-consuming, chancy process, requiring decades of crosses, selections, and culls to transfer the genetic instructions for a particular trait. This new-fashioned breeding, as some proponents call it, promises a way to transfer blight-resistance—or any number of other traits—with greater speed and efficiency. With a few snips and tucks of the molecular scissors and tweezers, you could potentially revise the genetic coding of a tree so that it grows faster or straighter, repels bugs or resists weed killers, weathers winter freezes or summer droughts. You could fashion the tree of a lumberman or paper manufacturer's dreams. You could design trees that pull toxic chemicals out of the soil or suck up excess greenhouse gasses from the atmosphere. And you could rescue an endangered species.

"There's a better future down the road for all trees with biotech, if it works," insists Darling, echoing a point Maynard and Powell also make. A better future. That's a can-do kind of outlook, one underpinned by an implicit faith in human ability to perfect and control technology. That may be a fine presumption when pondering an ambitious set of blueprints for a building or tunnel or bridge. But what about when your sights are set on something as extraordinarily complex and little-understood as the blueprint of a living organism, a master plan that has been billions of years in the making and is constantly being revised? Intrigued as I am by the possibilities offered by biotechnology "if it works," I can't help but wonder whether the real question is not if it can work, but whether I want it to.

A whiteboard in Powell's cluttered office is covered with a list of what look like nonsensical strings of letters and numbers. "WIN639-CPO-WIN6:39+355-NPTII," reads one; "P355-CPOT," another. Each, Powell explains, represents a gene—actually, a set of genes—he hopes will provide new weaponry to fill the fatal gaps in the American chestnut's own genetic arsenal. As of early 2006, he had eight genes on his list.

Powell, forty-eight years old, has sandy brown hair, a medium build, wire-framed glasses, and an open, expressive manner. He comes across as a bit of a science nerd, someone who enthusiastically describes this or that gene as "really neat" and who enjoys the arcane sport of geo-caching—scavenger hunts that rely on handheld GPS units and Internet clues. "I've always been interested in science," he says. "I was one of those kids that grew up with the Apollo missions, and that kind of stuff interested me." As he runs through the list of genes, describing the properties of each, Maynard listens attentively, occasionally throwing out elaborations or clarifications. The two are close collaborators, though it's a partnership that draws its strength more from their differences than their similarities.

Powell exudes high energy and speaks with rapid-fire delivery. Maynard, fifty-four years old, is a tall, affable man with thinning, curly black hair and squinty dark eyes who operates at a slower speed and plays his cards closer to the vest. Even Linda Polin McGuigan, his long-time lab technician, says she doesn't know much about what he does when he's not at work. (Not much, he admits, aside from watching TV and reading science fiction.) Maynard's office is orderly and has an all-business feel; few personal knickknacks are out for display. Powell's is awash in piles of papers, the walls plastered with posters, lists, and cartoons poking fun of scientists at work. Maynard tends to be cautious and methodical, while Powell is more of a charge-ahead, worry-the-details-later kind of guy.

"We don't see each other that much outside work," says Maynard.

"But I think we're very good colleagues," adds Powell.

They came to working on the American chestnut through very different routes. Maynard grew up in Des Moines, Iowa, the son and grandson of printers. While he spent weekends and summers working in the family business, he knew from a young age it wasn't for him. A lifelong affection for trees led him to forestry. He became interested in the emerging field of biotechnology while studying forest genetics and breeding at Iowa State University. He was intrigued by the possibilities the technology offered for the science of domesticating forest trees—"improving" them, as breeders call it. But he didn't have any specific trees in mind for genetic improvement when he arrived at SUNY-ESF in 1980. Several years later, he went to hear Phil Rutter speak about the newly formed American Chestnut Foundation. Maynard didn't know much about American chestnuts—he'd only seen one in his life, a raggedy specimen growing on the edges of the Iowa State campus. Listening to Rutter describe the foundation's chestnut breeding program, Maynard decided that the tree was a perfect candidate for bioengineering. Still, he lacked the expertise to tackle the project alone. Though he knew lots about growing and breeding trees, he knew only a little bit about molecular biology or gene-building technology. That's Powell's bailiwick.

The son of an Air Force mechanic, Powell spent much of his childhood on a series of military bases, including three years in Germany where his dad manned the silos containing nuclear missiles aimed at Eastern Europe. (If the elder Powell felt anything about the gravity of his responsibility, he never mentioned it to his son. All he said, Powell recalls, was that the job was "really boring. He'd read two books a night.") After high school, Powell followed in his father's steps, joining the Air Force so he could pay for college. He planned to become a veterinarian, but "after taking a few courses and having to dissect a few frogs, I decided I didn't like cutting up animals." He preferred biology on a much smaller scale—at the molecular level, which is where he focused his studies as a plant pathologist. He was introduced to the American chestnut in graduate school at the University of Utah, when he began working with Neal Van Alfen, one of the early researchers on hypovirulence. The job market took Powell to the University of Florida and dictated a shift in focus to a pathogen afflicting tomatoes. But he was eager to get back to the problem of chestnut blight and jumped at the chance to join Maynard at SUNY in 1989.

Their complementary scientific expertises make the two a perfect—and indispensable—fit. As Powell says, "Either one of us by ourselves would have a really hard time doing this project."

Consider what is involved in creating a genetically modified organism, such as the Roundup Ready soybean, which was introduced by Monsanto in 1996 and today accounts for about 75 percent of all U.S. soybeans. If you were to dismantle a Roundup Ready soybean down to its molecular studs and beams, you'd find buried in the DNA of every single cell the inserted gene that allows the plant to survive repeated applications of the weed killer Roundup, which is also produced by Monsanto. To create the Roundup Ready bean in the first place required two basic things: an herbicide-resistant gene to add to the chromosomes of soybean cells and a method for growing those genetically transformed cells into full-sized plants. The same requirements hold for bioengineering a blight-resistant chestnut. Each of those requirements calls on different scientific know-how. In their partnership, Powell is the gene guy, and Maynard has the task of growing the transformed cells. While Powell's job sounds more "sci fi," in fact, Maynard's job has been the more challenging—or at least, more frustrating—piece of the project.

Even before Powell arrived in Syracuse, Maynard had spent several years trying to work out a system for coaxing a cluster of chestnut cells to regenerate into a whole tree. "Some plants are ridiculously easy to regenerate," he explains. "You can take a leaf of tobacco, pop out a circle with a paper punch, put it on the right medium, and new tobacco plants will pop up all over." Hybrid poplars are also eager to please, so amenable to genetic transformation and regeneration that they have become the lab rat of forest biotechnology. In fact, the first transgenic tree, created in 1987, was a hybrid poplar outfitted with a gene to resist Roundup. It took so little time to produce that tree that when Maynard and Powell started working with chestnut, they were sure they'd have a blight-resistant tree within five to ten years.

But as everyone who works with it finds, chestnut is exasperatingly finicky. It inevitably balks at human efforts to fix it. "It's as if it wants to go extinct," scientists who've worked with the tree have joked. Maynard and his graduate students tried establishing plants in culture from tissue taken from all over the tree—from shoots, buds, and leaves. Nothing worked. The tree resisted every propagation method they tried.

While Maynard struggled with the problem of regeneration, Powell got busy looking for genes that could be deployed for blight resistance. The most obvious choice, of course, would be the genes that arm Asian chestnuts against the blight. But no one has yet identified or isolated those genes, and Powell had neither the resources nor the inclination at the time to start something as ambitious as a gene mapping project.* So he began perusing the scientific literature for genes that already had been culled from other organisms; genes that were foreign to both the chestnut tree and the blight fungus and so could provide wholly new ways for the tree to resist its foe. That way, the pair hoped, they could engineer a tree with even stronger blight resistance than the Chinese or Japanese chestnut—maybe even one that is completely immune to *Cryphonectria parasitica.*

Powell filled his shopping list with possibilities from a wide and sometimes surprising range of sources. African clawed frogs, for example, were inspiration for the first gene he worked with. Powell learned that the frogs' skin secretes antimicrobial peptides (tiny proteins) that fight infection. Actually all animals, including humans, produce these kinds of proteins, but since frogs live in such a miasma of microbes, the stuff their skin produces is particularly potent. The gene responsible for that antimicrobial effect would have been a good weapon against the blight, Powell thought, but he decided not to use it. Since his goal is a tree with edible nuts, he feared people might be put off by the presence of a frog gene in their food.

Instead, he studied the gene's structure and used that as a model to construct a similar gene from scratch. The resulting synthetic gene codes for tiny pieces of protein that poke holes in the outer membrane of fungal cells, causing an organism like *C. parasitica* to leak to death. As

---

*That effort is now under way. In mid-2006, the National Science Foundation awarded a $2.7 million grant for a team of scientists around the country to create genetic maps in the family Fagaceae, which includes beech, oak, and chestnut. Powell is one of the collaborators on the grant and is hopeful that the project may locate the Chinese resistance genes within a few years. "Once found, Chuck and I would be happy to try putting the Chinese resistance genes in American chestnut." But bioengineers wouldn't be the only ones to gain from a map of the *Castanea* genome. Those using classical breeding methods to restore the chestnut could benefit as well. The American Chestnut Foundation's breeders would be able to use molecular markers to identify the best, most resistant trees in any generation with much more precision and without having to wait until the trees are old enough to be challenged with a dose of blight fungus.

is common practice in bioengineering, in order to help control the outcome and minimize risk, Powell designed the gene product with two "safety features." The first was a "promoter," a kind of molecular on/off switch that would ensure the antimicrobial gene is activated only in the bark of the tree when and where the blight fungus attacks. But in case the antimicrobial enzyme is produced in the nuts as well, he made sure the gene could be quickly digested so that no harm would result to people or animals that ate them. Powell expected that the presence of two such fail-safes would boost confidence in the overall safety of the transgene.

To his and Maynard's disappointment, however, other chestnut researchers did not share their enthusiasm for the transgene. Some were frankly appalled. Albert Ellingboe, one of the science advisors to the American Chestnut Foundation, was dubious that it was really possible to control where the antimicrobial gene would be expressed or that it would really be safe for human consumption. "Even if you get a plant, what are you going to do with it? Because you and I can't eat the nuts," he told Powell and Maynard.

Another researcher, James Hill Craddock, was also skeptical that the gene would only swing into action in wounds where the blight attacked. He worried about the implications of a tree engineered to destroy fungal organisms. "That didn't seem to me a very good idea," he says. "If you make a plant that's completely fungus proof, it's not going to be part of the natural system" because trees coexist in symbiosis with various fungi, including the vital mycorrhizae that help trees absorb minerals from the soil.

Powell remains fond of the antimicrobial gene, convinced that it is the most effective and safest candidate he has found to date. After all, he says, "we know more about it [than any other possibilities] because we designed it from scratch." Still, he continued his hunt for other genes. The candidate now at the top of his whiteboard list—pVSB-OxO—is one he is sure will prove more acceptable, mainly because it comes from something people already eat: wheat.

"It's a really neat gene," Powell says enthusiastically as he describes how it works. The fight between parasitic fungi and their host plants is often a chemical war. Many fungi, including *Cryphonectria parasitica,* initiate their attack by releasing a potent chemical, oxalic acid. ("It's a good acid," Maynard chimes in. "It's one of the active ingredients in deck cleaners.") The oxalic acid lowers the pH along the front lines of the battle, killing the plant cells that are there. But many grasses, including wheat, have evolved a natural defense against this chemical assault. They release an enzyme, oxalate oxidase, that neutralizes the oxalic acid and breaks it down into harmless by-products. When Powell read that researchers had isolated the oxalate oxidase gene from wheat, he thought to himself, "Wow, this looks perfect."

But he didn't yet have a place to put it. Maynard was still trying to propagate chestnut tissue, and by this time had embarked on a new approach, using chestnut embryos. To explain, he pulls out a small chestnut from a bag of nuts behind his desk and carefully peels off the skin with a Swiss Army knife. Using the tip of the blade, he digs into the pointy end of the nut and extracts a tiny white nugget, barely the size of a grain of rice. This is the embryo. If it's extracted at just the right point in its development and pampered in just the right way, that single embryo will divide and multiply into dozens, hundreds of new embryos called somatic embryos. One embryo can generate a cell line— a colony of cells—that lives almost indefinitely.

At least that's the theory. In practice, it took years for him to success- fully generate viable plants from these clonally propagated somatic embryos. (And Maynard readily admits that much of his success was ultimately due to methods developed by the only other researcher try- ing to culture chestnut tissue, Scott Merkle, at the University of Georgia in Athens.) "I've got one slide I show people," he says. "I call it my $250,000 slide. It's got six boxes," each representing a stage in the process of growing plants from somatic embryos. "Each stage took one graduate student and two or three years at a time."

With more money and more grad students, the two insist the work surely would have gone faster. "We always work on a shoestring here," says Powell. They've gotten annual grants ranging from ten thousand to seventy thousand dollars from the American Chestnut Foundation's New York chapter, and for three years they got a hundred-thousand-dollar grant from New York State, until the response to the September 11, 2001, terrorist attacks dried up that money. They got a glimpse of what a big budget can accomplish when they visited one of Monsanto's biotech labs. "It was like we had died and gone to heaven," says Maynard. "They can just crank out transgenics," adds Powell. "We came back to our labs and it felt like we're playing here."

A variety of technical factors slowed Maynard's progress. For starters, the vast majority of embryos resist forming clones: only about one in every one thousand develops a fruitful cell line; the rest "grow into little disorganized lumps of nothing," says Maynard. He spent years discarding thousands of little disorganized lumps of nothing, until finally by 1995 he had a few cell lines ready for genetic transformation.

The actual mechanics of gene transfer is a weird mix of high- and low-tech. One approach is to use a gene gun—it's literally a gun—that shoots tiny gold particles coated with DNA into the tissue. It's a "brute force" kind of method, says Maynard, and in the case of chestnut, it didn't work particularly well. (Plus, on a few occasions the target tissue splattered all over the lab.) He and Powell opted instead for a more elegant transport system: using agrobacterium, a microbe that has evolved its own feat of genetic engineering in order to feed itself. The bacteria drill channels through a plant's cell walls and insert genes that travel into the nucleus, insinuate themselves into the plant's DNA, and instruct the cell to start producing food for the bacteria. "It's an almost unique natural system," says Powell admiringly, and one easily co-opted by human bioengineers, who outfit the agrobacterium with the genes they want to deploy. (That involves a complicated process of mixing the microbes in a flask with the desired DNA, which in this state, I'm told, "looks like snot.")

For their project, Powell and Maynard are equipping agrobacterium with a trio of genes: the one coding for oxalate oxidase, which contains a promoter (derived from soybeans) to ensure the oxalate oxidase is produced only in the tissues where the blight fungus attacks; a marker gene that allows them to see whether the gene transfer has worked by making the cells that have taken up the new gene look green under a special light; and an herbicide resistance gene, so they can use herbicide to kill off all the cells that haven't been "transformed." They pour a broth swimming with the gene-loaded agrobacterium over the chestnut embryos, and later check to see which have incorporated the transgenes. Through a microscope outfitted with a special light and filter, I look at a dish of treated cells. A clump of waxy, whitish balls comes into focus, and sure enough, a few knobs glow a ghostly green—the incandescent sign of success. Maynard picks out the cells that "glow and grow" and transfers them to new petri dishes that he marks with smiley faces.

As with every stage of the way from cell to plant, the yield is incredibly low: only about 1 percent of the cells that go through the agrobacterium bath come out glowing and growing. And only a fraction of the cells that glow end up growing in the way the researchers want. Among other factors, there's no way of controlling where in the chestnut DNA the new genes wind up. If the gene lands in the wrong spot, it may not be expressed in the right parts of the plant, or expressed in response to the fungus, or even expressed at all. For this reason, they have to repeat the process many, many times to find the transformed embryos that function correctly.

The most challenging part of the whole process has been getting the transgenic cells to grow into whole plants. Each step of the plant's development has been fraught with technical difficulties, demanding tedious trial-and-error experiments on such mundane but crucial matters as finding the right growth hormones to regenerate shoots or the proper soil mix for roots or the optimum humidity for tiny treelets. By 1997, Maynard had finally managed to generate whole chestnut trees—not yet genetically altered—from somatic embryos. That year, he and Powell proudly planted a dozen of the tissue-cultured trees at the university's experimental plantations and gave Darling six more to plant on his property in central New York.

But it would take at least another seven years to get to the same place with genetically transformed cells. At one lecture, Maynard summarized the setbacks in a slide that read: "Results: FRUSTRATION!"

The whole enterprise "is really more of an art than a science," says Linda Polin McGuigan, Maynard's laboratory manager.

"If we were doing this with hybrid poplar . . ." Powell starts to say.

"Oh, don't talk about hybrid poplar," Maynard interjects with a groan.

"You can go from transformation to a whole tree in four to five months," Powell continues. "With chestnut, the whole thing takes eighteen months."

"And that's if everything goes right," adds Maynard.

They're more familiar with what can go wrong. "I keep getting plants and then they die," says McGuigan. In the fall of 2004, the team finally had a few transformed treelets potted in soil and growing in Maynard's office. Members of the New York chapter of the American Chestnut Foundation came by to ooh and ahh. At last, it seemed all those years of effort were about to pay off. But within a few weeks, the treelets all died, victims of the overly dry air in Maynard's office.

A few months later, the team again had some newly transformed treelets. Once again, it seemed that they had rounded the corner. But asbestos removal at the university forced Maynard and McGuigan to evacuate their lab over the summer, and the treelets died. When they returned in the fall, McGuigan found herself back near square one. For six months she absolutely could not coax any of the transformed embryos to form shoots again even though, she says, "I was following the same procedures, using the same material."

"You forgot the magic spell," Maynard says, sparking a round of laughter. "We laugh," he continued, "but there's a lot of art to plant tissue culture. Some of the techniques can be learned, but a lot of it is a matter of magic fingers." Even in this high-precision, high-tech science, success can hinge on something as fuzzy and unscientific as a green thumb.

There's a certain irony about a project that is using the iconic technology of the twenty-first century to restore the iconic tree of a nineteenth-century way of life. Yet Maynard and Powell see themselves as fitting firmly into the tradition of scientists who have been struggling to rescue the chestnut tree for over a century. "I still consider myself a plant breeder," Maynard says emphatically. "We look at what we're doing as what plant breeders have been doing for a hundred years and what domestication has been doing for ten thousand years. We think we can extrapolate from [that experience]. . . . We're putting out there something that is no different than what could have evolved through natural selection and evolution." As he sees it, he and Powell are simply "giving natural selection more raw material to work with."

It's true different species do hybridize. Oaks are notoriously promiscuous, and the amiable pairing of different chestnut species is the linchpin of the American Chestnut Foundation's breeding program. Yet the chances that the oxalate oxidase gene in wheat could naturally find its way into the chestnut genome are infinitesimally slim. In fact, nature exerts a check on how far astray a species' genes can roam. If the pairing is too unlikely, the offspring are usually sterile. Think of mules. Genetic engineering breaches that natural barrier—not only across species and genera, but even across whole phyla.

It also bypasses the natural selective pressures that test the gene variants, or alleles, that give rise to new traits. Typically, new alleles arise in a population through mutation or migration (of seed or pollen). Either way, a new allele's arrival is a shy knock at the door, and whether it ultimately gains sway in a population depends on chance and on whether it has any selective advantage to offer. If it does offer an added edge in the fight for survival, then it will gradually become part of the population as it is passed through a chain of relatives over vast stretches of time. Bioengineering, however, circumvents that long process. With gene technology, a new allele busts through the door and pushes its way into the organism's genome like an aggressive party crasher. If multitudes of the transgenic organism are being produced in a lab, then a new population arises that has never been subjected to the tests of natural selection.

For that reason, some contend, you cannot compare conventional plant breeding with transgenic breeding, or extrapolate from experience with the former to predict what will happen with the latter. One prominent critic, David Suzuki, a geneticist retired from the University of British Columbia, calls it the difference between vertical and horizontal gene transfer. Thousands of years of experience have told us more or less what to expect when genes are transferred vertically from one generation to the next. Moving them horizontally with molecular gizmos moves us into new, uncharted terrain. Whether that's for better or worse remains an open question. Still, despite the many uncertainties, the rush is on to develop transgenic trees. And many are counting on the chestnut to lead the way.

Up until the mid-twentieth century, most of America's timber needs were supplied by native forests or lightly managed plantings of wild trees. Industrial tree science, such as it was, consisted mainly of finding ways to improve and strengthen wood after it was cut. It was a science of glues, resins, and kilns. Forestry offered guidance on how to plant trees for the best wood production, yet even in those human-tended forests, the trees remained untamed, undomesticated plants.

It wasn't until relatively recently that anyone contemplated cultivating forest trees in the way agricultural crops like corn or wheat or barley are cultivated. The process that transformed the tough, tiny nubs of ancient maize into the foot-long ears of sweet corn we eat today spanned ten thousand years and involved the combined selective pressures of humans and nature. As writer Michael Pollan points out, "Domestication has never been a simple one-way process in which our species has controlled others. . . . The plant in its wildness proposes new qualities, and then man (or, in the case of natural selection, nature) selects which of those qualities will survive and prosper." Where would bakers be today were it not for a natural, single-gene mutation that arose in wheat eons ago and prevented some stalks from spontaneously shattering and scattering their seeds? With their seed trapped on the stalk, those mutant plants could never have survived in the wild. But that mutation allowed humans to gather the seeds, plant them, and harvest a new crop containing more of these mutant seeds that could be sown, harvested, and ground into flour. And so began agriculture in the Fertile Crescent.

The effort to tame forest trees is barely fifty years old, not even the blink of an eye on the evolutionary time line. Yet the science serving as midwife to that effort renders the ancient timescale meaningless. Even without bioengineering, the domestication of forest trees has moved breathtakingly fast.

Drawing on advances in genetic theory and agricultural experience, breeders have been able to quickly exploit the inherent variability of valuable species to produce, say, Monterey pines that grow bigger and thicker or loblolly pines that are more easily pulped into paper. Modern methods of mass propagation allow forest companies to clone select specimens and then erect a wholly new kind of forest: vast plantations of trees growing in eerily orderly ranks, like some arboreal version of the old Soviet Army lined up for a May Day parade. In appearance, such plantations are as far removed from an old growth forest as my supermarket corn is from an ear of Mayan maize. Many are models of high-tech wizardry. Sprawling pipelines deliver water, fertilizer, and insecticides through automated "chemigation" systems that invert the normal scale between people and trees. "We control what the trees get almost as precisely as if they were on a petri dish in a lab," boasted the

research manager of a seventeen-thousand-acre hybrid poplar plantation in Oregon owned by timber company Potlatch. Such intensive,
mechanized plantations are sprouting all over the globe and already
supply the bulk of trees needed to satisfy the world's ever-growing
appetite for wood.

Still for all the high-tech pampering, those Potlatch hybrid poplars
contain essentially the same genetic blueprint as wild poplar trees. To
substantially change a tree's constitution through conventional breeding
(for example, to create a more pulpable loblolly or a faster growing
poplar) would take a long time—decades, if not centuries, given how
slowly trees grow. Gene-transfer technology offers a way to greatly
accelerate that process.

Bioengineering offers a way to "create the tree we want," as one leading researcher in the field has put it—a loblolly or poplar or sweet gum
Version 2.0, engineered to human specifications. By now, there are
dozens of different species of transgenic trees (most of them fruit, not
forest trees) growing in hundreds of test plots in the United States and
at least sixteen other countries. Transgenic trees are being field-tested
on every continent except treeless Antarctica. Almost none have yet
been commercially released. As of 2006, the USDA had given the green
light to only one: a papaya engineered to resist ring-spot virus, a scourge
that had threatened to wipe out Hawaii's papaya industry.

Most of the research has focused on relatively modest revisions:
adding a single gene to alter a single trait, like the herbicide-resistant
gene that was used to create the first transgenic tree in 1987. But taking
that utilitarian goal—the tree we want—to its logical conclusion, some
researchers have talked about a radical "rearchitecturing" of the basic
design of trees. Robert Kellison, of the Institute of Forest Biotechnology
in Raleigh, North Carolina, explains: "If it's lumber we want, the tree
we grow naturally today isn't the most efficient tree." Leaves, branches,
a soaring bole, and a sprawling root system may be valuable for organisms growing in the wild, but they're a waste of energy in a Forest
Version 2.0 whose occupants are all destined for the lumber mill. The

ideal plantation tree, according to Kellison, would be shorter and wider, with few branches and shallow roots—in other words, a giant block of wood. "Not that anyone's trying to genetically engineer that kind of tree today," he hastens to add.

Still, industry wish lists have largely set the research agenda in tree transgenics. One of the most hotly pursued areas is transgenic trees that contain less lignin, the cellular glue that holds wood fibers together and makes wood, well, woody. Lignin has to be removed to make paper, and that's a toxic and expensive process that costs the pulp and paper industry billions each year. (Conversely, since high lignin content makes for stronger lumber, there's also research focused on raising lignin levels.) Another top research area is the production of insect-resistant trees, mainly by lifting a gene from the common soil bacterium *Bacillus thuringiensis,* or Bt. Indeed, China has embraced this latter product wholeheartedly and has reportedly planted one million Bt poplars as part of an ambitious scheme to reforest some forty-four million acres by 2012. Ironically, as writer Michael Pollan points out, the use of sprayed Bt to manage pests was pioneered by organic farmers and gardeners, the very types of "greenies" most wary of biotechnology.

Though commercial interests may be driving the push for bioengineered trees, the technology does potentially offer environmental benefits, as advocates are quick to point out. Indeed, Powell says that's what got him interested in bioengineering in the first place: he hoped the development of insect-resistant transgenic trees could dramatically reduce reliance on polluting pesticides. Likewise, low-lignin trees could reduce the toxic messes generated by paper mills. Plantations of extra-fast-growing trees could act as sinks for atmospheric carbon dioxide, the heat-trapping greenhouse gas. One researcher hopes to use genetic technology to modify the structure and cell wall chemistry of trees to increase the amount of carbon dioxide they are able to store in their roots underground, boosting trees' natural capacity to help mitigate global warming. Transgenic trees might be used as potent bioremediators, like the yellow poplar that's being designed to pull mercury out of contaminated soil. University of Georgia researchers outfitted the poplars with a mercury-resistant bacterial gene that allows the trees to convert mercury in the soil to a less poisonous gas that can then be dispersed into the air. One place the trees are being tested is a site in Danbury, Connecticut, that was contaminated by dozens of hat factories, which historically relied on the poisonous mineral to cure pelts.

Advocates also contend that bioengineering offers a sustainable way to keep pace with the world's growing demand for trees. If we can fill plantations with the trees we need, that will reduce pressure on natural forests for the trees we want to save. Maude Hinchee, chief technology officer of a forest biotechnology company in South Carolina called ArborGen, described this technocratic vision of environmental balance to me: "The big picture is allowing people to grow trees more like crops. You can grow more wood on less land, so you don't have to go harvest old growth stands. So the potential is great for preserving forests for people and having these agricultural areas that are growing trees that are more product-focused."

Yet this tidy vision of sustainability ignores many messy realities, chief among them that it's still far from clear whether the potential environmental benefits of biotechnology outweigh the potential risks. For all the pretenses of precision, this remains a technology rife with uncertainties. The very act of gene transfer is itself unpredictable. Scientists still have no way of directing a new gene to a specific location on the genome. And since most genes code for more than a single trait, where the new gene takes up residence on the double helix and which genes are its neighbors can have implications for how it behaves over the long term.

"We really don't know very well what we're getting into when we start manipulating forest trees in this way," says Douglas Gurian-Sherman, who formerly reviewed transgenic crops and organisms for the Environmental Protection Agency and now is a senior scientist for the Center for Food Safety in Washington, D.C. "When you put a gene into a plant, it may interact in all kinds of unpredictable ways with the genome that is there."

A case in point is the Flavr-Savr tomato, genetically engineered to ripen more slowly than normal. Only after the tomato had been approved by the FDA did researchers discover that the same gene that delayed ripening also allowed the plant to accumulate large amounts of heavy metals from the soil. Some of the tomatoes could tolerate up to five times as much cadmium as normal tomatoes. Even conventional breeding has demonstrated the unpredictable ripple effects of new genes. In one famous case, corn breeders developed varieties of corn that were bred to be male-sterile. But the sterility had an unexpected side effect: the corn became extraordinarily vulnerable to a new strain of southern corn leaf blight, a pathogen that until then had been a minor pest.

No one yet can describe with certainty the long-term specific or environmental effects of a poplar that contains alien genes in every cell of its being that allow it to repel certain insects. Would it be more vulnerable to new pathogens or pests? Potatoes that were genetically transformed to resist the Colorado potato beetle came under attack by a growing population of a different nuisance, aphids. Would insects develop resistance to the new resistance trait? Experts consider this a virtual inevitability, given that the lifetime of a tree spans thousands of generations of bugs, allowing them ample time to evolve resistance. Could the new gene be dispersed through pollen or seeds into natural forests, potentially affecting the genome of wild poplar trees? Oregon researchers working on transgenic trees found transformed seeds in traps in cleared plots outside their study plantations, and discovered that up to 3.8 percent of seedlings in those cleared plots had been fathered by the plantation transgenics.

In answer to this last issue—the risk of "gene drift"—advocates of the technology summon an interesting defense, hearkening back to the same Darwinian rules that bioengineering sidesteps. They contend the new transgenes likely would be unable to gain a toehold in the wild because natural selection will work against them. "The main risks of using novel, highly domesticated trees will be to the growers and local economies, rather than to wild ecosystems, as highly altered trees are unlikely to be competitive in wild environments," writes Stephen Strauss, of Oregon State University, one of the leading researchers in forest biotechnology. Maynard agrees: "Evolution is a powerful force," he says. He maintains that bioengineered trees would have about as much chance in a wild ecosystem as lab rats released into a city sewer system: "The sewer rats would have them for lunch." Just in case, bio-engineers also are working to prevent the problem of gene drift by try-ing to develop trees that are sterile or have delayed flowering.

Such uncertainties galvanized opposition to genetically modified food crops. Arguably, the stakes are even higher with transgenic forest trees because trees have much longer life spans and dwell in far denser, richer ecosystems than the average soybean field. The lengthy list of unknowns is why environmental groups are pushing for a moratorium on the commercial development of transgenic trees until far more research and testing is done.

When I raise the risk of unintended consequences, Powell becomes exasperated. "That's the thing to bring up if you ever want to argue this, because there's no answer to that argument. Can you guarantee that when you drive your car to the airport you're not going to get into an accident?" It's a question of risk assessment, say Powell, Maynard, and other biotech advocates. They insist that through careful research and field trials, the uncertainties about the long-term risks of transgenic trees will be gradually whittled away. "The question is, how much test-ing do you need to do?" says Powell. He disagrees with critics who pro-pose tests on the order of decades. "What you do is a study for three to four years so you build up a history and can then predict [what will hap-pen] for one hundred years. . . . If you find a problem during the field trials, then it shouldn't be deregulated until it's resolved."

There's that can-do confidence again. Setting aside such issues as whether small field trials can predict large ecological effects or whether the current pro-market regulatory system will demand adequate risk assessments—two points some environmentalists dispute—I find myself troubled by Powell's deep faith in technology, by this certainty that we can predict and solve problems in natural systems that we still so little understand. Isn't this same assurance about our ability to direct nature toward our desired ends what got the chestnut in trouble in the first place?

In some ways, the chestnut represents a special case in the debate over transgenic trees. It probably poses relatively few environmental risks, because there are few chestnuts in the wild that could be affected by straying transgenes. It's even arguable that genetic engineering promises a less environmentally intrusive way to fix chestnut blight than conventional breeding: only a few genes would be added to the twenty-seven thousand to forty-five thousand genes thought to make up the American chestnut genome, whereas backcross breeding introduces not only those Asian genes that confer resistance but also an unknown number of others. Should it eventually be possible to target and transfer only the resistance genes from Asian trees, the resulting transgenic tree would be unquestionably "more American" than the 94 percent American chestnut the foundation aims to produce through backcross breeding.

And Maynard and Powell make a strong case that bioengineering would permit them to swiftly respond to any new pests that emerge as a threat to the chestnut. As Powell says, "We could start putting in genes for those pests in a couple of years, whereas backcross breeding would take another fifteen years or more."

So it's not surprising that even some of biotech's fiercest critics have second thoughts when it comes to a transgenic American chestnut, or any of the half-dozen or so other endangered species that are candidates for gene-transfer rescues. "To me, that's a much more compelling case than just trying to get trees to grow a little faster," says Faith Campbell, who authored a critical analysis of transgenic trees for the American Lands Alliance. "Restoring endangered species is to me a higher goal that's worth taking some of those risks for."

Still, noble as Maynard and Powell's ends may be, I would be less ambivalent about the means they have chosen were it not for the possibility that a transgenic American chestnut will be used to sell much broader applications of the technology. Robert Kellison is well aware of the chestnut's public relations value. A former academic forest geneticist, Kellison now directs the Institute of Forest Biotechnology, a nonprofit group formed by academic and industry interests specifically to prevent the nascent science from being stalled by the kind of political debates that embroiled agricultural biotechnology. Kellison sees the institute as a sympathetic watchdog, the "conscience of forest biotechnology": "We'd seen what was happening in Europe with the backlash against [genetically modified crops]. The conclusion was if that happened in forestry, it would set us back decades, if not longer."

Kellison frankly acknowledges that one way to score points in the coming debate is by emphasizing the potential social benefits of forest biotechnology. And what could be more beneficial than saving endangered trees? To that end, the institute has a special program supporting biotechnological research devoted to rescuing "heritage trees," including the European elm, the Fraser fir (a rare conifer that grows only in six locations in the Appalachians), and, of course, the American chestnut. Of the three, he believes the chestnut holds the greatest promise of furthering the interests of biotechnology.

Kellison is counting on Maynard and Powell to succeed soon enough that a Chestnut 2.0 will become the first transgenic forest tree to confront the regulatory gauntlet. (It would have to be approved by the USDA and the Environmental Protection Agency, which as of mid-2006 were still developing final rules regarding transgenic forest trees. And because the nuts are edible, it likely would also have to be approved by the Food and Drug Administration.) "We need to get something through the system so we can get an example," Kellison explains with startling candor. The chestnut would be a perfect test case—a relatively risk-free product that unlike, say, a more pulpable pine, is genuinely wanted by the public. It offers a chance to show society what can be accomplished by "working at the gene level," he says. "We can bring a species back that's near extinction. That's got tremendous value. Not from a business standpoint, but as a social value."

The precedent set by approval of a revived American chestnut could then smooth the way for those potentially higher-risk, "product-focused trees" that do have a business value.

The same debate now emerging over transgenic trees in general has been simmering, albeit at low volume, within the American Chestnut Foundation ever since New York joined as the group's first state chapter in 1990. The New Yorkers who formed the chapter were already committed to Maynard and Powell's vision, so the foundation's board of directors reluctantly agreed to let the chapter put all its eggs in the biotech basket. (Each of the thirteen chapters added since are required to hew to the backcross breeding program.)

But there's never been much enthusiasm at the national level for New York's program, much to the New Yorkers' frustration. The prevailing attitude among the foundation's leaders has long been that the group already has a workable and working method for transferring blight-resistant genes into the beleaguered tree—namely backcross breeding. "It's a plant improvement system that ain't broke, so why fix it?" asks Donald Willeke, longtime member of the group's board.

Still, the group's national leaders accepted the New Yorkers' devotion to biotech with the kind of irritated patience of a parent dealing with a willful child. There was even a sort of intramural rivalry between the two. The New Yorkers kept threatening to beat the breeding program to the goal of a blight-resistant tree, while the scientists involved in backcross breeding couldn't help but experience a certain schadenfreude in Maynard and Powell's repeated setbacks. Science advisor Albert Ellingboe recalls how in the early 1990s, one of the leaders of the New York chapter boasted to him that the chapter was going to "bury" the national effort by having a bioengineered tree within two years: "It was irritating to me because I knew it wasn't going to happen in two years. I knew there was a whole series of unknowns."

Although the leadership has tolerated the New York chapter's foray into gene-transfer technology, it was another story when the biotech company ArborGen came knocking in 2004. The company, a spin-off of several leading lumber and paper corporations with a sixty-million-dollar budget dedicated to forest biotech, wanted to partner with the organization to develop a bioengineered chestnut tree that would carry the foundation's seal of approval. The group's lead scientist, Fred Hebard, was instantly skeptical. "They're asking us to hold their lightning rod," he told members of the board. Why should the foundation set itself up for the inevitable flak the affiliation would draw, especially since bioengineering wasn't its primary focus?

Other board members agreed it was a risky proposition. Marshal Case, the foundation's president, feared an open embrace of biotechnology could shatter the shared focus that unites a membership sprawling across the political spectrum, from National Rifle Association members to Sierra Club stalwarts. He worried it might cost the group a third of its supporters. He and others also believed getting involved in biotechnology would be an expensive drain on the group's modest budget. But even had ArborGen offered buckets of money, Case says, "we would have turned them down." The decision was not made with public relations or budgetary considerations in mind, he insists: "The decision was based on science." In the end, the board decided that biotech had not yet proven it offered any advantage over traditional breeding in the race to save the American chestnut. Bioengineering proponents may keep promising a quick sprint to the finish line, but so far it looks like the lumbering tortoise of traditional breeding may well get there first.

The foundation didn't rule out a role for ArborGen down the line, however. Says Case, "If at some point it looks like a breakthrough is going on that could be beneficial to chestnut restoration, then we would consider how that would be brought into the program we are doing."

ArborGen, meanwhile, began granting fifty thousand dollars a year to support Maynard and Powell's research. "They saved the project," Powell says appreciatively.

"We're not just chestnut," Powell wants to make clear. He gestures to a printout taped to his wall bearing the headline "Infected Trees." It's a list of other forest trees currently threatened by alien pathogens: butternut, beech, hemlock, and dogwood. Each is potentially a candidate for the restorative powers of biotechnology, he says. "I like to think our work is restoring things, and chestnut is just the first thing."

Actually, in a sense, it's the second. While waiting for Maynard to master the problem of propagating chestnut tissue, Powell turned his attention to the American elm, veteran of a long-running battle with two fungal pests: Dutch elm disease and elm yellows. Elm proved much easier to work with than chestnut—happily regenerating from the mid-vein of the leaf—and in short order Powell had elm saplings equipped with the antimicrobial gene ready to be put in the ground.

Powell wanted to make a strong statement with the transgenic elms and plant them in a public place. The ever-cautious Maynard had reservations about the plan, but was pleased when Powell managed to convince the SUNY administration, as well as the USDA, to permit him to plant the trees in front of the College of Forestry library—the first transgenics ever set out in a public area in the United States. He and Maynard planted the trees in 2005, in beds filled with specially mixed, custom-designed soil. "We wanted them here purposely so people could see they're like any trees," says Powell. "The idea is for people to see they're all the same."

The five transgenic elms were planted alongside five unaltered elms, and in appearance they do all look the same: skinny, spindly, and on this winter day, bare of leaves. The only way to tell them apart would be by hopping over the decorative wrought iron fence and checking the little metal identifying tags twisted around the base of each tree. But that would set off the pair of infrared detectors that are trained on the trees and set to detect motion or body heat. A silent alarm would alert the campus security. The USDA insisted on the security precautions because a few years earlier extremist opponents of bioengineering had torched transgenic tree labs at Oregon State University and the University of Washington.

The arson left Powell and Maynard "darned nervous" says Maynard, but to date they've never had any problems. People may stop and read the explanatory plaques set up in front, but otherwise the trees draw little attention. The only complaint the researchers ever heard came from the chief librarian, who missed the cooling shade provided by the tall plane trees that were formerly in front of the library until disease forced their removal.

By the time of my visit in January of 2006, Maynard, Powell, and McGuigan are proud to show me yet another pair of transformed chestnut treelets potted in soil and growing in special humidity chambers set on a shelf in Maynard's office. Each is about three inches high and boldly brandishes a half-dozen or so tiny saw-toothed leaves, every cell in their being stocked with the wheat gene for oxalate oxidase. As we sit talking in Maynard's office, McGuigan jumps up several times to examine the treelets and fiddle with the valves that control the chambers' humidity. Her fussing is understandable, given the long years of hard work and delayed hopes that have gone into producing that pair of trees. Still, says Powell, "if you can get two you can get more."

Once again, the researchers are convinced they're finally coming into the home stretch. Assuming this pair of treelets survives—as well as a half-dozen others in earlier stages of growth—they and their New York supporters are for the first time giving serious thought to what comes next. Herb Darling has already been in contact with ArborGen to see if the company will lend its expertise and resources to the huge task of mass-producing transgenic chestnut trees. He, Maynard, and Powell are starting to think about the multiple intellectual property rights vested in these tiny trees. Other researchers own patents on the genes they've used; a key step used in treating the embryos is patented by Monsanto. Will an altruistic spirit guide the partitioning of those proprietary rights? And what will federal regulators require before OKing the release of the new and improved chestnut trees? Even under the best of circumstances, they expect it will be a good six years or more before any transgenic chestnuts see commercial release, which puts them on about the same time line as the American Chestnut Foundation's backcross bred trees.

But on this unseasonably warm winter day, Powell and Maynard are debating a more immediate question. Do they plant these new Chestnut 2.0s in test plots in the coming spring and let them grow bigger? Or do they risk killing them now by exposing them to blight to check whether the transgene provides adequate levels of resistance?

Maynard wants to get them in the field "just to say we did."

Powell thinks they ought to be tested soon for resistance. "My philosophy is if they die then it's not the plant we want." Finding that out may hurt, he admits, but he's not too concerned: "If it doesn't work, we have other genes waiting in the pipeline."*

---

*In June 2006, they planted two transgenic trees in a test plot near the university (after first getting permission from the USDA). They invited Darling and other New York chapter members to Syracuse for the ceremony and gave Darling the honor of planting one of the two trees. McGuigan planted the other. By the fall, one was thriving and the other appeared to have died. Tests had yet to definitely establish whether the transgene conveyed adequate blight resistance. "It is looking promising," Powell wrote me at the end of the year, "but there is more work to do."

NINE

Faith in a Seed

"Though I do not believe that a plant will spring up where no seed has been, I have great faith in a seed. . . . Convince me that you have a seed there, and I am prepared to expect wonders." So wrote Henry David Thoreau in one of his last works, an essay titled "The Succession of Forest Trees." It was intended as part of a larger work aimed at debunking the then-prevailing anti-Darwinian belief that plants can spring up spontaneously—unaffiliated with roots, cuttings, or seeds. Thoreau made his case, in part, by tracking the propagation of chestnuts, as well as other trees, in the countryside surrounding his Concord, Massachusetts, home, excavating the stashes of nuts buried by squirrels and mice to see how the seeds and "thus the chestnut wood advances."

Faith in a seed has propelled chestnut restoration for over a century, and it continues to sustain the two chief breeding efforts under way today: one devoted to the wondrous possibilities of combining the American chestnut with its sturdier cousins, the other dedicated to the potential of the American chestnut to save itself. By talking about faith, I don't mean to suggest that the efforts derive from unverifiable beliefs—both are firmly grounded in scientific theory and method. But at bottom, what's kept each going is an unswerving conviction that the future they envision can be eventually attained—even when skeptics have questioned that vision or nonbelievers have doubted its worth. It's a dream that has survived crushing disappointments and experimental dead ends—a dream that continues to animate the work of scientists and volunteers who know they won't live long enough to see their hopes confirmed. It's a faith worthy of Henry David Thoreau and his expectation of "wonders."

For those staking their faith in backcross breeding, Mecca can be found at the site Phil Rutter established, the American Chestnut Foundation's research farm in Meadowview, Virginia.* The ground is still wet from the rains the night before when I pull up to the ramshackle white farmhouse that serves as the farm's office. It's early on this June morning—barely 8 o'clock—but the office is already open and the day's crew is hanging out, awaiting marching orders. Danny Honaker and George Sykes, the two farmhands, and a volunteer—one of the many who come to work on the farm each spring—stand by the front screen door, debating whether things will dry out enough to continue pollinating trees today. Two visiting students sit on a sagging couch in what was once the farmhouse's living room; one stares into space, the other leafs through a paperback book. I browse the dusty bookshelves that line one wall; they're filled with an eclectic, though selective, array of texts: *Plant Anatomy, Wildflowers of West Virginia, The Nature and Properties of Soil, Shrubs of Michigan, Farm Tools, Dictionary of Fungi.* We're all waiting for the same person: Fred Hebard, who for the last sixteen years has run the farm and led the foundation's breeding operations.

Eventually, the back door slams open and there's a rush of commotion as three wet dogs tumble into the room followed by a tall, lean man

---

*Another destination for chestnut pilgrims might be the Connecticut Agricultural Experiment Station, where Sandra Anagnostakis has also used backcross breeding to produce blight-resistant American chestnuts. Her program, second only to the American Chestnut Foundation's, draws primarily on the blight resistance of Japanese chestnuts.

holding a cigarette in one hand and a sleek silver laptop in the other. He clomps through the room without a word and disappears into one of the front rooms. Ten minutes later, he reappears and stops in front of me, smiling shyly. He's wearing rubber boots, jeans, a gray T-shirt, and a cap bearing the words "Big M Farm Service Inc." Something about the wry expression on his face and the cocked eyebrow reminds me vaguely of a young Paul Newman. "You Susan?" he grunts. "This is Madeline," he adds, gesturing toward the panting golden retriever at his side. Then he's gone again. I'd been warned about Hebard's social skills.

But to be fair, this is Hebard's busiest time of year—the chestnuts are coming into bloom and there's a brief few-week window of opportunity in which to plan and execute the hundreds of matches that will advance the foundation's breeding program. Every year it's a mad rush: collecting the pollen of potential father trees and getting it onto the female flowers of earmarked mother trees, a laborious operation. And Hebard's worries aren't confined to the twenty-five-thousand-plus trees that by now have been planted in Meadowview's orchards. He's also providing pollen for the breeding efforts of the fourteen American Chestnut Foundation chapters spanning the eastern seaboard. (The Massachusetts chapter calls itself a "chestnut dating service.") In addition, Hebard and his crew have to get up into the mountains to collect pollen from the wild chestnut sprouts that they've scouted out. All this alongside the regular business of running a farm, where lofty thoughts about species restoration get pushed aside by such practical issues as a balky tractor, leaking irrigation lines, and uncooperative weather. "It's farming," says Hebard. "We're always playing it all the way to the bank."

At fifty-eight years old, Hebard has spent virtually his entire adult life thinking about chestnuts. He's not as fervid or expressive about his attachment as Rutter, Fulbright, or some of the other chestnut scientists I've met. "One of my great revelations was when I got poked in the eye by a chestnut twig." It was then he realized "that they didn't give a shit that I was trying to help them." Still, in his own diligent, single-minded way, Hebard has done more to advance the effort to save the American

chestnut than almost anyone else. "He is the single most important living chestnut breeder and probably will be remembered as the greatest
chestnut breeder to have lived," says James Hill Craddock, University
of Tennessee at Chattanooga professor and one of the leading evangel-
ists of the chestnut crusade.

Hebard grew up the youngest of six children in the wealthy
Philadelphia neighborhood of Chestnut Hill. His mother was a homemaker, a cultured woman who hosted bridge parties and tea parties
and mingled in Philadelphia society; his father was a lawyer and businessman whose avid interest in birding introduced Hebard to the natural world. He died when Hebard was just thirteen years old. The family was well off, thanks to the fortune his great-grandfather, Charles
Hebard, accumulated during the logging boom of the late nineteenth
century. The elder Hebard started out lumbering the forests of Pennsylvania in the 1840s. In the 1870s, he and partners established a sawmill
in northern Michigan and began cutting their way through the great
white pine forests there. In the early twentieth century, he turned his
sights back east and bought the 438,000-acre Okefenokee Swamp in
Florida for its vast stands of virgin cypress forest. (Decades later,
Hebard's more conservation-minded grandfather and father sold the
swamp to the federal government so it could be made into a wildlife
refuge.) Hebard tells his great-grandfather's story with no sense of
irony, growing irritated when I ask if there's any connection between
that ancestral history of forest exploitation and his lifelong devotion to
forest restoration. "I don't know what this 'exploitation' was," he says
peckishly. "Could they have cut less? Yes. But it was just—" he pauses,
searching for the words he wants "—careless philosophy. People exploit
what nature they can. If they have the means to exploit it, they'll exploit
it. I think it's universal in humans."

"And how much am I making up for the sins of my fathers?" he
asks. His sarcastic tone makes clear he firmly believes he is not.

Hebard's youth may have been decidedly upper crust—private
schools, debutante balls, summers sailing off the coast of Maine—but

few surface traces are left in the man he is today: a chain-smoking, cuss-prone, determinedly regular Joe who loves NASCAR racing and Old Milwaukee beer. "Fred has spent his whole life trying to overcome his background. I think he's done a pretty good job," jokes his wife Dayle Zanzinger, also a Philadelphia native, but from the other side of the tracks. He laughs hard when I tell him what Dayle said. "Yeah, we went from rich to poor in three generations." On the other hand, though I've heard him tell people he's "just a farmer," he's a farmer whose vocabulary is studded with words like "phenotype" and "homozygous" and who explains his downward mobility by saying, "I probably spent most of my patrimony on my education."

Hebard's detour from high society began in 1968, when after a year of studying English and history at the University of Virginia, he enlisted in the army. He didn't have the grades to avoid the draft, he explains. He spent "one year, one month, five days" in Vietnam, where he took part in some of the war's heaviest fighting, including the second Tet offensive. When he returned, he enrolled at Columbia University and started studying biology: "I read the Whole Earth catalogue; science seemed to be more useful than the humanities." Halfway through his sophomore year, he dropped out to follow a girlfriend to Connecticut, where he got a job working on a dairy farm. That's when he first learned about the American chestnut. As he has often told reporters, he was helping the farmer search the woods for stray heifers when they stumbled across an old chestnut sprout. The farmer told him about the blight and the billions of trees that had died. He always ends the tale with the same laconic summary: "I thought it would be nice to go back to school and learn about biology and try to do something about chestnuts. Little did I know it was a lifetime proposition."

During one visit to Meadowview, I try to get him to elaborate on what exactly it was about the chestnut that captivated his interest. He hems and haws and finally throws his arms in the air and laughs uncomfortably. "I don't know. I'm not in touch with that side of my head. I don't understand the psychology very well. But it gives me a mission." Others have told him he's lucky to have that sense of mission.

"Do you feel lucky?" I ask.

"Yeah," he says. "Or cursed."

After graduating from Columbia, he got a master's degree in botany from the University of Michigan, where his advisor told him to abandon any ideas about rescuing the chestnut; there was no money in the field. Hebard ignored the advice and went on to get a PhD in plant pathology at Virginia Polytechnic Institute and State University, where he worked with scientist Gary Griffin, who was seeking out and breeding the rare surviving American chestnut trees. "I never had anyone do as much reading on their own," Griffin recalls. "He's a guy of great intellectual curiosity." But, he adds, Hebard "also has a little bit of Dennis the Menace in him. He's not inhibited—or perhaps the word is restrained." With age, Hebard's tendency to let his opinions slip past his "diplomacy filter" has mellowed, but nearly every acquaintance can tell stories of arguments they have had with him at one time or another. For his dissertation, Hebard examined the biology of virulent and hypovirulent blight fungus and devised a method to screen surviving trees for resistance. It was, says Griffin, "perfect preparation for what he's doing now."

Unfortunately, when he graduated, there weren't any jobs for full-time chestnut rescue workers. So he moved for a year to Washington State to work on alfalfa disease and then took a three year post-doctoral position at the University of Kentucky to research hypovirulence. Then in 1989, he heard that the American Chestnut Foundation was looking for someone to run its newly established farm at Meadowview. "I jumped at the chance," he recalls—even though the salary was a mere twelve thousand dollars and it meant dragging his wife and two small daughters to a flyspeck farm community where there were few job prospects for Zanzinger, also a PhD plant pathologist. After months of fruitlessly searching for work in her field, she decided to go back to school and train to be a nurse practitioner.

But then, she'd known what she was getting into when she became involved with the fixated young scientist. She'd seen how absentminded he could be when thinking about work, how during conversations he'd drift off into "his own little world." Driving from Kentucky to Pennsylvania for their wedding, the couple stopped to visit friends, who gave the already-pregnant Zanzinger a bag of beautiful baby clothes. Before she had a chance to stop him, Hebard used the clothes to swaddle the potted chestnut trees he was also taking back east. "We have a picture of him watering the pots before the wedding," she recalls.

The move may have been hard on Zanzinger, but Hebard settled in readily to the local farm community. When we enter the Little Diner for lunch (one of two restaurants in town) several old-timers sitting at tables call out, "How're the chestnuts doing?" "Everything is early this year," he replies. We take a seat and he orders the meatloaf special. "You farming much?" he asks one old guy who's there with his grandson. "I'm not doing haying," the man answers. It's been too wet. The two compare rainfall measurements. This may not be a place where Hebard discusses the scientific complexities guiding his work, but he clearly enjoys the camaraderie.

Burnham and Rutter had laid out a clear road map for Hebard to follow at Meadowview. First would come the pairing of American and Chinese chestnuts—the match that would bring blight resistance genes into the American species' genome. Next, the successive backcrosses to American trees to gradually winnow out all the Asian genes but those conferring resistance. Hebard has doggedly stuck to the scheme, though he's found ways to whittle down the formidable time line that predicted it would take at least forty years to produce fully blight-resistant trees. He was able to leapfrog past the first Chinese-American cross, thanks to the existence of both a good hybrid bred by Arthur Graves decades ago and still-flourishing clones of the Clapper tree, the USDA's famed hybrid. And through careful cultivation he has been able to coax his trees to maturity far more quickly than the five to seven years it typically takes. Still, for the first several years as he diligently filled the fields at Meadowview with American, Chinese, hybrid, and early backcross trees, Hebard had no idea whether his labors would be totally in vain.

By 1993, he finally had some trees that were big enough to test for blight resistance. It wasn't just the trees being put to the test, but, in a sense, Burnham's whole hypothesis. Burnham's confidence in backcross breeding was largely based on inferences drawn from historical evidence and mathematical calculations. But was it really possible to breed away the American chestnut's fatal flaw? That June, Hebard carefully inoculated fifteen rows of first- and second-generation hybrids and backcrossed trees, as well as pure Chinese chestnuts that would serve as controls. With a cork borer, he punched holes in the saplings' slender, shiny trunks and then slathered on a paste teeming with *Cryphonectria parasitica* spores. It would take only a few months for the potent spores to go to work.

In early September, he returned to the trees to assess the results. The air was hot and muggy, and nettles poked his butt as he crawled along the ground between the long rows of trees, ruler in hand. He painstakingly measured the unsightly cankers on each tree and compared them to the small eruptions that had formed on the bark of the Chinese trees. He was so intent on recording the numbers that it was several days before he began to see a pattern. By week's end it was clear that a few of the hybrids were putting up a good fight: their cankers were as small as the ones on the Chinese trees. And the ratio of resistant to susceptible trees seemed to confirm the linchpin of Burnham's theory: that only two or three genes control resistance. The hypothesis had passed its first test. (It would gain further confirmation in later analyses, including a 1997 partial map of the Chinese chestnut genome, which linked resistance with three locations on the chromosome.) Until then, Hebard himself had been uncertain whether the trees' genetics would lend themselves to backcross breeding. Now here was evidence that the program might well work. "I was pretty pleased about that," he recalls with characteristic understatement.

Breeding is a slow slog, only rarely relieved by "aha!" moments. But this was one. He wrote Burnham, who was by then in a nursing home, and phoned Rutter with the good news. Rutter, too, was excited, though he restrained himself from whooping into the phone. But he says, "If I were five, I would have been jumping up and down and saying 'I told you so. I told you so.'"

It wasn't often that Hebard and Rutter were on the same page. Both are strong-minded men, and from the time Hebard started working for the foundation, they wrangled over control of the breeding program. As founder and president of the foundation and a tree breeder himself, Rutter thought he should be calling the shots. Hebard saw it differently. His job title may have been farm superintendent, but he never intended to limit his role to merely managing the farm or executing orders. Early on, for instance, the two had a heated disagreement over how to plant chestnut seedlings. Hebard wanted to plant them directly outdoors; Rutter wanted to grow them out in the greenhouse and then transplant them to the orchard. Hebard drew a line in the sand. "This is my call," he insisted. Rutter backed down. But, Hebard says, "it kind of soured our relationship."

By the time of Hebard's phone call, Rutter had already begun withdrawing from the organization. The official reason was his health. He'd developed chronic fatigue syndrome and simply couldn't continue the driving pace he'd maintained for nearly ten years. But he also sensed the foundation no longer needed him to the same degree. Thanks in good measure to his efforts, the group now had some money in the bank and the backing of a few committed donors (who could and did bail it out when funds got tight). There was a full-time director, several state chapters, and a growing corps of fantastically devoted members. The foundation had its own land in native chestnut country and thousands of trees in the ground. It had reached the point, he decided, "where I could leave and it would survive."

For a decade, Rutter had been the public face of the American Chestnut Foundation and the backcross breeding program. Now, Hebard assumed that role. It's sometimes an awkward fit: he's not a strong public speaker and he lacks Rutter's missionary zeal. But he's a caring pastor to his flock, ever ready to help members struggling to grow chestnuts and to provide advice and aid to state breeding efforts. His attention and kindness to one visiting couple led them in 1995 to donate a much-needed plot of land for the farm's growing operation. Every issue of the foundation's journal encouraged members to drop by for a tour of the farm, and they did. "All you had to do was find Meadowview and it was pretty easy to find someone to tell you where the farm was," says Zanzinger. At the time, the family still lived in the five-room farmhouse. More than once, Zanzinger emerged from the shower, her hair wrapped in a towel, to find her husband chatting with an excited group of chestnut pilgrims. "I remember once somebody showing up at 7:30 on a Saturday morning for a tour," she recalls, "and neither Fred nor I are morning people."

After ten years, the family moved to a home they built a few miles from the farm. Zanzinger refused to let Hebard plant any chestnuts on the grounds—she'd been stuck by burs too many times. The only thing chestnut in the house is a smooth block of blond wood over the fireplace that serves as a mantelpiece.

For a more demanding brand of faith, I travel two hours north along Virginia Interstate 81, a concrete ribbon stitched into the skirt trains of the Appalachian foothills. In Blacksburg, at Virginia Polytechnic Institute, is Hebard's former mentor, Gary Griffin, who for more than forty years has pursued his unwavering belief that American chestnuts themselves might hold the key to the species' survival. His conviction derives from the continued existence of a few hundred mature chestnut trees. They are neither escapees of the death wave that killed between three and four billion trees nor sprouts that are sure to succumb to its continuing deadly ripples, but veterans of the disaster, trees that against all odds have refused to die.

Researchers have been intrigued with such survivors since the earliest days of the pandemic, hoping to find among them that perfect tree: a truly blight-resistant American chestnut that could be used to resuscitate the entire species. To date, no one has ever found it. But there are some with enough fighting mettle to keep themselves alive. Just how many there are remains unclear. In 1963, after a decade of searching and weeding out false reports, USDA breeder Jesse Diller confirmed 180 large survivors across the chestnut's vast historic range, including a mammoth seventy-two-foot-tall tree in Chelsea, Michigan, which one writer described as "a really notable survival, like a dinosaur turning up in a backyard swimming pool." Later estimates pegged the number of significant-sized wild survivors at about 375 to 500. Griffin thinks those estimates are probably unduly low. He defines a large survivor as a tree that is at least ten inches in diameter at breast height, and he believes there are at least a hundred such veterans in each of the middle Appalachian states alone (that is, between Pennsylvania and North Carolina). North of Pennsylvania, the numbers drop off, but large survivors have turned up in New England and even as far north as Albany, New York. "And that's just the ones they find," he notes. How many more remain unfound? Indeed, in the spring of 2006, a wildlife biologist hiking near Franklin Roosevelt's "little White House" in Warm Springs, Georgia, stumbled upon a previously undiscovered stand of a half-dozen American chestnuts. The largest of the group was a good forty feet tall. The find was a little like coming across "Bigfoot or a black panther," the excited biologist recalled. The find made national headlines, but Griffin wasn't too impressed: he suspects the trees were simply blight escapees, rather than true survivors.

At sixty-nine years old, Griffin is a slender, unassuming man with gray hair, pale skin, and a long face. He's an avid outdoorsman who loves hiking, canoeing, fly-fishing, and grouse-hunting. (He named his two hunting dogs Chestnut and Timber "so when I'm in the woods I can go, 'Chestnut . . . Timber!'" he says, mimicking a lumberjack's call.) During any of those activities, he's always on the lookout for large surviving chestnuts. Technically he is retired from the VPI faculty, but you'd never know it from his daily schedule. He still arrives at his musty basement office every morning at 7:15 and works until 4:45. "I like science," he explains. "And I'm going to do science whether I get paid for it or don't get paid. . . . I'm not getting paid. But my retirement pay is good, so there's no problem with money." Like most chestnut scientists, he has an abiding affection and respect for the tree. Once, when he and Hebard were visiting an orchard in autumn, Griffin asked Hebard to shake the trees so he could experience what the old-timers were talking about when they described the nuts raining down. He stood there giggling in delight as the nuts and burs came tumbling over his head.

Though trained as a pathologist, Griffin much prefers fieldwork to sitting over a microscope in the lab. He'll happily sit in a spot in the forest from dawn to dusk, patiently tracking the trail of sunlight to better understand how it affects the tree growth there. "I've spent thousands of hours in the woods," he says. That experience has given him a rich understanding of the biology and ecology of both the chestnut and its fungal foe. His research suggests that the ability of some chestnuts to endure the blight is a complicated braiding of three factors. Most have some degree of innate resistance, though not enough to beat the blight alone. Their staying power comes from the fact that most also are infected with hypovirulent strains of the fungus—which gives them time to marshal their defenses to fight the blight—and are growing in conducive environments, where they don't have to grapple with the kinds of stresses that can sap a tree's ability to fight, such as drought, poor soil, or freezes. "Resistance is relative," Griffin contends, noting that even a Chinese chestnut's solid defenses against the blight can be broken by a hard frost. So his plan to restore *Castanea dentata* rests on what he calls "an integrated management program" that addresses all the factors that keep survivors going. He is picking out the toughest large survivors and breeding them with one another, in order to amplify that whisper of resistant DNA into a full-bodied shout. Then, through hypovirulence and careful cultivation, he hopes to sustain that shout across the canyons of time.

Even within the quixotic world of chestnut restoration, some think Griffin is tilting at windmills. Whatever genetic quirk has enabled some American chestnuts to resist the blight is just that: a quirk, a genetic windfall in which some genes that evolved to deal with another problem—a different fungal pathogen, perhaps, or climatic stress—just so happen to also confer protection against this newer threat of chestnut blight. But that doesn't constitute the reliably inherited defense system that Asian chestnuts developed through millennia of coevolution with *C. parasitica.* The genetic combination that allows one American chestnut to endure the disease may not be—and probably isn't—the same as that in another survivor. Nevertheless, Griffin contends that through a succession of crosses, it should be possible to gradually build up the complement of genes that contribute to blight resistance and to stack them so that eventually they form a reasonable bulwark against the deadly fungus. There's solid precedence for the approach, at least in an agricultural setting. Researchers, for instance, have managed to develop durably rust-resistant varieties of wheat starting with plants that had virtually no defenses against the disease. "It was like pulling resistance out of the woodwork," he says.

Although the theory may be sound, it's not the most efficient or practical route to restoration. The number of genes involved is simply unknown, and if each confers only a trace of resistance, then assembling the critical mass necessary to create the perfectly resistant tree could well require a staggering number of crosses—"more crossing than you can do in one guy's lifetime," says Hebard.* Even on the snail's pace

---

*Actually, Hebard favored Griffin's approach before he joined the American Chestnut Foundation and became immersed in backcross breeding. He still likes it well enough to maintain several thousand progeny of large survivors for intercross breeding.

timescale of tree breeding, Griffin's approach is considered dauntingly slow.

There have been others who shared Griffin's vision, including Al Dietz, who pursued the dream of inducing resistance through irradiation, and John Elkins, a West Virginia chemist who for decades has sought a quick chemical test for blight resistance, a goal most other researchers long ago abandoned as hopeless. In 1985, Griffin, Dietz, and Elkins formed the American Chestnut Cooperators' Foundation (ACCF) to provide a base for their "intercross breeding program" (an intercross is simply a cross between members of the same species) and to generate a steady source of funding for graduate student work on large survivors. Griffin and his colleagues were well aware of the American Chestnut Foundation, but they personally had little interest in the back-cross breeding approach. "We felt the potential for resistance in these large survivors was not being properly addressed or exploited, and we felt that we could do that," Griffin says.

Unlike the American Chestnut Foundation, which now has nearly six thousand members, a million-dollar-plus budget, multiple state chapters, four offices, and more than a dozen full-time staff, the ACCF remains a small volunteer organization. It has about six hundred members and a meager budget of fifteen thousand dollars, most of which goes to support graduate students and much of which, for many years, came from Griffin's own pocket. (Griffin says he and his wife "just felt that supporting this research is more important than a fancy steak dinner. I don't regret it.") The ACCF's goals are more modest than the American Chestnut Foundation's: rather than trying to restore chestnut across the historic range, the ACCF is focused solely on Virginia, West Virginia, and Tennessee.

Occasionally the two groups are portrayed as rivals, a comparison that upsets the resolutely noncontentious Griffin. "I think what they're doing is great," he says. "It needs to be done and we just have a different slant. You know, some people like steak and some like shrimp. It doesn't mean one's better than the other, it's just what you like. Both strategies, I think, have potential." Indeed, a number of chestnut enthusiasts belong to both groups.

Griffin admits the ACCF's approach may be more of a long shot than the American Chestnut Foundation's. But on the other hand, dealing only with American chestnut offers certain advantages. He doesn't have to worry about any unanticipated effects of introducing foreign genes into the American species genome. And if they're successful, there will be no quibbles about whether the products are truly American chestnuts. There are purists who object to the idea of reintroducing anything less than a 100-percent American chestnut.

Griffin and Elkins launched their breeding program in 1982 with four large survivors, one of which Griffin had found while hunting for grouse. They arranged various intercrosses between the trees and eventually tested the progeny for resistance. The results were a mixed bag. The most blight-resistant of the four turned out to be miserly about sharing its lucky genes; in Griffin's words, its genes don't "combine well" with those of other trees. However, the other matches went more smoothly, and about 5 to 10 percent of the progeny showed signs that they had inherited their parents' modest ability to fend off the blight. The results established that survivors can, indeed, pass on their extraordinary legacy, albeit at a rate few bookies would lay odds on. It was enough, however, to excite Burnham, architect of the backcross breeding program. Impressed by this proof of heritability, he encouraged Griffin to press on. Since then, Griffin and Elkins have continued to pursue those lines of intercrosses while adding new large survivors to the breeding program. By now, the group has several hundred first- and second-generation progeny growing in various test orchards, as well as a seedling orchard in West Virginia, and has distributed more than 135,000 nuts and seedlings to cooperating growers. Though follow-up is fairly loose, there are enough reports of progeny with some degree of blight resistance to keep Griffin heartened.

He estimates it will take at least four generations of intercrosses—and probably more—to end up with trees that are reliably more blight resistant than the average American chestnut. That's a process that will take at least another thirty years. "We're not going to be around," he cheerfully acknowledges. But he has faith that others will carry on the work.

Griffin takes me to see one of the ACCF's orchards, a small planting of chestnut trees near the Blacksburg airport. His wife, Lucille, waves hello as we pull up. She's a trim, gray-haired woman of sixty-seven, a nationally ranked master's swimmer with a hearty laugh and incredible stores of energy. Though a relative latecomer to the chestnut crusade— she spent most of the years of their marriage as a homemaker looking after their four children—she is, if possible, even more zealous about the mission than her husband. If Griffin is the group's guiding scientist, Lucille is its chief technician. Her official title is executive director, which means she's the one who tracks the correspondence, publishes the occasional newsletter, keeps in touch with members, and faithfully tends various plantings of their intercrossed trees. She brings to the task the deft touch of a longtime gardener, but little scientific background. "All I know about science I learned from him [Griffin] and working in the field and recording my observations," she genially admits, as she hands me a hat for protection from the noontime sun.

She also brings a certain homey touch to their enterprise. For instance, she found that the usual paper bags used to protect controlled pollinations tended to deteriorate after heavy rains. So she now sews cotton bags to protect the flowers that she has carefully pollinated by hand. "She made a lot of dresses for the girls growing up," Griffin explains. Now, "she considers these her babies." While most breeders identify their trees with codes referring to their lineage or provenance, Lucille refers to her trees by name—Heather, Vicky, Andy, Sandy—to underscore the individuality of each. She names her trees after family members, friends, or chestnut associates. The two best trees in the ACCF's breeding program are Miles and Ruth, whose namesakes donated land for one of the group's early plantations.

Lucille leads the way through the grove, bending down every so often to pull out weeds. There are American chestnuts of various ages here, from shy, slight sprouts to twenty-five-foot-tall juveniles reaching eagerly for the sky. The leaves are a deep vibrant green and larger than any I've ever seen. "See how big and nice the American chestnut leaves are," Griffin points out, gently fingering a leaf. Virtually all of these trees are grafts—clones grown from buds or stems taken from large survivors and spliced onto the old roots of blight-demolished chestnut trees. The Griffins are big on grafting. Even though it's a tricky technique that only works about 15 percent of time, grafting is a virtual necessity given the nature of their breeding program. There are so few large survivors that grafting is a way both to maintain and multiply their base population of blight-resistant trees and so sustain the shallow gene pool they are plumbing. (Hebard, by contrast, has a veritable ocean of genes to choose from, so he rarely uses grafts.) Grafting also has allowed them to bring together far-flung survivors in one locale for cross pollinations and to take the products of their breeding program back into the forest. By grafting first- or second-generation intercrosses onto the roots of bygone chestnut trees, they can study what kinds of natural conditions are most conducive to returning the species to the wild. They can simultaneously advance their breeding program and start the slow process of actual restoration.

Unlike Hebard, the Griffins don't expect to be able to breed an American chestnut that's as impervious to *Cryphonectria parasitica* as the Asian wing of the family. Nor do they need to. If the trees have moderate blight resistance, the ACCF can, as Lucille Griffin puts it, "manage them for survival." That means treating them with hypovirulent strains of the fungus—which is most effective in trees with some innate blight resistance—and making sure the trees are planted and maintained in the optimal environment.

To see the fruit of this approach, the next day we head a few hours north to a state forest near Lynchburg that has hosted repeated efforts at chestnut restoration. Lesesne Forest is where Dietz planted thousands of irradiated seeds (which invariably developed blight) and where Richard Jaynes planted thousands of American-Chinese hybrids. John Elkins joins us for the trip to Lesesne. A native of West Virginia, he is the only one of the ACCF's founders who grew up with the American chestnut. His grandmother, he recalls, cried when the blight swept through the chestnut woods near her farm. After her death, he found a newspaper column eulogizing the tree that she'd saved in the family scrapbook. He got interested in exploring the chemistry of blight resistance when he was in graduate school, continued the research as a chemistry professor at Concord College in Athens, West Virginia, and after retiring, set up a laboratory near his house to keep on looking. Bald, slightly pot-bellied, and wearing thick, black-framed glasses, Elkins is a garrulous story-teller and a big booster of his home state. All roads on his internal map lead back to West Virginia. Mention of the actor George C. Scott brings the observation that "Scott's favorite aunt was from Bluefield, West Virginia. And I lived in Bluefield, West Virginia, for a time. That was where John Nash is from. You know, from *A Beautiful Mind*. We West Virginians don't get much credit, but we're out there."

The Griffins and Elkinses have been grafting American chestnut intercrosses onto the root of Dietz's old trees for more than two decades. The star of their efforts and the proof of their faith is a towering American chestnut Griffin refers to as the "Thompson tree." It originated as two shoots taken from a veteran of the blight found in Appomattox County, Virginia, and grafted onto the roots of an old chestnut at Lesesne in 1980. Within two years, the tree began showing the telltale signs of its fungal assailant. The blight cankers were inoculated with hypovirulent strains of the fungus in 1982 and 1983. Then the tree was left alone. Tests in the 1990s confirmed the tree was blight resistant. Now the tree is about sixty-five feet tall and nearly twenty inches in diameter, with a broad healthy crown that shakes back and forth in the hot summer breeze, like a woman proudly tossing her hair.

There are still cankers on the tree, but they are the superficial sores that indicate the hypovirus has spread through all sites of infection, allowing the tree to successfully resist its microscopic enemy. Some of the wounds have even filled in with bark and wood so that the scars are as seamless as a good plastic surgeon's work. "That was cured," says Elkins, pointing to one closed-over canker on a branch. It's a phrase rarely used in chestnut circles.

The tree has also benefited by its prime location. The site is about 1,360 feet above sea level, which ensures the kinds of moderate temperatures in which chestnuts do best. "This is a remarkable success story, I think," Griffin says. The tree has achieved "almost complete disease control. It's the highest level of blight control of any existing American chestnut to my knowledge."

Breeding typically implies domestication of something that was once untamed. Whether working with corn, cattle, or cottonwoods, a breeder is manipulating the genes of an organism to make it more accommodating to human uses or desires. Hebard, on the other hand, is using the science and skills of domestication to create something that will be essentially wild. Captive breeding programs have been used to rejuvenate the populations of endangered animals such as the condor or Mexican gray wolf so they can be restored to the wild. But what does it mean to breed a wild tree?

For one thing, it is an infinitely more complicated enterprise than breeding orchard trees or even forest trees designated for a garden or a city street, as was the goal in the effort to save the American elm by developing varieties resistant to Dutch elm disease. It means creating a tree that will be able to last a hundred years or longer, beyond the helping hands of humans, confronted by threats known and unknown. The immediate goal may be blight resistance, but the tree has to endure not only the current incarnation of *Cryphonectria parasitica,* but also any of the inevitable future mutations of the fungus, not to mention other forest diseases, environmental stresses, and global warming. Hebard has taken several measures to try to ensure that the American Chestnut

Foundation's trees will be as strong as they can be. He vigilantly plots his matchmaking efforts, taking care to avoid inbreeding. He has resisted employing hypovirulence to sustain his trees. He wants to make sure they can stand up to the blight on their own. He culls the orchards ruthlessly, pulling out any trees that show less than stellar performance against the blight or the slightest deviation from the tall, erect form of American chestnut trees. In each generation, he chooses just one in one hundred trees.

Hebard's goal also means purposefully cultivating the kind of genetic diversity that would exist in the wild. The American chestnut's range sprawled over more than two hundred million acres, across a varied topography, a variety of soils, and wildly differing climates. Part of its value was its exquisite adaptability—a trait not easily replicated through breeding. The local wild chestnuts that Hebard uses to breed trees at Meadowview may thrive in temperate Virginia, but could they endure frigid Maine winters or broiling Georgia summers? That's one reason Rutter and others pushed for the foundation to form state chapters. They hoped that eventually the chapters would generate mini-Meadowviews: breeding orchards scattered every few hundred miles across the chestnut's historic range that could draw on the local stock of chestnut sprouts. Though there aren't quite that many breeding orchards, each of the state chapters has sought out wild mother trees in their vicinity and begun their own locally adapted lines of hybrid and backcross trees. All told, as of 2006, the state chapters had more than thirty thousand trees growing.

Breeding for the wild also means anticipating the pressures of natural selection. After more than a century of easy conquest, how will the blight fungus respond to suddenly encountering well-armed resistance? The answer, of course, is that the fungus will change. Over the course of a single tree's lifetime, thousands of generations of *Cryphonectria parasitica* will live, reproduce, and die, giving the fungus ample opportunity to evolve a way around any newly acquired fortifications. For the

first seventeen years of the foundation's breeding program, those fortifications were based on the genetic contributions of just three Chinese
ancestors—a cultivar imported by the USDA and the Chinese chestnuts Graves and Clapper used to make their hybrids. By 2006, it was
clear to Hebard and the group's other scientists that it was time to start
looking for other "sources of resistance" to incorporate into the breeding program. By that, they meant different species of *Castanea,* as well
as different Chinese cultivars that draw on other, as yet untapped, genes
to repel the blight. As one of the group's science advisors, plant geneticist Albert Ellingboe, explained, "We have to give that species lots of
material it can use to control the pathogen."

In other words, the end result of the breeding program will not be a
single perfect tree, but a panoply: a spectrum of perfection.

Even that may not be enough. Already it's clear there are other
pathogens and pests that have the chestnut in their sights. *Phytophthora
cinnamomi,* a root rot of Asian origin, in some ways poses an even bigger threat to the species than the blight. *C. parasitica* kills only the tree's
trunks and branches, but leaves the resilient root systems alone.
Phytophthora cinnamomi destroys the roots, chewing them into a pulpy
black mass. An outbreak of *Phytophthora* in the mid-nineteenth century
killed off most of the chestnuts across the South's Piedmont region. The
pathogen flourishes in moist areas and at low elevations. Griffin lost
one of the ACCF's best grafted survivors, a sixty-foot tree at the Lesesne
Forest, to *Phytophthora.* As Hebard presses forward in his efforts to
breed a chestnut that can withstand the blight, other scientists are starting to explore ways to cultivate resistance to *Phytophthora cinnamomi* in
American chestnuts.

There's also the Asian gall wasp, which arrived on illegally smuggled
budwood and was first reported in a chestnut orchard in Georgia in
1974. It has since spread through much of the tree's historic range. The
wasp lays its eggs in the leaf and flower buds of chestnuts and soon the
branches are stippled with the papery brown bulbs in which the larvae
grow. A heavy infestation can kill a tree, but even a moderate one can

cripple a tree's growth. The rows of trees that brought Hebard his first confirmation of the Burnham hypothesis are infested with gall wasps. He sees no solution beyond waiting out the infestation.

Other threats include the Ambrosia bark beetle, the gypsy moth, the two-lined chestnut borer, and possibly even another species of *Phytophthora* that has been laying waste to oaks in California. Every one but the chestnut borer was imported from abroad. If ever there was a poster child for the threat of invasive species, it is the American chestnut.

Tree breeding is an exercise in a kind of patience that seems archaic in the digital age. Aside from raising children, how many of us engage in enterprises that demand a decades-long wait? We parse time in ever smaller fractions, and our stores of patience are whittled away as well. Why wait the five minutes it takes to boil a kettle anymore when a thirty-second zap in the microwave will do? I drum my fingers impatiently when it takes longer than three seconds for my computer to download an image from the Internet.

I am continually moved by the patience and undying optimism of the chestnut scientists I've met; in their own way, they are as resolute as the tree itself. They spend years in what writer Noelle Oxenhandler has called "that precious 'while' when you have done your part, and surrendered the work of your hands to powers as great as sun, air, time." It sounds poetic. In reality, a lot of breeding work is mind-numbingly tedious. So while Hebard's scientific acumen has certainly been vital to the success of the American Chestnut Foundation's breeding program, his chief accomplishment may well be his sheer perseverance—his dogged return to the fields at Meadowview day after day after day: as of 2006, more than sixteen thousand days and counting of planning matches, pollinating flowers, spraying fertilizer, patching irrigation lines, harvesting nuts, digging holes, sowing seeds, testing trees for resistance, and bulldozing inferior specimens, plodding along on the slow march toward a perfect tree. Other scientists might have had the know-how to make that march, says fellow chestnut researcher Craddock, "but I'm not sure many people could have survived it. He worked alone for a lot of time and not much money and out of his personal vision."

Still, it's in the challenging ground of daily practice that a seed of faith blossoms and grows—from the isolated efforts of a handful of scientists to a movement several thousand strong; from devotion to a single species to a broader dedication to the natural world; from belief that it is possible to right one human-inflicted ecological wrong to the conviction that future wrongs must be prevented. In the case of the chestnut, faith in a seed has summoned a grace that is far-reaching.

Burnham had predicted it would take six generations of backcrosses and intercrosses to achieve an almost fully American blight-resistant tree. By 2004, the first group of sixth-generation trees had grown big enough for Hebard to assess. Once again, he carefully inoculated the trees and returned a few months later to measure the cankers that had opened up. This time, the results were disappointing. Fewer trees than he had hoped demonstrated adequate resistance to the blight. But he doesn't think the problem lies in the trees' genetics. The trees were young, and he hit them with a massive dose of blight fungus, a bigger blast than any tree would encounter in the wild. It could be he was just too hard on them; further tests will show. If necessary, he can extend the breeding program with another generation or two of crosses to try to boost resistance. Though worried, he remains optimistic that in the end he'll produce an improved American chestnut, a tree that is tougher than its diminished forebearer.

Indeed, in contrast to earlier breeding programs, he's already succeeded in producing trees that are, as Burnham predicted, virtually indistinguishable from the original American chestnut. That's true down to the most minute features of their appearance, as researchers reported in 2006. After examining third-generation backcross trees and Chinese chestnuts, comparing such fine details as the pointiness of the leaves, the color of the stems, the angle at which the buds attach to the stems, the researchers concluded that 96 percent of the backcross hybrids "resembled American chestnut and were distinctly different from Chinese chestnut."

Yet despite the close resemblance to the original American chestnut, the fact remains that Hebard's trees don't have fully American pedigrees. The final products of the breeding program will still have, on average, a genetic constitution that's about 10 percent Chinese. That matters more to some people than to others. "Fred hears 10 percent and thinks, 'Oh my God, that's almost completely American chestnut.' I hear 10 percent and think, 'Oh my God, that's a huge amount of exotic material,'" says Hugh Irwin, a forest ecologist who serves on the foundation's board. He'd like to see the backcrosses extended for a few more rounds to further dilute the component of Chinese genes. But no matter how many generations of backcrosses are performed, the end result will still be a chestnut with some quotient of Chinese genes.

The gap, however narrow, between the tree's phenotype—its appearance—and its genotype—its genetic composition—raises an interesting philosophical question: just what constitutes a species? By one definition, an organism is classified based on how much it looks like the original specimen that was used to name the species. If it looks like a duck, walks like a duck, and quacks like a duck, then some would say it's a duck, says Kim Steiner, head of the Pennsylvania State University Arboretum and one of the American Chestnut Foundation's science advisors. By that definition, the foundation's tree should qualify as *Castanea dentata*. But Steiner and others are reluctant to label it as such "because we know what it is." Instead of calling the group's tree an "American chestnut," they plan to come up with a new name that indicates its hybrid lineage. Steiner has suggested *Castanea × hebardii,* after Hebard, though an equally likely name might be something along the lines of "backcross American chestnut."

In the past few decades, efforts to save the chestnut have become so widespread, the science has advanced so far, and the flock of adherents grown so large, that the ever-optimistic Rutter insists, "The chestnut's coming back. There's no stopping it now." Hebard would rather be hog-tied than make such a brash prediction. If a certain kind of faith has kept him going all these years, he's also enough of an agnostic to admit that whether the chestnut can truly be restored to its former glory remains an open question. "Isn't it great to think you can die knowing that you were responsible for bringing back an entire species," an admirer once said to him.

"Yeah, it'll be great," Hebard replied. "If it works."

Still, it was clear just how far chestnut restoration had come on Arbor Day, 2005. In honor of the holiday, President George W. Bush planted an American chestnut on the White House's north lawn. Hebard supplied the tree—a sixteen-foot hybrid that is 75 percent American, which means that while it may be reasonably blight resistant, it probably won't ever achieve the dimensions of the classic old tree.

"This is our little part to help [the chestnut] come back," Bush told reporters during the brief planting ceremony. He pitched a few spadefuls of dirt around the roots of the green-leafed sapling and offered the bland pronouncement: "Our message is to our fellow citizens: plant trees—it's good for the economy and it's good for the environment."

Bush himself claims to have personally planted more than sixteen thousand trees at his Texas ranch. Yet the administration's dismal environmental record has made painfully clear that true stewardship of our natural resources means more than sticking a tree in the ground. At the last report Hebard got, a year after the planting, the White House chestnut wasn't doing too well: "I think they might have overwatered it."

Conclusion

The Comeback

In an essay discussing his environmental philosophy, the great conservationist Aldo Leopold described the vital importance of every part of what he called "the land organism." "You cannot love game and hate predators; you cannot conserve the waters and waste the ranges; you cannot build the forest and mine the farm." All are parts of one organic whole, he wrote. "Its parts, like our own parts, compete with each other and co-operate with each other," and only a fool would discard parts that he didn't understand or appreciate. "To keep every cog and wheel," he counseled, "is the first precaution of intelligent tinkering."

By the time he wrote those words, Leopold had already begun rescuing one of America's most distinctive native landscapes: the Midwestern prairie, which had been slowly disappearing under rows of corn and soybeans, highways and housing for over a century. In a two-square-mile planting at the University of Wisconsin Arboretum, Leopold began restoring the many cogs and wheels that made up the historic prairie, such as big bluestem, Indian grass, gentians, and goldenrod. This reconstruction of original Wisconsin, he said at the arboretum's dedication in 1934, "may be regarded as a place where, in the course of time, we will build up an exhibit of what was, as well as an exhibit of what ought to be."

Leopold's wise recognition that the past holds significant keys to a healthy environmental future has since inspired a host of projects around the world guided by a science now known as restoration ecology. The definition of restoration varies widely; one expert counted up nearly two hundred working definitions. Yet broadly speaking, restoration represents an effort to repair damage that humans have inflicted on an ecosystem by returning it to its pre-damage state, a goal that, in the United States, often implies a return to the conditions that existed before the arrival of Europeans. The goal is not to replicate the original—that would be impossible—but to restore the pieces, the cogs and the wheels that will allow some facsimile of the original ecosystem to develop and maintain itself.

Restoration projects run the gamut, from replenishing a pocket-size patch of city park to rejuvenating the eighteen-thousand-square-mile sauntering river of grass that is the Florida Everglades. The desire to save all the pieces has even inspired such provocative ideas as a recent proposal by scientists for "Pleistocene rewilding," introducing camels, cheetahs, elephants, and other modern-day versions of prehistoric large mammals to the Great Plains to approximate the environment that existed there thirteen thousand years ago. Given the countless number of degraded ecosystems around the planet, restoration has, not surprisingly, become big business, with projects now exceeding seventy billion dollars a year worldwide.

When the chestnut blight hit, scientists and laypeople alike certainly recognized the important role the American chestnut played in East Coast forests. To the mountain dwellers of Appalachia, it was the central cog of their ecosystem. And for the next hundred years, Americans focused their efforts on simply preserving that cog in some form or another. The twentieth-century fight to save the species consisted of finding a way to outwit its mortal enemy—be that through breeding, biological control, or biotechnology.

Success, on that front, may well be near. In the next few years, Fred Hebard hopes to harvest his first fully blight-resistant chestnuts. Hypovirulence experts are optimistic that they are homing in on ways to strengthen the blight-of-the-blight, while rapid advances in the science of genomics could well make it possible for Maynard, Powell, or other bioengineers to implant the precise genetic arsenal the American chestnut needs. Yet as anyone who works with chestnut knows, defeating the blight is only half the battle. The experts may make the most blight-resistant trees in the world, but getting them back in the woods is a whole other story.

With the twenty-first century comes the even harder task of releasing the tree from human care and returning it to nature's hands. That raises a host of questions, both practical and philosophical, which until recently no one concerned with saving the chestnut had to seriously consider. How do you return a species to a landscape that long since stopped missing it? What will it take for the species to take off in the wild? Or even more fundamentally: how do chestnuts grow and survive in the wild?

The blight decimated the tree in its natural range just as modern forestry and ecology were getting under way. As a result, experts know relatively little about the growing habits of chestnuts in the wild. The vestigial old stumps and young sprouts offer some clues, as does the one existing American chestnut forest in West Salem, Wisconsin. But there are still many unanswered questions. For instance, what types of soil does the tree prefer? What fungi make up the underground community that live in symbiosis with the tree? How does chestnut respond to drought? Or fire?

The issue of fire is controversial, but also especially important, as the U.S. Forest Service is increasingly using prescribed burns based on research indicating that fire played a critical role in shaping the pre-European forest. Paleobotanists Hazel and Paul Delacourt believe that Native Americans used fire to create pure stands of chestnut and other nut trees in the Appalachian uplands. They argue that those early peoples used fire so extensively that it fundamentally changed the forest ecosystem. Thus experts in the U.S. Forest Service now maintain that the careful use of fire—after decades of fire suppression—will improve the health of East Coast forests and benefit fire-tolerant species such as oaks or chestnut. But at least one critic, Quentin Bass, an archaeologist at the Cherokee National Forest, contends that the role of fire in the southern Appalachian forests has been grossly overrated and that prescribed burns will kill chestnut restoration plantings.

Another significant unknown is how the chestnut responds to sunlight. Scientists know chestnut loves sun but will tolerate shade. Will a shady environment provide enough sunlight to put the tree back in the forest canopy, or will it leave the chestnut a stunted "wanna-be" in an environment that has passed it by? Scientists have only recently begun exploring this question. Their answers will help dictate future forest plantings. If the tree needs full sunlight, then the trees can be planted only in clear-cut areas. Or, more controversially, other trees will have to be cut down to make way for chestnuts.

Regardless of its sunlight needs, restoring the chestnut to the forest means people will have to make room for it and take other measures to ensure its survival there. The East Coast forests of today in no way resemble their pre-blight predecessors. Logging and the legacy of fire left forests that were open enough for entire wagon trains to drive through; a single rider on horseback would have a hard time maneuvering through the dense underbrush and tight stands of trees that make up most eastern forests today. Nor did a chestnut in 1900 have to contend with the great scourge of tender young trees today: white-tailed deer. Deer fences will almost certainly be required. Even so, chestnut lovers may find themselves embroiled in the ongoing debate over deer hunting limits, caught on the horns of the unhappy dilemma of saving the chestnut or protecting Bambi.

"Restoring the chestnut is not going to be as simple as taking a two-year-old seedling from a nursery out into the woods, plugging it into the ground, and standing back as it takes over," says Douglass Jacobs, a Purdue University forestry researcher who works with the American Chestnut Foundation. "It's going to require some disturbance in the forest. And that means cutting trees, using herbicides, fire. And those are things that people in the culture at large resist." Indeed, environmental groups concerned about clear-cutting routinely challenge the Forest Service anytime it announces plans to cut trees, whether for commercial or ecological purposes. Of more than 3,700 challenges to U.S.

Forest Service plans filed with the U.S. Court of Appeals between 1997 and 2002, 139 concerned restoration projects.

Such culture clashes are common in restoration efforts. One famous example concerned a project known as Chicago Wilderness, an ambitious effort to restore seven thousand acres of native prairie landscape in suburban areas surrounding Chicago. The group wanted to remove trees from local forest preserves to resculpt the landscape into a tallgrass prairie and oak savanna. Local homeowners were appalled at the idea of cutting down trees to make way for what many perceived as weeds. Their protests eventually forced the group to curtail its plans. At the heart of such fights are differing notions of nature and its value to people. To the homeowners, what mattered was the natural world that was there when they arrived a generation or two ago: the shady green oases in which they hiked and biked and picnicked and found welcome relief from the pollution and noise of urban life. But to the restorationists, looking back much further in time, the hundred-year-old forest preserves are interlopers on a more authentic natural landscape—one composed of a rich array of grasses and wildflowers that are in danger of being lost forever. Prairie grasses might not provide shade or cleanse the air, but to the restoration crew, the rarity of the plants gave them a value superseding any others.

Will the chestnut's supporters be able to persuade local communities that chestnut restoration should trump competing natural landscapes?

Restorationists start out with a vision of the landscape they wish to restore: the sinuous line of a river before it was dammed, a Midwest prairie circa 1870, or a pre-blight chestnut forest. Yet there's also a recognition that once the original cogs and wheels are set back in place they may turn in unexpected, unpredicted directions. How can it be otherwise? The ultimate goal is not to create a static museum display or a perfect tree that will last unchanged into perpetuity. It's to restart the chaotic choreography of natural change itself—to reopen evolutionary pathways that were knowingly or carelessly disrupted when humans entered the scene. The aim "is precisely to set in motion processes we neither fully control nor understand," as Steve Packard, a leading figure in the field, has put it. "A restorationist, like a parent, needs to protect an unsteady being from certain great insults to its health or existence. . . . The goal is to help some life go forward on its own—and in the process become more truly itself." Like parenting, restoration is a perpetual tug between control and letting go.

That tension between control and letting go has simmered within the American Chestnut Foundation since its earliest days, when the PhD scientists who founded the group were reluctant to entrust its all-too-scarce breeding materials to members who were amateurs. For the most part, the members have willingly deferred to the group's scientific leaders. But in the late 1990s, control issues threatened to break the organization apart. The source of the trouble was a legal document that the foundation's leaders wanted local members to sign. The agreement was designed to protect the "germplasm" of the American Chestnut Foundation's backcross chestnuts, that is, any part of the tree that could be used for propagation: seeds, pollen, scion wood, or roots. Among other provisions, it prevented members from selling or giving any germplasm to a third party. The group's leaders wanted to prevent unscrupulous breeders from hijacking the backcross trees and selling them as their own, which not only would deprive the group of revenue but also might jeopardize restoration plans if the trees weren't yet fully blight-resistant. They also wanted to ensure that all the members were following the same breeding protocol. "It was mainly to keep everyone rowing in the same direction," Hebard recalls.

But some local members felt they were being handcuffed to their oars; they believed that the agreement was overly restrictive. Bob Leffel, a leader of the Pennsylvania chapter and a former USDA plant breeder, chafed at the provision that forbid members from "making selections."

What else does a breeder do? he complained. "Plant breeding is mostly selection." Surely he knew as much as Hebard about how to choose the right trees to advance through the breeding program. He and his wife, Ann, also were frustrated that the wording of the agreement prevented local chapters from cooperating with various public agencies, such as state forestry departments. They, like other dissenters, felt the national leadership was being too controlling over the work of the volunteer members.

Debate over the document escalated. The Leffels refused to sign it, as did other Pennsylvania members. Soon the entire chapter was threatening to secede. "We called it 'the germplasm wars,'" recalls foundation president Marshal Case.

Eventually a special committee hammered out a new agreement, adopted in 2003, that softened some of the most restrictive provisions, such as the prohibition on making selections. It was enough to mollify the Pennsylvania chapter, and though the Leffels still objected to the agreement, they agreed to a ceasefire.

Even some outside the organization objected to the agreement. Sandra Anagnostakis, at the Connecticut Agricultural Experiment Station, considered it a bad idea, because, among other things, the restriction on seed distribution prevents her from cooperating with the foundation. Perhaps because she works for a public organization, she feels no pressure to control the fruits of her efforts; she freely gives away any nuts or pollen her breeding program produces. "I don't care what people do with it," she says. "Eventually chestnut's going to sort it out for itself in the real world."

Control versus letting go. The tug-of-war is on again as the foundation starts to lay plans for its first few crops of fully blight-resistant chestnut seeds. Given the fervor of chestnut fans, there will no doubt be great public clamor for those seeds. Anyone who has cared about the tree will want a chance to plant them. But after devoting two decades to fortifying the American chestnut against the greatest insult to its health or existence, the foundation's leaders are feeling understandably protective (and proprietary; after all, the group has invested considerable time and resources in the seeds and rightly sees them as a potential source of revenue for the organization). Having cultivated the tree for a comeback, they want to do all they can to make sure that its return is successful.

To that end, the group has adopted a detailed protocol for testing those first few generations of fully resistant trees. The protocol calls for state chapters, cooperating agencies, and scientists to establish test plantations in forest plots, abandoned farm fields, and other areas that are likely to be conducive to the trees' growth. It prescribes precisely how the plantations shall be planted (in a square grid, with eight-by-eight-foot spacing between each tree, and with a mix of pure Americans, Asian trees, and backcross hybrids from various lineages) and cared for, as well as what kinds of measurements testers should make and the records they should keep. The stewards of the plantations are required to maintain them for at least five years, though the document acknowledges it will really take closer to ten years to come to any definitive conclusions about the tree's "performance." Assuming the trees perform well, what then?

Then comes the trickier issue of letting go: planting backcross chestnuts in the wild so the species may start the unpredictable process of going forward on its own. The hows, whens, wheres, and what-ifs of that process are sources of continuing debate. At one end are scientists like board member Hugh Irwin, an ecologist, who is urging the group to take its time, given that approximately one-sixteenth of the trees' genes are of nonnative origin and that breeding programs have a hard time maintaining "hereditary wildness," the ensemble of traits that occur in the wild. Even if the trees start out looking and growing like American chestnuts, Irwin believes it will take at least twenty-five to fifty years to determine if they express some of the more subtle, yet important, traits of the species, such as the capacity to survive for long periods as sprouts in the understory.

His concern is not only that the hybrids won't thrive, but that they might thrive all too well, before it's been determined whether they are up to snuff as a replacement for the original tree. An inadequate hybrid that flourishes in the forest could become yet one more introduced exotic threatening native species. The chestnut is, after all, an extraordinarily aggressive tree, capable of beating out any other hardwood in the race to the forest canopy. A backcross chestnut unhampered by the blight could well muscle aside oaks, poplars, red maples, and other natives and take over whole swaths of forest. It could even drown out the tenacious sprouts of pure American trees, threatening the valuable reservoir of the species' native genes. That concern is one reason the National Park Service has yet to commit to planting backcross chestnuts on its lands, even though places like the Great Smoky Mountains National Park were once strongholds of the American chestnut's former kingdom. Even if the hybrids do prove a desirable replacement for the original tree, some scientists have expressed concern that the perfect tree could be too perfect. As longtime chestnut researcher Scott Schlarbaum told me, only half-facetiously, "In one hundred years people could be saying, 'What the heck did we do? We want oaks and black cherry and we've got chestnut.'"

Others are less concerned about the impact of releasing this or any other iteration of the backcross chestnut tree, considering the magnitude of actual restoration. "It's going to take so long to restore the species, we're going to be beyond debating whether fifteen-sixteenths is pure enough by the time we are done," says Kim Steiner, another member of the foundation board and director of the Pennsylvania State University arboretum. The foundation has calculated that by 2025, its various breeding orchards should be able to produce twenty million seeds a year for planting. That sounds like a lot, until you consider that the blight wiped out an estimated three to four billion trees. Even if foundation volunteers are planting twenty million seeds a year, it would take many decades to create a population capable of replacing the chestnut forests that existed before the blight. And that's assuming the group has the one hundred million dollars a year Steiner estimates it would take to plant so many seeds. On the restoration time line Steiner envisions, there will be ample time for the foundation—and future generations of chestnut devotees—to continue perfecting the tree through further refinement of the breeding program or biotechnology.

Even as chestnut scientists debate the issue, they know it will soon enough be made moot by the tree itself. Out in the forests, the backcross trees will cross with one another and with pure American trees, chinquapins, various hybrids that have developed over the years, and other stray members of the *Castanea* family. Eventually new variations of American chestnut may well arise as the tree restores itself. As Anagnostakis says, "What we do is only a drop in the bucket of what will be done by natural evolution."

For one vision of how that process may be set in motion, I travel to eastern Kentucky, to the highlands of the Cumberland Plateau where American chestnut once held sway. There, on a bright May morning, I find myself in a landscape as desolate-looking as the moon. The dusty, flat expanse on which I am standing used to be capped by a high round peak that rose 1,847 feet high and was known as Bent Mountain, until Addington Mining Inc. arrived here in 2004. Then all parts of the mountain that were not coal—trees, shrubs, topsoil, layers of sandstone—were cut, blasted, pulverized, and scraped off into the valley below by gigantic earth-moving machines—the same ones now lumbering across another flattened tier cut into the mountain several hundred feet away. In place of the lush forest of oaks, hickories, pines, and maples that once hosted life here, there is now a barren plain of gray and brown rock. I have trouble grasping the scope of the change.

"There was a mountain here?" I ask Patrick Angel, my guide for the day. He's a native of the area and a longtime inspector for the federal Office of Surface Mining.

"There was a mountain that came up and back down," he replies, drawing an arc in the air to illustrate the missing topography.

Still, it's hard to imagine how a whole mountaintop could disappear until I turn and walk to the edge of this plateau and see, off in the middle distance, another partially digested peak. It looks like a crude depiction of a mountain cross-section. A thickly forested slope rises and then abruptly drops off into a steep, sheer wall of shale and sandstone. There are still trees growing right up to the edge of the ledge that marks the mammoth bulldozers' last bite into the mountainside. A thin black seam of coal is visible in the cut-away wall. Presumably, the bulldozers eventually will return to finish the job and consume the rest of the mountain.

In the doleful saga of America's extractive industries, mountaintop removal mining will surely end up counting as one of the sorriest chapters. It accomplishes what neither the blight, fire, industrial logging, underground mining, conventional strip mining, nor other assaults on the region's natural resources achieved—the total dismantling of an ecosystem.

The ecological wound on this site is so severe, the land seems beyond recovery. But, Angel eagerly explains, although the mountain can't be restored, the land can be healed—through reforestation. And he sees the American chestnut playing a pivotal role in that process. Amazingly enough, researchers have found that trees will grow and thrive in the "spoil," the mix of rock and dirt chunks that is excavated in a mining operation. Spread thick rows of spoil over a mine site, plant seedlings in them, and the trees will grow twice as fast as seedlings in their native forests. "Research has shown you can grow trees like gangbusters," says Angel. "You can grow trees so fast that if you lean over them, they'll poke you in the eye." The trees flourish because their roots can dig down deep and spread wide in the loose rock. Based on that research, the federal Office of Surface Mining has teamed up with seven coal-mining states to form the Appalachian Regional Reforestation Initiative

(ARRI), an organization devoted to putting forests back onto abandoned, as well as active, surface mines. Angel is providing ARRI's forestry expertise. Among the hardwood trees he envisions ARRI will plant is the American chestnut.

University of Kentucky researchers already have started test plantings here. We clamber down the side of the plateau to a boulder-strewn area that looks as if it had been tilled by Paul Bunyan. Poking out from between the chunks of rock, improbably enough, are dozens of little seedlings—ash, white oak, sycamore, and yes, American chestnut. I pause by one chestnut sprouting from a pile of broken-up sandstone. It's encased in a plastic tree shelter to protect it from browsing deer, and after one growing season is already about eighteen inches tall. With its scrawny stem and large floppy leaves, it's as gawky as a big-eared kid. Because the tree is a pure American chestnut, no doubt it will eventually be done in by the blight. But once the American Chestnut Foundation starts releasing blight-resistant trees, Angel hopes they will be planted all over abandoned surface mines in the region. The cost would be borne by the mine operators, who are required by federal law to restore or remediate the land they've damaged. That makes the planting of American chestnut a "win/win situation for everyone," Angel says enthusiastically. "The Appalachian coal fields and the native range of the American chestnut overlap perfectly. So as ironic as it sounds, surface mines may make the best springboard to get the American chestnut back into its native range."

It's a vast springboard. According to author Erik Reece, who chronicled the dismantling of another mountain in this area, there's so much abandoned, unreclaimed mine land that the Office of Surface Mining doesn't even try to account for it in terms of acreage. The few studies done to date suggest the ever-adaptable chestnut grows very well on former surface mines, provided the area is not grossly contaminated—a caveat that could well eliminate many potential sites. Still, they offer such a promising stage for the chestnut's comeback that the American Chestnut Foundation is an active ARRI partner and has forged an agreement with one of the country's largest mine operators, Peabody Energy, to conduct a test planting of four hundred thousand hybrid trees on five abandoned mine sites in Kentucky.

Such projects are controversial, however. While environmental groups support the idea of reclamation, many also fear the projects allow mining companies to justify the fundamentally unjustifiable practices of mountaintop removal. That's why many Appalachian environmental organizations seeking a moratorium on mountaintop removal mining have been cautious about publicly embracing ARRI. Angel understands the caution, but finds it frustrating. "We're not about promoting more strip mining," Angel says repeatedly as we tour the Bent Mountain site. "If they are going to do this horrible thing to the earth, then let's make sure we reclaim it."

Angel's is hardly the only vision of how to restore the chestnut to its native range. Given the vast territory the tree once covered, the trees will be planted in a variety of locales, from existing forest tracts to the empty farm fields that are often used to incubate stands of hardwood trees. There will be plantings not only on public lands—the U.S. Forest Service and some state forests have already pledged to cooperate with the American Chestnut Foundation—but also on private lands and even at tourist attractions and historic sites. (Indeed, to promote its cause over the years, the foundation has planted hybrids at places such as the Biltmore estate, Jimmy Carter's presidential library, George Washington's Mt. Vernon home, and even Dollywood.)

Later, as I think about Angel's plans, I remember the first recorded reference to the American chestnut: an observation by a member of Hernando de Soto's historic expedition through the southeast and the Blue Ridge Mountains. De Soto and his men were the first Europeans to lay eyes on the imposing towers of wood that dominated so much of the region's forest. "Where there are mountains, there are chestnuts," wrote the chronicler known only as the Gentleman of Elva in 1540. Now, five centuries later, there's the prospect that where there once were mountains, there will be chestnuts.

How much does it matter that the mountains are missing? Or that the chestnuts Angel hopes to plant won't be identical to the species that once flourished in this region? Or that any forest that emerges will be, at least initially, a human-made artifact?

Some would argue it matters a great deal. The restoration literature is filled with debates over the issue of authenticity. In a provocative 1982 essay, Australian environmental philosopher Robert Elliott blasted the practice of restoration as "faking nature." Elliott contends that restoring a landscape is akin to forging a work of art. Just as a copy of the *Mona Lisa,* however perfect, will never be as valuable as the original, so even the most faithful restoration of a wild place cannot reproduce the value of the original wilderness, for that value lies in its intrinsically non-human nature, the fact that it exists free of human influence. American philosopher Eric Katz extends the argument. He calls the notion that damaged natural systems can be restored "the big lie," arguing that ecological restoration is merely another form of human domination over nature. "The idea of restoration is the same kind of 'technological fix' that has engendered the environmental crisis—the notion that science and technology will repair and improve natural processes. On a deeper level, it is an expression of an anthropocentric world view, in which human interests shape and redesign a comfortable natural reality. . . . Cloaked in an environmental consciousness, human power will reign supreme."

Their objections are more abstract than practical. Neither Elliott nor Katz is calling for environmentalists to abandon efforts to restore damaged ecosystems. Rather, they are drawing attention to the dangerous presumption that nature is infinitely repairable. Like the environmental groups that are wary of publicly endorsing ARRI's reforestation program, they fear that presumption will only serve to justify further outrageous assaults on the environment: what's the problem with making a mess if we can clean it up?

Underlying such objections is a view of nature as something fundamentally other than and apart from human culture. As defenders of restoration efforts have argued, this can be an equally problematic presumption, and one that in some ways has hamstrung the effectiveness of the environmental movement. If nature is only good to the extent that it is unsullied by human contact, where does that leave people? If we can only be apologetic about our presence on this lovely blue and green orb, how can we ever begin to take constructive action to help it? If the only nature that matters is an untrammeled wilderness that few people ever see, how do we learn to care about the tamer slices of nature—the parks, rivers, bits of woods, prairie, or desert—that we encounter daily?

The expansive land ethic embraced by Leopold emphatically denies any such divide between humans and nature. Instead, as Leopold famously wrote in *A Sand Country Almanac,* we are plain members and citizens of the broad biotic community with which we share our planet. As such, we have an obligation to respect our fellow community members and the community as well. Conserving the community and restoring parts we have despoiled are essential acts of citizenship.

When we plant a seed, we are extending a handshake to nature. When we take on the far more challenging task of restoring a native landscape, we can reach beyond that handshake to develop a deep and meaningful relationship with the natural world, as William Jordan, one of the leading thinkers in the field, has argued. In his book *The Sunflower Forest,* Jordan contends that restoration offers an opportunity to become actively engaged in the natural world—to be participants, rather than mere observers or appreciators of nature. It also provides a way to compensate for our destructive impact on the landscape; indeed, nearly everyone who becomes involved in chestnut work talks about their desire to right the ecological wrong that occurred when humans introduced the blight to its unwitting victim. As Jordan writes, "The restored ecosystem is perhaps as close as we can come to paying nature back in kind for what we have taken from it."

By now, our takings from nature have brought us to a perilous point. The world is losing species faster than we can save or restore them. To be sure, species have come and gone throughout the 3.5 billion years that life has existed on earth. Sometimes the vanishings have been cataclysmic, as at the end of the Permian period 250 million years ago, when nearly every organism on Earth was extinguished. But even between the jolts of five such episodes of mass extinctions, the fossil record indicates that species died off at a fairly stable rate of about one in a million per year. Because that rate of loss was slower than the evolution of new species, biodiversity on the planet continued to grow. But since the emergence of one species, *Homo sapiens,* others have disappeared at a vastly accelerated rate. The human imprint on Earth has expanded to the point that we are now losing an estimated fifty thousand species a year; that's 137 a day, or one every ten minutes. Not diminished, like the American chestnut, but gone. Forever. Most are fungi, invertebrates, and plants— little organisms little noticed by humans, but nonetheless cogs and wheels in their particular ecosystems. Such a rapid and profound erosion of the planet's biodiversity threatens to produce what Harvard entomologist Edward O. Wilson has called "the greatest extinction spasm since the end of the Mesozoic era, 65 million years ago."

The leading causes of species extirpation include global warming, pollution, destruction of habitat, and the problem that to this day is best symbolized by the plight of the American chestnut: invasive species. *Cryphonectria parasitica* was not the first destructive pathogen to arrive unbidden in this country, but its disastrous impact introduced Americans to this dark consequence of global commerce. With the escalating pace of global trade and travel, what once was a trickle of ocean-hopping, border-jumping organisms has become a flood. U.S. government inspectors now intercept about fifty-three thousand pathogens, insects, or noxious plants each year—and those inspections only cover about 2 percent of all the incoming cargo and baggage. Just a minuscule fraction of those that slip past the inspectors take hold and prove harmful. But those that do tend to be really harmful—to the tune of approximately $137 billion a year in losses, damage, and associated costs. The fight to contain the exotics that have become established costs the United States approximately $100 million a year.

By now more than twenty exotic pathogens and 360 harmful nonnative insects have become permanently ensconced in North American forests and woodlands. Generally they have arrived through one of three routes: on imported live plants, on lumber or logs, or in pallets and other solid wood packing material. Few wreak havoc on the scale of the chestnut blight, but a significant number threaten some of the country's most commercially valuable and best loved trees. The casualty list includes Fraser firs, dogwoods, beeches, butternuts, white pines, wild elms, larches, and Port Orford cedars, a fragrant tree that grows only in southern Oregon and Northern California. Eastern hemlocks are so endangered by a tiny insect known as the woolly adelgid that the U.S. Forest Service has planted specimens abroad to preserve the species. Likewise, ash trees are under such heavy attack by a recently arrived beetle that the USDA has arranged to store the species' seeds for potential future restoration efforts.

The most worrisome disease to surface since the days of the chestnut blight appeared in 1995 in Northern California. Sudden oak death—a misnomer, because the disease is neither sudden nor confined to oaks—is caused by a newly discovered microorganism, *Phytophthora ramorum,* which belongs to the same family of water molds that attack the roots of chestnut trees, decimated eucalyptus forests in Australia, and caused the Irish potato blight. By the time scientists identified the pathogen, thousands of trees in Northern California had already died. But what has really given experts the heebie-jeebies is *P. ramorum*'s ability to spread quickly via airborne spores, plus its wide-ranging appetite. To date, researchers have found it can infect more than a hundred species of trees and shrubs, including rhododendrons, huckleberries, bays, madrones, Douglas firs, redwoods, and the red oaks and pin oaks that dominate eastern forests and make up a substantial part of the region's timber industry. Most of the victims suffer only minor damage—including, to California's relief, redwoods—but greenhouse tests suggest it may be deadly to several species of oaks. The big unknown is whether it can have the same lethal effect outside the laboratory, on oaks in the wild.

The unfolding of the sudden oak death story is a discouraging replay of the chestnut blight saga, suggesting that the lessons of that earlier disaster still have yet to be learned. *P. ramorum* is most likely a native of Asia and is thought to have arrived in California on imported rhododendrons. It soon spread from infected trees in nurseries or people's yards to nearby forests. By the time anyone noticed its presence, it was too late to contain it—at least in Northern California. A quarantine was applied to the Northern California counties afflicted by ailing trees. But soon there were sightings of the disease in Oregon and Washington, where despite ongoing eradication efforts, it has yet to be squelched. Then in, early 2004, infected camellias were found near Los Angeles in the state's largest nursery, Monrovia Growers, a business that ships its trees and plants all across the country, including to the Appalachian states where oaks have replaced American chestnuts as the dominant tree in the forest canopy. With the aid of your friendly express shipper, there was now the danger that the microbe had nimbly skipped its way past every natural barrier—the Rockies, the Great Plains, the Great Lakes—to threaten the susceptible oak forests on the opposite side of the continent. Indeed, three weeks after the Monrovia discovery, inspectors tracking the company's shipments found infected camellias in five nurseries in Georgia.

By then, the USDA had broadened its quarantine, ordering a ban on interstate sales of all host plants from California until they have been inspected and given a clean bill of health. Still, as of this writing in 2006, infected trees have been found in twenty states. In every case, the trees have been located in people's yards or in nurseries, suggesting the disease has yet to spread into the wild. Experts are still uncertain whether the disease could explode into a pandemic on the order of the chestnut blight. But the Forest Service and the USDA aren't taking any chances. While the USDA has been inspecting nurseries, for the last three years, the Forest Service has been intensively surveying eastern forests that have the types of trees and shrubs and cool, moist conditions that *P. ramorum* favors. They're further ahead of the curve than the experts battling chestnut blight a century ago ever were. But whether they end up being more successful remains an open question.

Many cultures contain a notion of a cosmic tree, its roots reaching deep to the underworld, its branches raised high to the heavens. There's a reason trees often are employed as metaphors for life itself. In the forest, trees are the flywheels on which the whole complex, interlocking system of life turns. They are sources of food and shade, nests and burrows; provisioners of soil; holders of land; shapers of streams. Consider the shaggy eastern hemlocks that line the banks of streams like a solemn crowd of dark-coated undertakers. Their heavy branches shelter virtual microclimates: cool, dim places in which dozens of birds and small mammals nest, no fewer than fourteen kinds of salamanders and other amphibians wriggle, and brook trout trawl for bugs. The woolly adelgid has caused such a severe decline of hemlocks in the Delaware Valley Water Gap National Recreation Area that the National Park Service has warned of "massive adverse effects on the ecological, aesthetic and recreational value of the park." Stripped of the tree's cooling shade, the streams may run warmer, carry less water, and be more prone to drying up during summer droughts. The changing microclimate and loss of habitat could reduce the overall variety of species in hemlock strongholds by a third or more. The dead trees that tumble into the streams could interfere with water flow and create conditions that raise the chances of flooding. If the disappearance of just one tree species, one cog, can leave a forest less productive and resilient, how much more impoverished will our forests be after the nibbling onslaughts of hundreds of pests and pathogens?

Unfortunately, it's easy to overlook the change. Diseases and insects spread slowly. The losses they produce accumulate over time, without any obvious beginning or end. By the time the chestnut forests were gone, there were whole new generations who didn't know anything was missing. "One of the penalties of an ecological education is that one lives alone in a world of wounds," Leopold wrote. But in an era when there's talk of a widespread "nature deficit disorder," how many of us have the expertise to recognize the wounds that are being inflicted? It's easy for someone like me, a city dweller with an untrained eye, to look out over a forest vista—as I did in Patrick County, Virginia—and naïvely be reassured by the rolling waves of green. That took place early in my research for this book, and at the time, I did not yet understand that the scene I was admiring was far from a picture of health. In just one example of the troubles now plaguing the southern Appalachian woods, the oak trees that filled the chestnut's place in the forests are themselves in the midst of a major die-back caused by a complicated disease complex known as oak decline. And as those oaks die, they are being replaced by trees like red maple that have even less value to wildlife. As one forest ecologist told me, "When you have tree species after tree species disappearing, what worries me is there will still be trees and shrubs and people will think their forests are beautiful. But to those who knew what the forest once looked like, it will look like the ruins of an ancient civilization."

Just as the chestnut blight introduced Americans to the threat of invasive species, the fight to save the tree now offers a promising template for rescuing other threatened trees. Chances are, if the pest or pathogen originated overseas, there are either individual members of the species or close relatives that harbor resistant genes that can be tapped for backcross breeding. Scientists are beginning to explore that avenue for beleaguered butternuts, dogwoods, and beech trees. But it will surely take more than science to make such efforts work. Efforts to save the chestnut would have languished in researchers' labs and green-houses were it not for the thousands of dedicated nonscientists who never stopped missing their perfect tree.

I started this book with a question: what happens when a species disappears? There is by now a vast and ever-growing amount of scientific literature concerning that question: studies documenting the eclipse of this butterfly or that wildflower, analyzing the effects when a particular niche is emptied or detailing how ecosystems unravel when some critical proportion of the flora and fauna die off. There is, however, surprisingly little writing about the emotional impact of such losses. Ecologist Phyllis Windle is one of the few, outside literature, to tackle the subject. In a lovely essay titled "The Ecology of Grief," Windle discusses her sorrow over the demise of dogwoods (from the anthracnose fungus) and the difficulties for scientists (like her), trained in rational, dispassionate discourse, to admit or express such sentimentalities. "I am tempted to dismiss my feelings for dogwoods as irrational, inappropriate, anthropomorphic," Windle writes. "My arguments go like this: another tree will take the dogwoods' place; death is part of productivity too; evolution removes as well as adds species." Though the arguments were all true, Windle found she could not escape an equally compelling truth: "I am in mourning for these beautiful trees." Gradually, she came to realize that there was a great value in acknowledging her grief. It wasn't some embarrassing hindrance to her work, but part and parcel of it. What made her care about the fate of the dogwood trees was the same passionate interest in other organisms that had led her to become an environmental biologist.

Appalachia mourned the loss of the chestnut because it was, for mountain dwellers, a true and trusted member of their community. But today most of us don't live in the kind of culture that explicitly acknowledges how the fate of the human community is entwined with the fate of the broader biotic community. Can we cultivate such an awareness? Can we survive if we do not? As the late Stephen Jay Gould pointed out, "We cannot win this battle to save species and environment

without forging an emotional bond between ourselves and nature ...
for we will not fight to save what we do not love."

There's no question that people's deep feelings for the American chestnut are in part a product of nostalgia, a keening for a time and place that can never again be. But if nostalgia sparked the drive to save the chestnut, an energetic pragmatism has kept it going. Restoration of the chestnut "is going to recharge the health of our forests," insists American Chestnut Foundation president Marshal Case. He's spent a lifetime on environmental causes and education, including a stint with the International Crane Foundation, a group dedicated to saving the fifteen species of endangered cranes. But he sincerely believes that chestnut restoration has more potential than any other cause he has ever been involved in—that returning the tree to the forest can help redeem a host of human errors. "The chestnut just touches so many aspects of the environment, from the air to the soil to water to wildlife," he says.

As a practical matter, the chestnut's reintroduction would add a layer of diversity to forests that are becoming desperately impoverished. The trees would help wildlife populations rebound, those annual crops of nuts making them more prodigious benefactors than oaks or any other forest tree. Chestnuts grow so rapidly that they could be virtual vacuums of greenhouse gases, pulling carbon dioxide out of the atmosphere and sequestering it in their wood. Chestnuts planted in river bottoms may improve the health of streams, as their deep root systems appear to be capable of filtering pollutants out of the water. Some experts even speculate that the tree is so adaptable it may be better able than many other forest trees to weather the climate changes portended by global warming.

There could be economic benefits as well. Chestnut plantations grown on old mine sites could provide new opportunities for Appalachia once King Coal is exhausted. Chestnut could be used for new, clean biomass fuels, some have suggested. The rot-resistant wood offers a source of lumber that need not be treated with toxic chemicals. "If we can bring this species back right now it would be as if a new species dropped from the sky on us," says Dennis Fulbright, longtime chestnut researcher and fan. "It would be just like getting a gift from the heavens."

But the real gift could be something even more important. It's easy to despair of our ability to ever solve the vast environmental messes we have created, yet that sense of hopelessness only sinks us deeper. The American chestnut, successfully restored, would confirm that we have the power to make things right. As Phil Rutter has written, "There is no better brace for our collective will than a big win: something to demonstrate that we can, really can, make a difference."

If the day comes when our descendants can venture with wonder into chestnut forests, we will have gained back more than a perfect tree. We will have gained a new reason for hope.

NOTES

INTRODUCTION

1 *"Chestnut defined the region"*:
Charlotte Ross quoted in Peter Friederici, *Nature's Restoration: People and Places on the Front Lines of Conservation* (Washington, D.C.: Island Press, 2006), 55–56.

3 *"the country is . . . on the verge"*:
Theodore Roosevelt, "Seventh Annual Message to Congress, 1907," *State of the Union Addresses* (Whitefish, MN: Kessinger Publishing, 2004), 236–93.

6 *America was known as the "wooden country"*:
James Hall, *Statistics of the West* (Cincinnati: H. W. Derby, 1848), 100–101, in Michael Williams, *Americans and Their Forests: A Historical Geography* (New York: Cambridge University Press, 1989), 5.

ONE. WHERE THERE ARE CHESTNUTS

12 *Patrick County's southern border:*
Patrick County Historical Society, *History of Patrick County, Virginia* (Stuart, VA: 1999), 1.

13 *"Up here there was a world of chestnuts":*
Transcript of interview with W. Noel Weaver, Feb. 20, 1981, Patrick

County Project, Special Collection, Newman Library, Virginia Polytechnic Institute and State University, Blacksburg, VA.

13 *Chestnuts . . . grew all over Laurasia:*
Steven Nash, "A Man and His Tree," *Washington Post Magazine,* July 25, 2004.

14 *Allegheny chinquapin:*
There is another type of chinquapin in North America, the Ozark chinquapin, but taxonomists disagree over whether it is a separate species or a subspecies of the Allegheny chinquapin.

14 *flavorful nuggets of nutrition:*
Melinda Hemmelgarn, "NUTrition and Your Health: Missouri Chestnuts," and Sandra Anagnostakis and Peter Devin, "Nutrients in Chestnuts," *Journal of the American Chestnut Foundation* 18 (Spring 2004): 35–41.

15 *induced peasants "to laziness":*
Antoinette Fauve-Chamoux, "Chestnuts," in *The Cambridge World History of Food,* ed. Kriemheld Conee Ornelas and Kenneth F. Kiple (Cambridge: Cambridge University Press, 2000). Accessed online at http://www.cup.org/books/kiple/chestnuts.htm. The chapter is a rich source of information about the role of the chestnut in Europe.

15 *one of the pillars of civilization:*
According to Fauve-Chamoux, "Chestnuts," the Romans and Greeks also believed that chestnuts provided protection against dysentery, poisons, and the bite of a mad dog.

15 *J. Russell Smith asked one villager:*
J. Russell Smith, *Tree Crops: A Permanent Agriculture* (New York: The Devin-Adair Company, 1953), 131.

15 *places with chestnut in their names:*
SongLin Fei, "The Geography of American Tree Species and Associated Place Names," *Journal of Forestry* 16 (March 2007): 84–90. Fei used the U.S. Geological Survey's Geographic Names Information System database to perform his analysis. Clint Neel, a member of the Tennessee chapter of the American Chestnut Foundation, came up with 1,035 "chestnut" place names by searching the Web site http://www.topozone.com.

16 *When colonial Americans began planting chestnut orchards:*
Sandra Anagnostakis, "An Historical Reference for Chestnut Introductions into North America," *The Annual Report of the Northern Nut Growers Association* 80 (1989): 132–43.

16   *source of the expression "a chestnut":*
Don C. Seitz, "The Chestnut Tree's Struggle to Survive," *The Outlook,*
Aug. 11, 1926, 511.

16   *a single tree might bear as many as six thousand nuts:*
Pennsylvania chapter of the American Chestnut Foundation, "The
American Chestnut Tree in the Eastern U.S," http://www.patacf.org/
history.htm.

16   *huge drives of wild turkeys:*
Donald Edward Davis, *Where There Are Mountains: An Environmental
History of the Southern Appalachians* (Athens: University of Georgia
Press, 2000), 26.

17   *a rich source of remedies:*
Paul Hamel and Mary U. Chiltoskey, *Cherokee Plants and Their Uses—
A 400 Year History* (Sylva, NC: Herald Publishing, 1975), in Ann Frazier
Rogers, "Chestnut and Native Americans," *Journal of the American
Chestnut Foundation* 16 (Fall 2002): 24.

17   *"Hodadenon and the Chestnut Tree":*
Annie Y. Bhagwandin, *The Chestnut Cookbook: Recipes, Folklore and
Practical Information* (Tucson, AZ: Hats Off Books, 1996), 12–13.

17   *"If ever there was a place defined by a tree":*
The quote is from a talk Ross delivered at the annual meeting of the
American Chestnut Foundation, Oct. 29–31, 2004.

17   *One Goliath in Francis Cove, North Carolina:*
Samuel P. Detwiler, "The American Chestnut Tree," *American Forestry*
21 (Oct. 1915): 957. An article in an 1876 edition of *The Kentucky Argus*
tells of a nine-foot diameter, 230-year-old chestnut that was split into
seven hundred rails. Cited in *Journal of the American Chestnut Foundation* 16 (Spring 2003): 15.

18   *"a sea with white combers":*
Donald Culross Peattie, *A Natural History of Trees of Eastern and Central
North America* (Boston: Houghton Mifflin, 1991), 189.

18   *population pressures . . . forced many residents:*
Davis, *Where There Are Mountains,* 93–108. Davis provides a good
description of how Europeans settled the region and created their
farms.

18   *"the bare bones" of the mountains:*
Richard C. Davids, *The Man Who Moved a Mountain* (Philadelphia:
Fortress Press, 1970), 2.

18 *"hard-shell" Baptist sects:*
By the 1930s, church membership had fallen off and the county had one of the state's lowest percentages of residents who were church members. These days, residents of Patrick County are again a churchgoing breed; the county boasts one hundred churches covering multiple denominations, one for every 190 residents. Patrick County Historical Society, *History,* 228.

19 *to make a rail fence:*
Ralph H. Lutts, "Like Manna from God: The American Chestnut Trade in Southwestern Virginia," *Environmental History* 9 (July 2004): 500.

19 *"white oak acorn":*
J. Russell Smith, in *The Pennsylvania Chestnut Blight Conference Proceedings,* ed. The Pennsylvania Chestnut Tree Blight Commission (Harrisburg, PA: C. E. Aughinbaugh, 1912), 145.

19 *"There was one time of year when we had food":*
Davids, *The Man Who Moved a Mountain,* 17.

19 *Chestnut leaves . . . could be brewed into a broth:*
Indeed, between 1873 and 1905, chestnut leaves were known to pharmacologists as *extractum Castanea fluidum* and were considered so valuable they were included in the U.S. Pharmacopeia. Alice Thomas Vitale, "Leaves in Myth, Magic and Medicine," excerpted on the American Chestnut Cooperators Foundation Web site, http://ipm.ppws.vt.edu/griffin/lore.html.

19 *No one needed to buy land:*
David Cameron, "The Drovers of Appalachia," *Journal of the American Chestnut Foundation* 15 (Spring 2002): 10. Because the forests were used for open grazing and foraging, chestnut fences that zigzagged across the mountains were intended not to pen livestock in but to keep open-grazing herds out of fields and vegetable gardens.

19 *"There wasn't no kind of game":*
Jake Waldroop, "Memories of the American Chestnut," in *Foxfire 6,* ed. Eliot Wigginton (New York: Doubleday/Anchor, 1980), 402.

20 *"The chestnut mast is knee-deep":*
The quotes are from immigrants' letters Ross described at the annual meeting of the American Chestnut Foundation, Oct. 2004.

20 *They'd tend the trees:*
Lutts, "Like Manna from God," 511–12.

20 *"a better provider than any man":*
Quoted in Davids, *The Man Who Moved a Mountain,* 5.

20 *"had little or no cash value":*
Lutts, "Like Manna from God," 502.

21 *lumber barons were now casting their eyes:*
For information on the Appalachian lumber boom, see Davis, *Where There Are Mountains;* Chris Bolgiano, *The Appalachian Forest: A Search for Roots and Renewal* (Mechanicsburg, PA: Stackpole Books, 1998); Michael Williams, *Americans and Their Forests: A Historical Geography* (Cambridge: Cambridge University Press, 1989).

21 *it was the arrival of a railroad line in 1884:*
For a discussion of the Dick and Willie and its impact on the chestnut trade, see Lutts, "Like Manna from God," 506; also Patrick County Historical Society, *History,* 278–79.

21 *nut collection had become a major industry:*
Lutts, "Like Manna from God," 502. The extent of the trade varied, depending on how widespread chestnuts were in a given area, how good the local transportation systems were, and how much people needed that extra income.

22 *The nuts didn't bring a lot of cash:*
Robert L. Youngs, "'A Right Smart Little Jolt': Loss of the Chestnut and a Way of Life," *Journal of Forestry* 98 (Feb. 2000): 19. Youngs claims retailers were making twelve dollars a bushel, the equivalent of about twenty-four cents a pound.

22 *It was the same story all over the mountain:*
Recollections come from Patrick County Oral Histories, held in Patrick County Library; Youngs, "'A Right Smart Little Jolt,'"; and Noel Moore, "Memories of the American Chestnut," in Wigginton, *Foxfire 6,* 403–4.

23 *At the height of the season:*
Lutts, "Like Manna from God," 504, 506.

23 *The trade was also a boon to Stuart's railway stationmaster:*
Ibid.

23 *Patrick County produced more nuts:*
Ibid., 505, 507. That total may also have included a small number of chinquapins and walnuts.

24 *"the forest was only dented":*
Bolgiano, *Appalachian Forest,* 76.

24 *typically held fewer than two hundred acres:*
Davis, *Where There Are Mountains,* 179.

24 *Scottish Carolina Land Company:*
Ibid., 166–67.

25   *"Virtually no stand of timber":*
Ibid., 167.

25   *Such a winning combination of traits:*
P. L. Buttrick, "Commercial Uses of Chestnut," *American Forestry* 21 (Oct. 1915): 961. The article describes many of the contemporary uses of chestnut that are listed.

25   *Sturdy chestnut ties:*
The railroads' need was staggering. On Dec. 14, 1885, the *New York Times* reported that the railroads were consuming 225,000 acres a year to cut the twelve to fifteen million ties used annually. Later, according to Buttrick, "Commercial Uses," the railroads determined the wood didn't hold up well enough under heavy traffic and relegated the chestnut ties to light rail or little-used lines.

26   *over two-thirds of tannic acid produced:*
Buttrick, "Commercial Uses," 964.

26   *Champion Paper and Fibre Company:*
Andrew Owen, "Waste Nothing—Sell the Same Wood Twice," *Journal of the American Chestnut Foundation* 19 (Spring 2005): 13–16.

26   *chestnut pulp was being used for all sorts of low-grade paper:*
Buttrick, "Commercial Uses," 964.

26   *"chestnut has the largest cut":*
Ibid., 960.

26   *most of the profits:*
Youngs, "'A Right Smart Little Jolt,'" 20.

26   *peaking in 1909:*
Bolgiano, *Appalachian Forest,* 80.

27   *In a report submitted:*
Message from the president of the United States, transmitting a report of the secretary of agriculture in relation to the forests, rivers and mountains of the southern Appalachian region (Washington, D.C.: U.S. Government Printing Office, 1902), quoted in Bolgiano, *Appalachian Forest,* 77, 79–80.

TWO. A NEW SCOURGE

28   *"hungerless sleep" of a spore:*
The phrase is Alan Burdick's from *Out of Eden: An Odyssey of Ecological Invasion* (New York: Farrar, Straus and Giroux, 2005), 198.

29 *"in its natural condition":*
Annual Report of the New York Zoological Society 9 (1905): 43.

29 *The collection included chimpanzees:*
Annual Report of the New York Zoological Society (1905) and Brief History of the Bronx Zoo—the zoo was renamed in 1993—from the Bronx Zoo Web site, http://bronxzoo.com/bz-about_the_zoo/bzhistory.

29 *the park drew residents of Manhattan's crowded Lower East Side tenements:*
Ogden Tanner and Adele Auchincloss, *The New York Botanical Garden: An Illustrated Chronicle of Plants and People* (New York: Walker and Co., 1991), 57.

30 *Then spray the trees with "Bordeaux mixture":*
C. Lee Campbell, Paul D. Peterson, and Clay S. Griffith, *The Formative Years of Plant Pathology in the United States* (St. Paul, MN: APS Press, 1999), 144. Ironically, Bordeaux mixture (*bouille bordelaise*) was developed to fight a fungal pathogen (*Plasmopara viticola*) that was imported to France from the United States, according to Christy Campbell, *The Botanist and the Vintner: How Wine Was Saved for the World* (Chapel Hill, NC: Algonquin Books of Chapel Hill, 2004), 191.

30 *Merkel set about trying to treat his sickened trees:*
Merkel described his discovery and efforts in "A Deadly Fungus on the American Chestnut," *Annual Report of the New York Zoological Society* 10 (1906): 97–103.

31 *would return at night to make sure all was well:*
William Alphonso Murrill, *Autobiography* (Gainesville, FL: N.p., 1945), 74; this book offers a rich portrait of Murrill. Information on Murrill also comes from two articles published in *Mushroom: The Journal of Wild Mushrooming*—David W. Rose, "William Alphonso Murrill: The Legend of the Naturalist" (Dec. 2, 2002), and James W. Kimbrough, "The Twilight Years of William Alphonso Murrill" (Summer 2003)—from a lengthy obituary by George F. Weber in *Mycologia* 53 (Nov.–Dec. 1961): 543–57; and from author interview with James Kimbrough, June 2005.

31 *"The sights and sounds of the fields":*
Murrill, *Autobiography*, 7.

31 *"great uplifter of the race":*
Ibid., 37.

32 *he collected a staggering seventy-five-thousand-plus botanical specimens:*
Kimbrough, "The Twilight Years."

32 *"With a splendid heritage of health":*
Murrill, *Autobiography,* 37.

32 *a son . . . died in infancy:*
Kimbrough, "The Twilight Years."

33 *"I am wedded to science":*
Murrill, *Autobiography,* 45.

33 *"To be strong and independent, a man doesn't have to drive his lawn-roller":*
Murrill, *Autobiography,* 47.

34 *"a charming Southern gentleman":*
Rose, "William Alphonso Murrill."

34 *Murrill set to work in his lab:*
Murrill described his research in several articles, including "A Serious Chestnut Disease," *Journal of the New York Botanical Garden* 80 (June 1906): 143–53; "Further Remarks on a Serious Chestnut Disease," *Journal of the New York Botanical Garden* 81 (Sept. 1906): 203–11.

36 *"Mycelium inserted beneath the bark":*
Murrill, "A Serious Chestnut Disease," 146.

36 *"There is no mistaking the blight":*
"Mysterious Blight Kills Chestnut Trees by Thousands," *New York Times,* Oct. 2, 1910, part 5, 2.

36 *"as though scorched by fire":*
Ibid.

37 *He presumed infection took place through wounds:*
Murrill, "A Serious Chestnut Disease," 152.

37 *repeated resprouting . . . sapped a tree's strength:*
Ibid., 153.

37 *a parasite with far more destructive habits:*
Murrill, "A New Chestnut Disease," *Torreya: A Monthly Journal of Botanical Notes and News* 6 (July 1906): 187.

37 *It would be reassigned yet one more time in 1978:*
William Lord, *"Cryphonectria parasitica,* Stealth Invader," *Journal of the American Chestnut Foundation* 11 (Summer 1997): 32–37.

37 *native to the East Coast:*
Murrill, quoted in "Mysterious Blight," 2.

37 *"vigilance and care should largely control the disease":*
Murrill, "A Serious Chestnut Disease," 153.

38 *he was shocked by how rapidly the plague had spread:*
Murrill, "Further Remarks," 203, 207.

38 *"Chestnut Trees Face Destruction":*
    New York Times, May 21, 1908, 4.

39 *"The chestnut trees are our special friends":*
    "The Chestnut Trees Going," *American Forestry* 18 (July 1912): 457.

39 *"all New York goes a-nutting":*
    Henry David Thoreau, *Wild Fruits,* ed. Bradley Dean (New York: Norton and Co., 2000), 213.

39 *People flocked to chestnut groves:*
    "A Good Place for Nutting Parties," *New York Times,* Oct. 13, 1901, SM15.

39 *the New York lawyer who died:*
    "G. S. Bonner's Injuries Fatal," *New York Times,* Oct. 4, 1902, 9.

39 *In the outskirts of Philadelphia:*
    Clarence Weygandt, *A Passing America: Consideration of Things of Yesterday Fast Fading from Our World* (New York: Henry Holt and Co., 1932), 180–83. Thoreau, on the other hand, didn't have the stomach for such a savage way of collecting nuts. He worried that clubbing or throwing stones wounded the trees. "It is not just so to maltreat the tree that feeds us," he wrote in a journal entry that was published in a newspaper article titled "A New Volume by Thoreau," *New York Times,* Sept. 19, 1892, 3. Roaming his beloved Lincoln woods, he preferred to gather up nuts that had already fallen to the ground or to pinch from the stockpiles of squirrels or wood mice.

40 *"I love to gather them":*
    Thoreau, *Wild Fruits,* 210.

41 *All told, he estimated, five to ten million dollars' worth:*
    "Chestnut Trees Face Destruction," *New York Times,* May 21, 1908, V9.

42 *European chestnuts . . . were also susceptible:*
    "The Costly Blight of the Chestnut Canker," *New York Times,* May 31, 1908, V9.

42 *"There should be a law":*
    "Chestnut Trees Face Destruction," V9.

42 *The city's rich and famous beseeched him for help:*
    "Mysterious Blight," 2.

42 *It was said a tree could be saved:*
    "All Chestnut Trees Here Are Doomed," *New York Times,* July 30, 1911, 6.

43 *people who saw the blight in apocalyptic terms:*
    Ibid.

43 *the disease highlighted the dangers of permitting people to hunt native birds:*
"Chestnut Trees of State Dying of Cancer," *The New York World,* n.d.

43 *A Philadelphia florist insisted that it was caused by a small black beetle:*
"What Kills the Chestnuts," *New York Times,* August 5, 1911, 3.

44 *As Secretary of Agriculture James Wilson declared:*
Annual Reports of the Department of Agriculture, 1900 (Washington, D.C.:
GPO, 1900), quoted in Paul D. Peterson and Clay S. Griffith, "Herman
von Schrenk: The Beginnings of Forest Pathology in the U.S," *Forest
History Today* (Fall 1999): 30.

44 *an "appallingly vast army":*
"Parasites Threaten White Pine Trees and Potatoes," *New York Times,*
April 21, 1912, SM11.

44 *"It is no exaggeration":*
Haven Metcalf, "The Immunity of the Japanese Chestnut to the Bark
Disease," *Bureau of Plant Industry Bulletin* 121 (Feb. 10, 1908): VI: 6,
reprinted in James Wilson, *Chestnut Tree Blight: Letter from the Secretary
of Agriculture* (Washington, D.C.: Government Printing Office, 1912), 6.

44 *Bessey had been among the first botanists:*
Campbell et al., *Formative Years,* 100–101.

45 *Metcalf joined the USDA's Bureau of Plant Industry:*
Ibid., 271.

45 *"it's a waste of money":*
"Costly Blight," V9.

45 *the trees one knows "will never be forgotten":*
Murrill, *Autobiography,* 100.

45 *"The chestnut canker was just another timely round":*
Ibid., 70.

46 *"If this disease continues":*
Murrill, "The Chestnut Canker," *Torreya: A Monthly Journal of Botanical
Notes and News* 8 (1908): 111–12.

46 *"Certain trees . . . are too sensitive":*
"Urge States to Act to Save Shade Trees," *New York Times,* Aug. 29,
1909, 8.

46 *"There is no contagious disease known that does not yield":*
Wilson, *Chestnut Tree Blight,* 4.

46 *a resource worth at least three to four hundred million dollars:*
"In Aid of Chestnut Trees," *New York Times,* Nov. 12, 1911, 11. Current
value based on the Consumer Price Index.

46   *"The stake for which we are fighting":*
"All Chestnut Trees in America Threatened," *The Sun,* Jan. 14, 1912.

THREE. LET US NOT TALK ABOUT IMPOSSIBILITIES

48   *"It seems unthinkable that a disease of this character":*
Programme of the Conference Called by the Governor of Pennsylvania to Consider Ways and Means for Preventing the Spread of the Chestnut Tree Bark Disease (Harrisburg, PA: C. E. Aughinbaugh, 1912), 16; hereafter referred to as *Conference Proceedings.*

49   *a bill . . . committing the grand sum of $275,000:*
The calculation to determine present value of that amount is based on the Consumer Price Index. The entire state budget for fiscal year 1911–1912 was about $31 million, according to *Smull's Legislative Handbook and Manual for the State of Pennsylvania* (Harrisburg, PA: 1912), 1904. Pennsylvania's intense interest in the blight made sense: chestnuts comprised about a fifth of the state's forests, and the state was also home to a thriving orchard industry. Yet the push to fight the blight didn't come from rural areas or orchard owners, but from the affluent Main Line suburbs of Philadelphia, where nearly every town had a Chestnut Street and homes flanked by gorgeous ornamental chestnut trees. The prime force behind the commission was an energetic businessman named Harold Peirce, who had discovered blight on the chestnuts around his home in Haverford in 1909 and quickly alerted the state's Department of Forestry. When the state assigned only one consultant to survey the entire southeast region, Peirce and fellow members of the Main Line Citizens' Association swung into action. The group hired forestry inspectors to survey properties along the Main Line for signs of the disease, which was found to be too widespread to be contained through local efforts alone. The well-connected Main Line group then lobbied the governor and the legislature for a statewide initiative. Peirce was appointed secretary of the resulting Chestnut Tree Blight Commission. I. C. Williams, "A History of the Early Effort to Combat the Chestnut Bark Disease," in *Final Report of the Pennsylvania Chestnut Tree Blight Commission, Jan. 1 to Dec. 15, 1913* (Harrisburg, PA: William Stanley Ray, State Printer, 1914), 19–23.

49   *inaugurated in a burst of patriotic fanfare:*
     George Hepting, "Death of the American Chestnut," *Journal of Forest History* 18 (July 1974): 634.

50   *the scouts soon discovered it had already hopped that watery barrier:*
     Report of the Pennsylvania Chestnut Tree Blight Commission, July 1 to December 31, 1912 (Harrisburg, PA: C.E. Aughinbaugh, 1912), 20.

50   *Murrill . . . considered it pure folly:*
     "States Are to Act on Chestnut Blight," *New York Times,* Feb. 18, 1912, 6.

50   *In one of his first bulletins on the chestnut bark disease:*
     William A. Murrill, "The Spread of the Chestnut Disease," *Journal of the New York Botanical Garden* 9 (Feb. 1908): 30.

51   *only two chestnuts remained of the park's original 1,500:*
     "Only Two Chestnuts Left," *The Evening Post,* Jan. 8, 1912.

51   *"It has swept like a tidal wave":*
     "States Are to Act," 6.

51   *Metcalf concluded he had succeeded:*
     Haven Metcalf and J. F. Collins, *The Control of the Chestnut Bark Disease,* USDA Farmer's Bulletin 467 (Washington, D.C.: GPO, 1911), 11.

52   *Metcalf saw it more as a smoldering wildfire:*
     Haven Metcalf, quoted in "What Shall We Do about the Chestnut Blight?" *Country Life in America* (Sept. 1, 1911): 93.

52   *"We have discovered that if these advance spots of infection can be located":*
     "All Chestnut Trees in America Threatened," *The Sun,* Jan. 14, 1912.

52   *the federal government had no authority:*
     Metcalf and Collins, *Chestnut Bark Disease,* 11.

52   *"the largest and best chestnut forests":*
     Ibid., 2.

52   *In December 1911:*
     "States Are to Act," 6.

52   *By early 1912, bills to that effect were pending:*
     "All Chestnut Trees." The federal bill passed in August, according to "To Check Chestnut Blight," *New York Times,* Aug. 9, 1912, 7.

53   *growing tension between . . . the "progressives" . . . and the "reactionaries":*
     "After Insurgents in War on Blight," *The [Philadelphia] Evening Bulletin,* Feb. 12, 1912.

54   *To do nothing "is un-American":*
     Conference Proceedings, 20.

54 *"My views are so much at variance":*
Franklin Stewart's testimony in ibid., 40–45.

56 *Connecticut's George Clinton:*
Ibid., 76–77.

56 *"One continued negation":*
Ibid., 109.

56 *"Whenever I hear a man talk about 'impossibilities'":*
Ibid., 163.

57 *"It is unlikely the chestnut will be exterminated":*
Ibid., 45.

57 *Williams proclaimed that he would "go after" any visitor:*
"After Insurgents."

57 *the gentlemanly Virginian finally rose to speak:*
Conference Proceedings, 194–95.

57 *Williams castigated the scientists:*
Ibid., 196–99.

58 *His response, however, was measured:*
Ibid., 201–202.

58 *There was only one recorded dissenter:*
"Checking Tree Blight," *New York Times,* Feb. 22, 1912, 7.

59 *it had been "the battle of his career":*
Murrill, *Autobiography,* 70.

59 *his career soon took a tragic turn:*
The story of Murrill's post–New York years is told in Kimbrough, "The Twilight Years," and Rose, "William Alphonso Murrill." Also author interview with James Kimbrough, June 2005.

60 *Carleton, the USDA expert on foreign-plant introductions:*
Campbell et al., *Formative Years,* 275.

60 *"one of the big men of the department":*
Haven Metcalf, letter to Harold Peirce dated May 13, 1912, from the Pennsylvania State Archives.

60 *Carleton had already changed the agricultural habits of America's breadbasket:*
The story of Carleton's effort to introduce Russian wheat to the United States is taken from an excellent biographical sketch of Carleton by Paul de Kruif in *Hunger Fighters* (New York: Harcourt, Brace and World, 1928), 3–30.

61 *what attracted him . . . was "the prospect of a good scrap":*
Metcalf letter to Peirce, May 13, 1912.

61 *The sheer magnitude of the task was daunting:*
    Report of the Pennsylvania Blight Commission 1912, 29.

61 *the law . . . granted Carleton and his men "the power":*
    Conference Proceedings, 131. The commission's activities were exten-
    sively documented in a series of reports issued from 1912 to 1914.

62 *As Carleton explained it, his field agents had to be:*
    Report of the Pennsylvania Blight Commission 1912, 24–25. Carleton also
    got an infusion of enthusiastic recruits when the Boy Scouts of America
    rallied to the commission's call for help. Boy Scout leaders saw it as a
    great opportunity for their young charges who, unlike boys in the past,
    no longer had many chances "to get acquainted with nature and outdoor
    life without special guidance and training," as one Scout leader ex-
    plained. "Of course," another assured, "the boys will not cut down or
    burn any tree that they find infected. They will simply report it to the
    proper authorities." The Pennsylvania troops did such a fine job locating
    blighted trees that the first head of the U.S. Forest Service, Gifford
    Pinchot, put together a manual on other tree pests and pathogens for use
    by scout troops across the country. He viewed the Boy Scouts as an army
    more than half a million strong that could help protect the nation's be-
    leaguered forests ("Boy Scouts to Save Trees," *New York Times,* July 1,
    1912, 5; "War Call to the Boy Scouts to Fight Nature's Pests," July 21,
    1912, SM12).

62 *The ever-skeptical Murrill questioned the value of the cure:*
    William A. Murrill, *Mycologia* 5 (Jan. 1913): 90.

63 *There were more than thirty commercial uses of chestnut:*
    Conference Proceedings, 136.

64 *"the blight will practically be wiped out":*
    "State News," *American Forestry* 19 (Jan. 1913): 55. Though eradication
    was the centerpiece of the commission's campaign, it wasn't the only
    item on its agenda. The commission also supported scientific research
    both to gain further insight into the way the disease spread and in search
    of a cure. Scientists conducted experiments such as blowing bellows on
    infected trees to determine how far the wind could carry the fungal
    spores and injecting trees with various remedial solutions to see if any
    deterred the fungus's spread. None did.

64 *As Charles Darwin observed:*
    Quoted in Burdick, *Out of Eden,* 7.

64 *farmers . . . have sought out exotic additions . . . "with ludicrously little knowledge":*
Yvonne Baskin, *A Plague of Rats and Rubbervines: The Growing Threat of Species Invasions* (Washington, D.C.: Island Press, 2002), 21.

64 *the queen of Egypt was sending ships down the African coast:*
Ibid., 22–25.

65 *Some of today's most notoriously destructive plants . . . were intentionally introduced:*
Ibid., 37.

65 *"Ballast lots sprouted":*
Burdick, *Out of Eden,* 200.

65 *USDA scientists warned farmers in 1912:*
P. Spaulding and E. Field, *Two Dangerous Imported Plant Diseases,* Farmer's Bulletin 489 (Washington, D.C.: GPO, 1912), 5, quoted in Campbell et al., *Formative Years,* 277. This book provides an excellent succinct summary of the scientific and political concerns that led to the passage of the Plant Quarantine Act and other regulations on the importation of plant materials.

66 *American authorities relied instead "on a loosely organized . . . practice of inspection":*
Campbell et al., *Formative Years,* 277.

66 *Meyer was a Dutch-born, mostly self-taught botanist:*
Isabel Shipley Cunningham, *Frank N. Meyer: Plant Hunter in Asia* (Ames: Iowa State University Press, 1984). The book quotes extensively from Meyer's journals.

66 *"skim the earth for things good for man":*
Ibid., 272.

66 *During one earlier trip to China, he had come across groves of chestnut:*
David Fairchild, "The Discovery of the Chestnut Bark Disease in China," *Science* 38 (Aug. 29, 1913): 297.

67 *"This blight . . . does not do as much damage":*
Ibid., 298–99, quoting Meyer. The Chinese, Meyer explained, ascribed the ailment to caterpillars, grubs, and ants; to combat it, they scraped the bark clean every winter or early spring.

67 *When Metcalf received the Chinese specimen:*
David Fairchild, *The World Was My Garden: Travels of a Plant Explorer* (New York: Charles Scribner's Sons, 1938), 405–6. Fairchild also

tells the story of the discovery of the fungus's origin in "Discovery," 297–99.

67   *one last link would be added:*
C. L. Shear and Neal E. Stevens, "The Discovery of the Chestnut-Blight Parasite (*Endothia parasitica*) and Other Chestnut Fungi in Japan," *Science* 48 (Feb. 4, 1916): 173–76.

68   *"Any or all of those Japanese imports could have carried blight":*
Interview with Sandra Anagnostakis, who has carefully tried to track chestnut importations. See also Sandra Anagnostakis, "Chestnuts and the Introduction of Chestnut Blight," *Annual Report of the Northern Nut Growers Association* 83 (1992): 39–42; "An Historical Reference for Chestnut Introductions into North America," *Annual Report of the Northern Nut Growers Association* 80 (1989): 132–43.

68   *New York City just happened to be the first place:*
Actually, there were reports of some type of fungal disease afflicting chestnuts as early as 1902, according to Anagnostakis in "Chestnuts and the Introduction of Chestnut Blight."

68   *political machinations . . . brought the . . . Commission's grandiose effort to a close:*
Minutes of the Pennsylvania Chestnut Tree Blight Commission, June 27, 1913, Pennsylvania State Archives.

69   *Carleton tried to put the best gloss he could:*
Mark Carleton, "The Fight to Save the Chestnut Trees; Final Report of the General Manager," in *Final Report of the Pennsylvania Chestnut Tree Blight Commission, Jan. 1 to Dec. 15, 1913* (Harrisburg, PA: William Stanley Ray, State Printer, 1914), 28.

69   *Commission chairman Winthrop Sargent was more blunt:*
Winthrop Sargent, "Letter of Transmittal," in *Final Report of the Pennsylvania Chestnut Tree Blight Commission, Jan. 1 to Dec. 15, 1913,* 9–13.

FOUR. A WHOLE WORLD DYING

71   *A Whole World Dying:*
The title of the chapter comes from a phrase used by Donald Davis in *Where There Are Mountains: An Environmental History of the Southern Appalachians* (Athens: University of Georgia Press, 2000), 192.

71 *Chestnut extract . . . the antidote for despair:*
From the Web site of the Dr. Edward Bach Centre in Mt. Vernon, England, http://www.bachcentre.com/centre/38/swchest.htm.

73 *Chestnut products brought in some $2.5 million a year:*
Flippo Gravatt, *The Chestnut Blight in Virginia* (N.p.: Commonwealth of Virginia, 1914), 3. The present value is based on the Consumer Price Index.

73 *In 1912, the legislature voted to set aside funds:*
Ibid., 5. See also "A History of Plant Pathology in Virginia: The Reed Era (1908–1915)," University Archives of Virginia Tech, accessed online at http://spec.lib.vt.edu/arc/ppws/reed.htm.

74 *The disease "had a firm foothold" in the northern part of Virginia:*
According to Gravatt, in two cases the outbreaks were caused by imports of infected trees. In a nursery in Henrico County, near Richmond, an outbreak that "was causing great destruction among young chestnut trees" was thought to have gotten its start from trees imported from "the orient." And in Bedford County, near Roanoke, Gravatt believed the disease arrived on the scions of grafted trees brought from "the northern states." Gravatt, *The Chestnut Blight in Virginia,* 6.

74 *The infection rate skyrocketed:*
Ibid., 8.

74 *"Every year's delay . . . means a year longer to market chestnut products":*
Ibid., 4.

74 *"the chestnut stand of the southern Appalachians was doomed":*
G. F. Gravatt, "The Chestnut Blight in North Carolina," *Chestnut and the Chestnut Blight in North Carolina,* North Carolina Geological and Economic Survey: Economic Paper No. 56 (Raleigh, NC: N.p., 1925), 15.

75 *This "death wave":*
P. L. Buttrick, quoted in Arthur Graves, "The Future of the Chestnut Tree in North America," *Popular Science Monthly* 84 (June 1914): 559.

75 *In the years after the Civil War:*
Bowen S. Crandall, G. F. Gravatt, and Margaret Milburn Ryan, "Root Disease of *Castanea* Species and Some Coniferous and Broadleaf Nursery Stocks Caused by *Phytophthora cinnamomi,*" *Phytopathology* 35 (March 1945): 166. The article remains one of the best sources of information on *P. cinnamomi* and was a primary source for this chapter.

76   *about twenty-four miles a year:*
      Gravatt, "Chestnut Blight in North Carolina," 15.

77   *"When from a mountain top one looks over thousands of acres":*
      Ibid.

77   *New Jersey . . . experts . . . turned up only about twenty living trees:*
      "Chestnut Tree Is Facing Doom," *Los Angeles Times,* Nov. 3, 1924, 6.

77   *In Connecticut . . . when scientists . . . needed a peck of nuts:*
      C. F. Korstian, "The Tragedy of the Chestnut: How an Uncontrollable
      Pest Is Exterminating a Valuable Hardwood Species," *Southern Lumber-
      man* 117 (Dec. 20, 1924): 180–81.

77   *Pennsylvania was forced to bid farewell:*
      "Huge Chestnut Felled by Dynamite," *American Forestry* 25 (Nov. 1919):
      1484.

77   *"What was formerly a majestic, soul-inspiring landmark":*
      Charles F. Thurston, "Good Bye, Chestnuts," *American Forestry* 29 (Dec.
      1923): 733.

77   *"Will eating chestnuts by crackling log fires":*
      "Chestnut," *Los Angeles Times,* July 4, 1926, B4.

78   *"You could just almost see [the trees] a'dyin' ":*
      Jake Waldroop, quoted in Wigginton, *Foxfire 6,* 409.

78   *"we could hear a heart rendering . . . 'thud' ":*
      William Banks, "My Life with the Chestnut," *Journal of the American
      Chestnut Foundation* 19 (Spring 2005): 19–20.

78   *a two-mile "graveyard of giant trees":*
      Cited in Lutts, "Like Manna from God," 514. Lumbermen used the
      blight in a last-ditch effort to defeat the creation of the Great Smoky
      Mountains National Park, arguing without success that "certainly noth-
      ing could be more unsightly than the gaunt and naked trunks of these
      dead trees standing like skeletons in every vista to which the eye turns."
      Margaret Brown, *The Wild East: A Biography of the Great Smoky Moun-
      tains* (Gainesville: University Press of Florida, 2000), 100.

78   *an area covering thirty-three million acres:*
      Gravatt, "The Chestnut Blight in North Carolina," 17.

79   *there was still an estimated fifteen billion board feet available for salvage:*
      D. V. Baxter and L. S. Gill, *Deterioration of Chestnut in the Southern
      Appalachians,* USDA Technical Bulletin No. 257 (Oct. 1931), 1. A 1958
      timber resources review put out by the U.S. Forest Service estimated the
      volume of timber killed by the blight at eighteen billion board feet, less

than six billion of which was salvable, reported the *Asheville (N.C.) Citizen* on Dec. 9, 1958. At the then-prevailing stumpage prices, that represented fifty million dollars' worth of timber lost.

79 *The trees could be used for their tannins even longer:*
Gravatt, "The Chestnut Blight in North Carolina," 22.

79 *The extract companies had . . . found ways to glean tannin:*
Flippo Gravatt, *Chestnut Blight,* USDA Farmer's Bulletin No. 1641 (Washington D.C.: Government Printing Office, 1930), 13–15.

80 *by 1930 there were twenty-one plants:*
Ibid. See also Korstian, "Tragedy," 181.

80 *Champion's operation hummed along until 1951:*
"Chestnut Extract: A Champion Milestone," *Champion Log* (1951): 2. According to this in-house publication, at the height of operations, the plant was producing three hundred barrels of extract every twenty-four hours; over the course of its forty-three-year history, the plant produced more than 2.5 billion pounds of extract.

80 *Some urged the chestnut-using industries to adopt systematic logging plans:*
E. Murray Bruner, "The Marketing and Utilization of the Remaining Stand of Chestnut in North Carolina," *Chestnut and the Chestnut Blight in North Carolina,* 18–23.

80 *"The best thing to be done is to chop down the good remaining chestnut trees":*
"Chestnut Trees Doomed," *New York Times,* Oct. 13, 1926, 10.

81 *The leader of a New Jersey Boy Scout troop responded:*
"Chestnut Blight Not Yet Checked," *New York Times,* Sept. 12, 1926, X14.

81 *How many more might there have been?:*
One Rutgers University professor reported in 1924 that he had seen signs of healing and recovery among both saplings and mature chestnuts, and that the condition was "common" in southeastern Pennsylvania. He recognized the trees' improved condition might be due simply to the reduced amount of spores then circulating. "These trees, however, which seem most likely to survive and produce seed are in danger of extinction, since the public has been educated to believe that cutting of all chestnut trees from a woodlot is a virtue. Instead living ones should now be preserved. It might prove advisable to locate the best groves and to protect them from cutting and from fire," he wrote. Arthur Pierson Kelley, "Chestnut Surviving Blight," *Science* 40 (1924): 292–93.

81 *A map produced by Gravatt in 1943 showed the scope of the pandemic:*
Russell Clapper and G. F. Gravatt, "The American Chestnut: Its Past, Present and Future," *Southern Lumberman* 167 (Dec. 15, 1943): 227–29.

82 *Enough trees to fill nine million acres:*
That estimate was made by Jesse D. Diller, "Chestnut Blight," USDA Forest Pest Leaflet 94 (March 1965), 1.

82 *"You just can't imagine how much it changed the looks of the mountains":*
Jake Waldroop, quoted in Wigginton, *Foxfire 6,* 414.

82 *when the chestnut trees tumbled:*
John Jay Morgan and Sara H. Schweitzer, "The Importance of Chestnut to the Eastern Wild Turkey," *Journal of the American Chestnut Foundation* 8 (Winter 1999–2000): 24–25.

82 *a widespread affliction known as oak decline:*
Steve Oak, "From the Bronx to Birmingham: Impact of Chestnut Blight and Management Practices on Forest Health Risks in the Southern Appalachian Mountains," *Journal of the American Chestnut Foundation* 16 (Fall 2002): 32–41. Also author interview with Oak, June 6, 2006.

83 *Researchers who compared the amount of mast:*
Seth J. Diamond, Robert H. Giles, Jr., Roy L. Kirkpatrick, and Gary Griffin, "Hard Mast Production before and after the Chestnut Blight," *Southern Journal of Applied Forestry* 24 (2000): 198–99.

83 *"the worst thing ever happened to this country":*
Walter Cole, interview by Charles Grossman, 1965, Oral History Collection of the Great Smoky Mountains National Park.

83 *"We've never had a honey crop":*
Noel Moore, quoted in Wigginton, *Foxfire 6,* 403.

83 *the dearth of chestnuts has hindered efforts to restore various animals:*
Davis, *Where There Are Mountains,* 194.

83 *The creatures thought to have been most severely threatened . . . are seven species of moths:*
Paul Opler, "Insects of American Chestnut: Possible Importance and Conservation Concern," in William L. MacDonald, Franklin C. Cech, John Luchok, and Clay Smith, eds., *Proceedings of the American Chestnut Symposium* (Morgantown: West Virginia University Books, 1978), 83–85.

84 *"We didn't have no other way of bringing in nothing":*
Transcript of interview with Curtis Fain, June 11, 1981, Patrick County Project, Special Collection, Newman Library, Virginia Polytechnic Institute and State University, Blacksburg, VA.

84 *"a right smart little jolt":*
Transcript of interview with Walter Thomas Dudley Hopkins, Nov. 1980, Patrick County Project, Special Collection, Newman Library, Virginia Polytechnic Institute and State University, Blacksburg, VA.

84 *"Man, I had the awfulest feeling":*
Quoted in Davis, *Where There Are Mountains,* 196.

84 *leading Virginia to establish a eugenics program:*
Bill Baskerville, "Virginia Governor Apologizes for Forced Sterilization under Eugenics Law," Associated Press, May 2, 2002.

85 *"You can't even sell a egg":*
Transcript of interview with Dennis Hall, 1981, Patrick County Project, Special Collection, Newman Library, Virginia Polytechnic Institute and State University, Blacksburg, VA.

PART TWO

91 *The spores attach themselves to the bark:*
Jesse Diller, *Chestnut Blight,* Forest Pest Leaflet 94 (Washington, D.C.: USDA, 1965), 2.

92 *A writer in the* New York Times *cheered:*
"Chestnut Blight Not Yet Checked," Sept. 12, 1926, X14.

FIVE. ROLLING THE DICE

96 *Graves spent months in 1911 touring Massachusetts:*
Conference Proceedings, 21, 221.

96 *the only solution was to "outwit" it:*
Arthur Graves, "Making New Chestnut Trees," *Yankee Magazine* (Sept. 1946), reprinted in *Journal of the American Chestnut Foundation* 12 (Autumn 1998): 18–21. Other useful articles covering the early breeding efforts are Charles Burnham, "Historical Overview of Chestnut Breeding in the United States," *Journal of the American Chestnut Foundation* 2 (Dec. 1987): 6–9; Charles Burnham, "The Restoration of the American Chestnut," *American Scientist* 76 (Sept.–Oct. 1988): 478–86.

96 *the blight brought a "summary termination" . . . to his experiments:*
Van Fleet, quoted in Graves, "The Future of the Chestnut Tree," 566.

96 *various species of chestnut were quite amenable to pairing up:*
Actually, people had been interbreeding chestnuts long before Van
Fleet. The vaunted orchards that the Pennsylvania Chestnut Tree Blight
Commission tried so hard to save were filled with a hybrid cultivar
known as the Paragon. Indeed, Sandra Anagnostakis contends that the
woods throughout the chestnut's native range are filled with wild hybrid
trees, the products of spontaneous intercrosses between American chestnuts, chinquapins, and stray European or Chinese chestnut trees.

96 *"The most hopeful indications for chestnut in North America in the future":*
Graves, "The Future of the Chestnut Tree," 566.

97 *After choosing a mother and father tree:*
Graves described the breeding methods in "Forest Tree Breeding,"
Economic Botany 2 (1948): 293–95.

98 *For those first crosses:*
Information about Graves's early efforts comes from Hans Nienstaedt
and Arthur Graves, *Blight Resistant Chestnuts, Culture and Care* (New
Haven, CT: Connecticut Agricultural Experiment Station, 1955), 4–5;
Arthur Graves, "Breeding Work toward Development of a Timber
Type of Blight-Resistant Chestnut: Report for 1940," *Bulletin of the
Torrey Club* 68 (1941): 667–74; and author interview with Richard
Jaynes, April 2005.

98 *"success would mean a shrieking genetic miracle":*
J. C. Furnas, "New Chestnuts for Old," *American Forests* (Jan. 1963): 47.

98 *Graves wasn't the most meticulous of breeders:*
Interview with Sandra Anagnostakis, April 2005.

98 *the number of surviving mature trees or flowering sprouts was diminishing:*
Graves developed a grafting trick that allowed him to keep hybrids alive
even after they were attacked by blight. Since blight-infected trees tend
to sprout suckers from their roots, he would graft the suckers onto a part
of the trunk above where the fungal cankers had erupted; in effect, the
graft bypassed the infection. He could keep infected trees alive and
available for breeding for years. Graves, "Forest Tree Breeding."

99 *blight-resistant trees owed their good fortune to at least two genes:*
The exact number of genes involved in resistance is still not known.

99 *Graves . . . began seeking "cooperators":*
Arthur Graves, "Breeding Work," 672.

99 *He'd describe each in lovingly rich language:*
Arthur Graves, "Some Outstanding New Chestnut Hybrids I," *Bulletin*

of the Torrey Botanical Club 87 (May 1960): 192–203; Arthur Graves, "Some Outstanding New Chestnut Hybrids II," *Bulletin of the Torrey Botanical Club* 89 (May–June 1962): 161–70.

100   *"He never had a shadow of a doubt":*
Jaynes described Graves's last years in an interview with the author, April 2005.

100   *Beattie sent back 250 bushels of nuts:*
Jesse Diller and Russell Clapper, "Asiatic and Hybrid Chestnut Trees in the Eastern United States," *Journal of Forestry* 67 (May 1969): 328. The article describes the program and how the trees fared.

101   *Chinese chestnuts assumed even greater importance during World War II:*
Amanda Ulm, "The Chinese Chestnut Makes Good," *American Forests* 54 (Nov. 1948): 491.

101   *Over thirty-five years, the USDA breeders joined chestnuts in every direction:*
Russell Clapper, "Chestnut Breeding, Techniques and Results I: Breeding Material and Pollination Techniques," *Journal of Heredity* 45 (May–June 1954): 109.

101   *They produced some ten thousand hybrids:*
Frederick Berry, "Chestnut Breeding in the United States Department of Agriculture," in MacDonald, Cech, Luchok, and Smith, *Proceedings of the American Chestnut Symposium,* 40.

101   *Diller began planting promising trees on fifteen different cleared forest plots:*
Ibid. See also Diller and Clapper, "Asiatic and Hybrid Chestnut Trees"; Burnham, "The Restoration of the American Chestnut."

101   *One lot grew so fast:*
Amanda Ulm, "Remember the Chestnut," *American Forests* 54 (April 1948): 190–92.

102   *crossing first-generation Chinese-American hybrids with Chinese trees:*
G. Flippo Gravatt, "Chestnut Blight in Asia and North America," *Unasylva* 3 (Jan.–Feb. 1949): 6.

102   *By the time Clapper and Diller tallied the final results:*
Jesse Diller and Russell Clapper, "A Progress Report on Attempts to Bring Back the Chestnut Tree in the Eastern United States, 1954–1964," *Journal of Forestry* 63 (March 1965): 186–88. By 1980, USDA breeder Fred Berry found that 27 percent of 705 hybrid trees from the Connecticut Agricultural Experiment Station and 12 percent of the 500 hybrids from the USDA program in Maryland were still surviving in the fifteen test plots Diller had established. Cited in Gary Griffin, "Blight

Control and Restoration of the American Chestnut," *Journal of Forestry* 98 (Feb. 2000): 24.

102 *The government breeders had run into the same catch-22:*
Graves and the USDA breeders were stymied by another obstacle, as well: a poor selection of trees to draw from for that all-important base population. The breeders did not have very many varieties of Chinese or Japanese chestnuts to use in their programs—and what they did have were mostly orchard cultivars, meaning they were even shorter and shrubbier than wild Asian chestnut trees. Likewise, the most available source of American chestnut pollen was from young sprouts, so the breeders couldn't tell whether they were selecting for the tallest, most timber-worthy trees (see Berry, "Chestnut Breeding").

102 *Clapper paired a Chinese-American hybrid with its American parent:*
It was one of the few times the USDA scientists crossed a hybrid back to an American parent. Their failure to pursue that strategy was later deemed one of the reasons the USDA breeding program failed. That approach would become the linchpin of a later, far more successful breeding program.

102 *The reserve manager logged it in as B26:*
The tree's story is told in Shelly Stiles, ed., "Diary of the Clapper Tree," *Journal of the American Chestnut Foundation* 11 (Summer 1997): 15–22.

103 *"hopeful forerunner of a great new crop":*
"What Goes on Here!" *Women's Day* (May 1965): 24–25.

103 *a poetic tribute, parodying Longfellow's classic poem:*
Stiles, "Diary of the Clapper," 19.

103 *Roy Owen, an eighty-four-year-old man from Terre Haute, Indiana:*
The correspondence is reprinted in "Roy J. Owen's Letters on the Clapper Tree," *Journal of the American Chestnut Foundation* 11 (Summer 1997): 22–24.

103 *it had also been struggling with the blight for some five years:*
The refuge manager wrote Diller in 1968 to inform him that the tree showed signs of blight infestation: "I can appreciate your disappointment as we all had high hopes for this tree." Scion wood from the tree was grafted onto chestnuts at the Connecticut Agricultural Experiment Station and would play an important role in later breeding efforts. Stiles, "Diary of the Clapper," 20–21.

104 *The agency had long since shut down its breeding program:*
The decision to end the program upset Diller and Gravatt, who cam-

paigned people within the agency and outside it, urging them not to destroy the various field test plots of hybrid chestnuts. "I am writing this letter to express the hope that these plots be kept in order and they be followed up to locate the best trees," Gravatt wrote in one letter. (Correspondence from the Gravatt archives at Scientists' Cliffs, Maryland.)

104 *The breeding stock and hybrids . . . were all destroyed:*
Burnham, "The Restoration of the American Chestnut," 480.

104 *One of the oddest efforts was undertaken by Ralph Singleton:*
Information on Singleton's irradiation program comes from Essie Burnworth, "A Brief History of the Efforts by Stronghold Inc. to Restore the American Chestnut, 1969 to the Present," unpublished manuscript prepared for Stronghold Inc., August 2002; E. F. Rodger, "Atomic Energy and the American Chestnut," *Virginia Wildlife* 30 (1969): 10–11; W. Ralph Singleton, "The Use of Radiation to Produce Blight Resistant Strains of the American Chestnut, *Castanea dentata*," *Annual Report of the Northern Nut Growers Association* 63 (1972): 61–65; and interview with Gary Griffin, June 2004. Actually, Singleton wasn't the only scientist pursuing "mutant" chestnut breeding. A similar irradiation program was initiated by Eyvind Thor, a professor of forestry at the University of Tennessee.

105 *Singleton irradiated the seeds:*
Burnworth, "A Brief History," 11.

105 *his best source was a Wisconsin grove:*
Ibid., 7.

105 *Dietz and Singleton had about eighteen thousand viable seedlings:*
Griffin, "Blight Control," 25.

105 *this was the longest shot of all:*
Some experts are still not entirely willing to write off Singleton's theory, because interesting things continue to happen with the irradiated seeds Singleton and Dietz planted at a private farm in Maryland owned by the Stronghold Corporation. The entire first generation of trees that grew from the seeds all died, but subsequent sprouts are showing some degree of resistance—in a weird way. Within a clump of sprouts growing from a single root system, some appear resistant and others seem susceptible to the blight. Though they share the same root system, the stems are showing differing responses to the blight. "In other words," researchers who visited the site wrote, "each stem seems to represent an unrelated separate event—like those induced through mutations" (Burnworth, "A Brief

History," 17). A few researchers, including Fulbright, have begun investigating the Stronghold trees in an effort to figure out whether the apparent resistance is real and due to some genuine genetic transformation.

105   *botanist Richard Jaynes was continuing Graves's breeding program:*
The story of Jaynes and his efforts is based largely on an interview with Jaynes, April 2005. See also Richard Jaynes, "Project Village Smithy," *Annual Report of the Northern Nut Growers Association* 62 (1971): 26–28.

106   *"the largest experimental planting of chestnut":*
Jaynes, "Project Village Smithy."

106   *the hybrids initially showed great potential:*
Interview with Tom Dierauf, March 2006. In a 1981 survey covering half of the trees, only eight showed the desirable growth, form, and blight resistance (American Chestnut Cooperators' Foundation, "Breeding for Blight Resistance," http://www.ppws.vt.edu/griffin/breed.html).

SIX. EVIL TENDENCIES CANCEL

108   *"Evil Tendencies Cancel":*
Robert Frost, *A Further Range* (New York: Henry Holt and Co., 1936), 70.

109   *"like admiring the Boston Strangler":*
Fred Hebard, quoted in Steve Nash, "A Man and His Tree," *Washington Post Magazine,* July 25, 2004, W18.

110   *Some say it arrived on chestnut mine timbers:*
Rudolph Chelminski, "A Fungus Beats the Chestnut Blight at Its Own Game," *Smithsonian* 10 (June 1979): 97.

110   *it sneaked in on chestnut trees planted in botanical gardens:*
This is Fulbright's belief.

110   *the Laboratory of Biological Struggle:*
Chelminski, "Fungus," 97.

111   *Or actually, as later research established, a virus:*
Discovery of the agent responsible for affecting the fungus came many years later. Researchers isolated particles containing double strands of RNA, which is the hallmark of viruses that afflict fungi. Sources for this chapter include author interviews with Fulbright, Oct. 2005; Sandra Anagnostakis, 2005, 2006; Fred Hebard, 2004, 2005, 2006; William MacDonald, 2004, Dec. 2005; Neal Van Alfen, Aug. 2005; Richard Jaynes, April 2005; Michael Milgroom, Dec. 2005; and Donald Nuss, Dec. 2005.

111 *within ten years the blight epidemic there had ground to a halt:*
John E. Elliston, "Hypovirulence and Chestnut Blight Research: Fighting Disease with Disease," *Journal of Forestry* 79 (Oct. 1981): 657–60.

111 *"The blight has been defeated by nature, not me":*
Quoted in Chelminski, "Fungus," 97.

112 *Anagnostakis had begun working on her doctorate:*
Anagnostakis's story comes largely from an interview with the author, April 2005. See also Sandra Anagnostakis, "Chestnut Blight: The Classical Problem of an Introduced Pathogen," *Mycologia* 79 (Jan. 1987): 23–37.

114 *The research team reported their findings in a landmark article in 1975:*
N. K. Van Alfen, R. A. Jaynes, S. L. Anagnostakis, and P. R. Day, "Chestnut Blight: Biological Control by Transmissible Hypovirulence in *Endothia parasitica,*" *Science* 189 (Sept. 1975): 890–91.

115 *It is no wonder one forest researcher declared:*
R. Phares, "New Challenges in Chestnut Research," in MacDonald, Cech, Luchok, and Smith, *Proceedings of the American Chestnut Symposium*, 29.

116 *There were similar old groves:*
D. W. Fulbright, W. H. Weidlich, K. Z. Haufler, C. S. Thomas, and C. P. Paul, "Chestnut Blight and Recovering Chestnut Trees in Michigan," *Canadian Journal of Botany* 61 (1983): 3164.

116 *One of the most heartening sites was a small woodlot:*
Sources for the story of the Michigan trees are M. Ford Cochran, "Back from the Brink," *National Geographic* (Feb. 1990): 138; Mike Toner, "Is This the Chestnut's Last Stand," *National Wildlife,* Oct.–Nov. 1985, 25–27; Fulbright et al., "Chestnut Blight," 3164–71; D. W. Fulbright and W. H. Weidlich, "Interactions of American Chestnut and *Endothia parasitica* in Michigan," *Annual Report of the Northern Nut Growers Association* 74 (1983): 74–81; interview with Fulbright, Oct. 2005.

119 *the blight-of-the-blight is a far more complex system than initially supposed:*
Based on interviews with Fulbright; Anagnostakis; MacDonald, Dec. 2005; and Nuss. See also Anagnostakis, "Chestnut Blight"; Michael G. Milgroom, "Biological Control of Chestnut Blight with Hypovirulence: A Critical Analysis," *Annual Review of Phytopathology* 42 (2004): 311–38; Joseph R. Newhouse, "Chestnut Blight," *Scientific American* (July 1990): 106–11.

120   *One way the virus is transmitted:*
The virus also is spread through *C. parasitica*'s asexual spores. As the spores are moved by the rain or by passing birds, mammals, or insects, they carry the virus to new locations, either on the same tree or other trees.

120   *a new avenue for the virus to spread:*
Normally, those spores don't inherit the virus because the virus renders the female fungus infertile.

122   *a remarkable stand of chestnut trees growing in West Salem, Wisconsin:*
The story of the West Salem stand is based on interviews with Fulbright, Jane Cummings-Carlson, Oct. 2005; Ron Bockenhauer, Oct. 2005; Dolores Bockenhauer, Oct. 2005.

123   *The first virus strain used:*
Fulbright had his doubts all along about that particular strain, but says the choice was dictated by the researchers' limited resources. They needed to pick a hypovirus with a powerful enough effect that it could be quickly recognized when it was cultured, since they didn't have the resources for expensive molecular analyses. He notes that chestnut researchers are nearly always strapped for funds. "I hope you get that in," he tells me. "I'm probably luckier than the others to have some funding. A lot of these people are paying for this research out of their own salaries."

123   *This strain spread more readily:*
Forest Health Conditions in Wisconsin: Annual Report, 1997 (Madison: Wisconsin Department of Natural Resources, 1997), 67.

123   *By 2002, approximately six hundred trees in the stand were infected:*
Jane Cummings-Carlson, personal communication, Feb. 3, 2006.

126   *its promise as a biological control is built on "a lot of hype":*
Milgroom, "Biological Control," 330; interview with the author, Dec. 2005.

SEVEN. LET US PLANT

129   *he hated being called Charlie:*
Interview with Phil Rutter, June 2004.

130   *The era became known as "the golden age of plant genetics":*
Interview with Ronald Phillips, plant geneticist at the University of Minnesota, June 2004.

130   *"He'd be out in the field at daybreak":*
      Interview with Larry Inman, June 2004.

130   *Years after his retirement, he still liked to putter around the university library:*
      Burnham tells the story of how he became interested in the chestnut in
      "A Minnesota Story: Restoration of the American Chestnut," *Journal of*
      the American Chestnut Foundation 6 (1991): 82–90.

131   *the tree's prospects . . . were, in fact, "discouraging":*
      Frank H. Kaufert, "Prospects for American Chestnut (*Castanea dentata*)
      Plantings in Minnesota and Neighboring Upper Mississippi Valley
      States," *Minnesota Agricultural Experiment Station Miscellaneous Report*
      144 (1977): 5.

131   *"I could not believe what I was reading":*
      Burnham, "A Minnesota Story."

132   *Burnham called his colleague Norman Borlaug:*
      Interview with Norman Borlaug, March 2006.

134   *Nut tree crops, Rutter contends, can feed the world:*
      Rutter lays out his idea in an essay, "Why Is the Future of the World
      Nuts?" http://www.badgersett.com/future%20why.html. Interestingly,
      one of his sources of inspiration was the influential 1950 book *Tree*
      Crops: A Permanent Agriculture by geographer J. Russell Smith (New
      York: Devon-Adair Co.), who spent a lifetime trying to convince
      Americans to emulate Europeans and plant chestnut trees. In the early
      twentieth century, Smith was one of the chestnut's most ardent fans.
      He had a farm in Virginia where he watched the blight's rampage
      with dismay. In 1912, he attended the Pennsylvania Chestnut Blight
      Commission conference, where he made a passionate appeal to other
      states and the federal government to join Pennsylvania in fighting the
      blight.

138   *In early 1981, Burnham called Rutter:*
      The account of their early collaboration is based on author interviews
      with Phil Rutter in 2004 and 2005 and e-mail correspondence in 2006, as
      well as on interviews with Richard Jaynes, April 2005; Larry Inman,
      June 2004; and Ronald Phillips, June 2004. See also Burnham, "A
      Minnesota Story."

139   *The Chinese trees' ability to fight the blight derived from two or three genes:*
      Or more precisely, alleles. Alleles are the alternative forms of a gene; for
      example, "straight" and "curly" are two alleles of the gene that codes for
      hair.

139   *The Chinese chestnut's genetic baggage:*
Though all Chinese chestnuts are resistant to the blight, some trees seem better equipped to shrug off an infection than others, which suggests those trees have more powerful resistance genes.

140   *they surely would have tried backcross breeding:*
Charles Burnham, "Historical Overview of Chestnut Breeding in the United States," *Journal of the American Chestnut Foundation* 2 (Dec. 1987): 9–11.

143   *he couldn't resist tweaking the young Turks:*
Charles R. Burnham, "The Restoration of the American Chestnut."

144   *In 1981, Burnham published a letter:*
Charles R. Burnham, "Blight Resistant American Chestnut: There's Hope," *Plant Disease* 65 (June 1981): 459–60.

144   *"You're wasting your time":*
Interview with Donald Willeke, May 2004.

144   *each tree yielded two precious nuts:*
Burnham, "A Minnesota Story."

145   *By 1983, Burnham and Rutter had backcross hybrids growing:*
The best source of information on the early years of the breeding program (and through to the present day) is the *Journal of the American Chestnut Foundation,* which the group began publishing in 1986. Every issue contains at least one article summarizing the progress and experience of the program. Gradually, the journal also began including articles on the history, culture, and ecology of the American chestnut.

145   *"the preservation and restoration of the American chestnut":*
D. W. French, *Prospectus, American Chestnut Foundation,* undated.

146   *It needed to start recruiting members:*
Willeke and Rutter described the debate over the membership issue in interviews with author.

147   *"When the time comes . . . we can turn the blight resistant trees loose":*
Philip A. Rutter, "The President's Message," *Journal of the American Chestnut Foundation* 1 (Aug. 1986): 13.

147   *To get just one fully resistant tree:*
That figure was based on standard probability equations. If, as Burnham hypothesized, resistance is the product of three genes, it would take sixty-four rolls of the dice—sixty-four Chinese-American hybrids—to get one fully resistant tree. But that's an average figure. To secure a 95 percent chance of success actually requires 190 rolls of the dice—or the creation of 190 nuts.

148   *"It was an enthralling talk":*
Author interview with Jennifer Wagner, April 2006.

149   *With just a thin curtain of privacy:*
The description is drawn from former foundation director John Her-rington's description of Burnham's living situation in "Tributes to Charles Burnham and Angus McDonald," *Journal of the American Chestnut Foundation* 9 (Fall–Winter 1995–96): 11–12.

149   *When friends and colleagues gathered for his ninetieth birthday:*
Dean Rebuffoni, "He Wouldn't Give Up: Geneticist's Plan to Save American Chestnut Trees Finally Taking Root," *Minneapolis Star-Tribune,* Jan. 17, 1994.

150   *"Dearly beloved!":*
Text of his talk provided by Phil Rutter. See also Phil Rutter, "President's Message," *Journal of the American Chestnut Foundation* 4 (1990): 4.

EIGHT. CHESTNUT 2.0

151   *Herb Darling stands out:*
Darling's story is based on an interview with Herb Darling, Feb. 2003.

152   *they're counting on Charles Maynard and William Powell:*
Maynard and Powell work closely with another scientist, Scott Merkle, of the University of Georgia in Athens, who is also interested in bio-engineering a blight resistance. The information about Maynard and Powell's work is based largely on interviews with them and with Powell's laboratory manager, Linda Polin McGuigan, Jan. 2006.

155   *the Roundup Ready soybean:*
"Roundup Unready," *New York Times,* Feb. 19, 2003.

156   *the first transgenic tree, created in 1987:*
Scott A. Merkle and C. Joseph Nairn, "Hardwood Biotechnology," *In Vitro Cellular Development and Biology—Plant* 41 (Sept.–Oct. 2005): 602–19.

161   *he and Powell proudly planted a dozen of the tissue-cultured trees:*
Some of the trees produced from cultured tissue have a tendency to grow weirdly. They grow like branches, sprouting in several directions, rather than branching off a main stem. Maynard can't explain the effect, but has found that if he cuts the saplings back to the ground, they'll grow back following normal chestnut form.

163 *Oaks are notoriously promiscuous:*
Author interview with Douglas Gurian-Sherman, Jan. 2006.

163 *Typically, new alleles arise:*
Rowland D. Burdon and Christian Walter, "Exotic Pines and Eucalypts: Perspective on Risks of Transgenic Plantations," in *The Bioengineered Forest: Challenges for Science and Society,* ed. Steven H. Strauss and H. D. Bradshaw (Washington, D.C.: Resources for the Future Press, 2004): 67.

164 *Industrial tree science:*
Robert L. Youngs, "Wood Science and Technology in North America," *Forest Products Journal* 53 (Nov./Dec. 2003): 12–20.

164 *Forestry offered guidance on how to plant trees:*
Alan Lucier, Maude Hinchee, and Rex B. McCullough, "Biotechnology and the Forest Products Industry," in Strauss and Bradshaw, *The Bioengineered Forest,* 15.

165 *"Domestication has never been a simple one-way process":*
Michael Pollan, *The Botany of Desire: A Plant's-Eye View of the World* (New York: Random House, 2001), 196. I am indebted to Pollan for his clear discussion on natural selection and genetic technology.

165 *a natural, single-gene mutation that arose in wheat:*
Jared Diamond, *Guns, Germs, and Steel: The Fates of Human Societies* (New York: W. W. Norton and Co., 1999), 120.

165 *Modern methods of mass propagation:*
Not all species lend themselves to cloning, but poplars and a few species of pines do.

165 *"We control what the trees get":*
That quote and the description of the Potlatch plantation and the spread of plantations worldwide is from Charles C. Mann and Mark L. Plummer, "Forest Biotech Edges Out of the Lab," *Science* 295 (March 1, 2002): 1626. As of 2000, it was estimated that tree plantations covered over 185 million hectares worldwide. About 60 percent of that land is in temperate regions and around 40 percent is in the tropics, according to Brian Johnson and Keith Kirby, "Potential Impacts of Genetically Modified Trees on Biodiversity of Forestry Plantations: A Global Perspective," in Strauss and Bradshaw, *The Bioengineered Forest,* 192.

166 *Bioengineering offers a way to "create the tree we want":*
H. D. Bradshaw, quoted in Mann and Plummer, "Forest Biotech." Any transgenic tree is not only an improved plant but also intellectual prop-

erty, its genome owned by its creator and protected by patents and proprietary rights that potentially determine who can use it and what it will cost. The products of conventional breeding are rarely candidates for patents. That's arguably less of an issue in the case of trees than food crops, which have to be planted from seeds. Still, it's worth noting.

166 *Transgenic trees are being field-tested on every continent:*
As of 2006, the list of countries field testing transgenic trees includes France, Italy, Indonesia, the United States, Belgium, Spain, Canada, New Zealand, Chile, Germany, Japan, Portugal, Uruguay, South Africa, and Australia, according to Neil Carmen, who is leading the Sierra Club's opposition to genetically modified trees. Author interview with Carmen, Jan. 2006.

166 *As of 2006, the USDA had given the green light to only one:*
There were also two other transgenic fruit trees in the regulatory pipeline: another virus-resistant papaya and a plum tree engineered to resist plum-spot virus, according to John Cordts of the Biotechnology Regulatory Services of the Animal and Plant Health Inspection Service of the USDA. Author interview with Cordts, Jan. 2006.

167 *in other words, a giant block of wood:*
The image comes from Karen Charman, "The Shape of Forests to Come," *World-Watch,* May–June 2005, 24.

167 *China has embraced this latter product:*
Mark Clayton, "Now, Bioengineered Trees Are Taking Root," *Christian Science Monitor,* March 10, 2005, http://www.csmonitor.com/2005/0310/p14s02-sten.html.

167 *the use of sprayed Bt to manage pests was pioneered by organic . . . growers:*
Indeed, organic growers fear widespread use of Bt will lead to the evolution of Bt-resistant insects, which, as Pollan notes, "would ruin one of the safest insecticides we have and do great harm to the organic farmers who depend on it." Pollan, *The Botany of Desire,* 198, 213.

167 *One researcher hopes to use genetic technology:*
Hillary Rosner, "Turning Genetically Engineered Trees into Toxic Avengers," *New York Times,* Aug. 3, 2004.

168 *a site in Danbury, Connecticut:*
Ibid.; author interview with Scott Merkle, May 2004, who has helped develop the trees.

169 *A case in point is the Flavr-Savr tomato:*
Interview with Gurian-Sherman. The maker of the tomato, Calgene

Inc., was bought out by Monsanto in 1996, and by 1998 the tomato was removed from the market.

169 *breeders developed varieties of corn that were bred to be male-sterile:*
Burdon and Walter, "Exotic Pines," 64.

169 *Potatoes that were genetically transformed:*
Ahmad Ashouri, Dominique Michaud, and Conrad Cloutier, "Unexpected Effects of Different Potato Resistance Factors to the Colorado Potato Beetle (Coleoptera: Chrysomelidae) on the potato Aphid (Homoptera: Aphididae)," *Environmental Entomology* 30 (June 2001): 524–32. See also Johnson and Kirby, "Potential Impacts," 199.

169 *Oregon researchers working on transgenic trees found transformed seeds:*
Faith Campbell, *Genetically Engineered Trees: Questions without Answers,* American Lands Alliance, July 2000, http://www.americanlands.org/archive.php?articleNo=old_1092427489.

169 *"The main risks of using novel, highly domesticated trees":*
Steven H. Strauss and Amy M. Brunner, "Tree Biotechnology in the Twenty-First Century: Transforming Trees in the Light of Comparative Genomics," in Strauss and Bradshaw, *The Bioengineered Forest,* 92. Pollan notes this same irony in *The Botany of Desire.*

170 *Setting aside such issues as whether small field trials can predict:*
In early 2006, the USDA's Office of Inspector General issued a report finding that the agency had failed to adequately regulate field trials of genetically modified crops, raising the risks of unintended environmental effects. According to an article titled "Lax Oversight Found in Tests of Gene-Altered Crops" in the *New York Times* on Jan. 3, 2006, the report said that weakness in regulations and in the agency's internal management controls "increase the risk that genetically engineered organisms will inadvertently persist in the environment before they are deemed safe to grow without regulation." Agency officials and biotech spokespeople said the problems cited in the report had already been fixed before the report was published.

171 *the American chestnut genome:*
The exact size of the chestnut genome is unknown, but it's thought to fall somewhere between the smallest plant genome (that of *Arabidopsis,* which has twenty-seven thousand genes) and one of the larger genomes (such as rice, which has around forty-five thousand genes). William Powell, personal communication, Nov. 2006.

171 *endangered species that are candidates for gene-transfer rescues:*
Researchers are looking at such species as bald cypress, dogwood, Fraser fir, and other trees threatened by imported pests or pathogens.

174 *it was another story when . . . ArborGen came knocking:*
The story about ArborGen's courtship of the American Chestnut Foundation is based on author interviews with Charles Maynard, Jan. 2006; William Powell, Jan. 2006; Fred Hebard, 2004, 2005, 2006; Marshal Case, Aug. 2003, April 2006; Hill Craddock, Feb. 2006; Donald Willeke, April 2006; and Maude Hinchee, Feb. 2006.

175 *ArborGen, meanwhile, began granting fifty thousand dollars a year:*
The company is giving the same amount to University of Georgia researcher Scott Merkle, who also has been working on ways to propagate chestnut from somatic embryos.

175 *Powell turned his attention to the American elm:*
Although he used the same transgene that caused such consternation among chestnut scientists, there were no complaints about putting it in elm because elm trees don't bear fruit.

175 *the first transgenics ever set out in a public area:*
Whether the trees have anything more than symbolic value remains to be seen. It's difficult to test for resistance against Dutch elm disease in young trees. "We won't know if we have resistant trees until they're four or five years old," says Maynard.

176 *extremist opponents of bioengineering had torched transgenic tree labs:*
Laura Tangley, "Words (and Axes) Fly over Transgenic Trees," *Science* 292 (April 6, 2001): 34–37; Robert F. Service, "Arson Strikes Research Labs and Tree Farm in Pacific Northwest," *Science* 292 (June 1, 2001): 1622–23.

NINE. FAITH IN A SEED

178 *"Though I do not believe that a plant will spring up":*
Henry David Thoreau, "The Succession of Forest Trees," *Excursions: Writings of Henry David Thoreau,* vol. 5 (New York: Houghton Mifflin, 1906), 203.

178 *"thus the chestnut wood advances":*
Henry David Thoreau, *Faith in a Seed: The Dispersion of Seeds and Other Late Natural History Writings* (Washington, D.C.: Shearwater Books,

1993), 128. The book contains the unpublished writings that continued the argument begun in "The Succession of Forest Trees." Thoreau also fretted that the trees were rapidly disappearing from the area because of the demand for chestnut timber by railroads and industry: "There is danger, if we do not take unusual care, that this tree will become extinct here."

180 *"One of my great revelations was when I got poked in the eye":*
Quoted in Steve Nash, "A Man and His Tree," *Washington Post Magazine,* July 25, 2004. The magazine edited out the profanity.

184 *Burnham and Rutter had laid out a clear road map:*
Information about Hebard's breeding efforts is based on author interviews with Fred Hebard, 2004, 2005, 2006; Phil Rutter, 2005, 2006; Paul Sisco, geneticist for the American Chestnut Foundation, 2004, 2006; and science advisors Hill Craddock, 2006; Albert Ellingboe, Oct. 2005; Hugh Irwin, June 2006; Kim Steiner, June 2006; and Tom Kubisiak, July 2004, as well as reports published in the *Journal of the American Chestnut Foundation* from 1986 to the present day.

185 *It would gain further confirmation in later analyses:*
Thomas L. Kubisiak, Frederick Hebard, et al., "Molecular Mapping of Resistance to Blight in an Interspecific Cross in the Genus *Castanea,*" *Phytopathology* 87 (1997): 751–59.

188 *In 1963, after a decade of searching:*
J. C. Furnas, "New Chestnuts for Old," *American Forests* (Jan. 1963): 23.

188 *Later estimates pegged the number of significant-sized wild survivors:*
Hugh Irwin, "The Road to American Chestnut Restoration," *Journal of the American Chestnut Foundation* 16 (Spring 2003): 7.

189 *the ability of some chestnuts to endure the blight:*
Information about Griffin's approach is drawn from author interviews with Gary Griffin, June 2004, April 2006; Lucille Griffin, June 2004; John Elkins, June 2004; and Fred Hebard, 2006. See also the American Chestnut Cooperators' Foundation Web site, http://www.ppws.vt.edu/griffin/accf/html; Gary Griffin, "Blight Control and Restoration of the American Chestnut," *Journal of Forestry* 98 (Feb. 2000): 22–27; Gary Griffin, "Blight Resistance in American Chestnut," *Annual Report of the Northern Nut Growers Association* 73 (1982): 66–73; Gary Griffin, "Survival of American Chestnut Trees: Evaluation of Blight Resistance and Virulence in *Endothia parasitica,*" *Phytopathology* 73 (1983): 1084–92; Gary Griffin, *Integrated Use of Resistance, Hypovirulence, and Forest Management to*

Control Blight on American Chestnut, paper presented at Restoration of American Chestnut to Forest Lands conference and workshop, Asheville, NC, May 4–6, 2004.

194 *The Griffins are big on grafting:*
The Griffins also encourage American Chestnut Cooperators' Foundation members to do nut-grafts, in which a piece of scion wood (an active bud or stem) is embedded into a chestnut seed. That nut graft can be planted anywhere, Griffin explains. "You can plant it on the moon if you want." Talk about extending the tree's range.

195 *The Griffins and Elkinses have been grafting American chestnut intercrosses:*
Equally important to the effort was Tom Dierauf, a Virginia Department of Forestry forester who was responsible for chestnut research at Lesesne and who helped the cooperators do the first grafts on the Dietz trees.

197 *purposefully cultivating the kind of genetic diversity that would exist in the wild:*
That can be a particularly difficult task. As Scott Schlarbaum, of the University of Tennessee in Knoxville, pointed out to me, breeding for disease resistance can diminish genetic diversity. The U.S. Forest Service program to develop blister-rust resistant white pines used only one hundred parent trees for reintroduction, and the resulting seedlings, though rust-resistant, were less fit and less adaptable to a variety of sites.

198 *time to start looking for other "sources of resistance":*
To that end, in 2006, the group hired a second breeder who is supposed to focus on finding other resistant chestnut species and cultivars that may help broaden the base of the breeding program and take advantage of any useful information that comes out of the gene-mapping project.

198 *An outbreak of* Phytophthora:
Crandall, Gravatt, and Ryan, "Root Disease."

199 *"that precious 'while' when you have done your part":*
Noelle Oxenhandler, "Fall from Grace," *The New Yorker,* June 16, 1997, 65–68. Quoted in William R. Jordan III, *The Sunflower Forest: Ecological Restoration and the New Communion with Nature* (Berkeley: University of California Press, 2003), 77.

201 *After examining third-generation backcross trees:*
Matthew Diskin, Kim Steiner, and Fred Hebard, "Recovery of American Chestnut Characteristics following Hybridization and Backcross Breeding to Restore Blight-Ravaged *Castanea dentata,*" *Forest Ecology and Management* 223 (2006): 439.

201   *a genetic constitution that's about 10 percent Chinese:*
In theory, after three backcrosses the trees should be, on average, nearly 94 percent American, but in the real-world shuffling of genes that takes place through the backcrosses and later intercrosses, some trees will have less and some trees will have more, leading to experts' estimate that the trees will, on average, have a genetic base that's about 90 percent American genes.

CONCLUSION

205   *"You cannot love game and hate predators":*
Aldo Leopold, *Round River* (New York: Oxford University Press, 1993), 145–46.

205   *"we will build up an exhibit":*
Quoted in Peter Friederici, *Nature's Restoration: People and Places on the Front Lines of Conservation* (Washington, D.C.: Island Press, 2006), 90–92.

205   *one expert counted up nearly two hundred working definitions:*
Interview with John Cairns, a restoration ecologist at Virginia Polytechnic Institute, June 2006.

206   *"Pleistocene rewilding":*
Josh Donlan, Harry W. Greene, et al., "Re-wilding North America," *Nature* 436 (Aug. 18, 2005): 913–14.

206   *restoration has . . . become big business:*
Mark Clayton, "Eco Firms See Growing Profits," *Christian Science Monitor,* April 7, 2005.

207   *The vestigial old stumps and young sprouts offer some clues:*
One limitation is that many of those stumps have by now disappeared and sprouts are no longer to be found in every part of the historic range. For instance, there are no more sprouts growing in southern Indiana, according to Purdue forestry professor Douglass Jacobs.

207   *The issue of fire is controversial:*
This debate was played out in the pages of the *Journal of the American Chestnut Foundation.* See Quentin Bass, "Talking Trees: The Appalachian Forest Ecosystem and the American Chestnut," *Journal of the American Chestnut Foundation* 16 (Fall 2002): 42–54. In response to Bass's arguments, forester John Perry and forest archaeologist Cecil Ison weighed in with "The Impact of Fire on Chestnut in the Central Hardwood Region," *Journal of the American Chestnut Foundation* 17 (Fall 2003): 34–41.

208 *If the tree needs full sunlight:*
There are precious few clear-cut areas to be found. The U.S. Forest Service has indicated that it can make available at most four hundred acres of clear-cut land a year for chestnut plantings, according to both Douglass Jacobs and Kim Steiner.

208 *Of more than 3,700 challenges to U.S. Forest Service plans:*
R. W. Malmsheimer, D. Keele, and D. W. Floyd, "National Forest Litigation in the US Courts of Appeal," *Journal of Forestry* 102 (March 2004): 20–25.

209 *One famous example concerned a project known as Chicago Wilderness:*
Friederici, *Nature's Restoration,* 115–25. The full story of the Chicago prairie restoration project is told in William K. Stevens, *Miracle under the Oaks: The Revival of Nature in America* (New York: Simon and Schuster, 1995).

210 *"A restorationist, like a parent":*
Quoted in Stevens, *Miracle under the Oaks,* 290.

210 *The source of the trouble was a legal document:*
Information on the agreement and the debate over it comes from author interviews with Marshal Case, 2006; Hill Craddock, 2006; Bob Leffel, Dec. 2006; Ann Leffel, Dec. 2006; and Sandra Anagnostakis, Dec. 2006.

211 *It was enough to mollify the Pennsylvania chapter:*
The debate over the agreement was wrapped up with a broader dispute over the structure of the organization. Some members were angry that the bylaws deprived the state chapters of being represented on the board of directors or having any significant say in the running of the organization. The group's bylaws were ultimately revised to give the chapters more of a voice in decision making.

212 *To that end, the group has adopted a detailed protocol:*
"TACF Adopts Guidelines for Testing Blight-Resistant American Chestnuts," *Journal of the American Chestnut Foundation* 18 (Spring 2004): 7–11.

212 *The hows, whens, wheres, and what-ifs:*
While some would like to see plantings limited to the species's historic range, Paul Sisco, the foundation's regional science coordinator, notes that the boundaries of any tree's native range are not set in stone: "Tree species are constantly on the move and not always well-adapted to the places where they happen to be at any given moment in time. It is warmer now than it was when the blight was introduced and *Phytoph-*

thora cinnamomi has spread to more places. Chestnuts may be better adapted to more northerly and westerly regions now. They do well in the Pacific Northwest, and the largest American chestnut tree still alive is in Sherwood, Oregon, a suburb of Portland. It was planted in 1890, and is at the home of a direct descendant of Daniel Boone." Personal communication with the author, March 2007.

212 *breeding programs have a hard time maintaining "hereditary wildness":*
Hugh Irwin, "The Road to American Chestnut Restoration," *Journal of the American Chestnut Foundation* 16 (Spring 2003): 10.

212 *His concern is not only that the hybrids won't thrive:*
Friederici, *Nature's Restoration,* 71–72.

213 *the National Park Service has yet to commit:*
Ibid., 74.

213 *Even if foundation volunteers are planting twenty million seeds a year:*
By way of comparison, Steiner notes that about ten million oak seedlings are planted a year, and oaks are a far more commercially important tree that chestnut ever was or ever will be.

215 *In the doleful saga of American's extractive industries:*
As Erik Reece notes in his wrenching account of mountain top removal: "Those ecosystems are the most diverse on this continent. What compounds the tragedy of mountain top removal in central Appalachia is that this disappearing forest, the mixed mesophytic, is home to nearly eighty different species of trees. It is the rain forest of North America and it is falling fast." Erik Reece, *Lost Mountain; A Year in the Vanishing Wilderness: Radical Strip Mining and the Devastation of Appalachia* (New York: Riverhead Books, 2006), 4.

215 *Spread thick rows of spoil over a mine site:*
Ibid., 218.

216 *It's a vast springboard:*
Ibid.

216 *The few studies done to date:*
One study of chestnut planted on reclaimed mine lands in Ohio found that despite harsh site conditions and a prolonged period of drought, 70 percent of the trees planted were still alive after the third growing season. Douglass Jacobs, "The Potential Use of American Chestnut for Reclaiming Mine Lands," *Journal of the American Chestnut Foundation* 19 (Fall 2005): 35.

217 *Angel's is hardly the only vision of how to restore the chestnut:*
For a good general discussion of the current thinking and status of chestnut restoration, see the proceedings of a conference sponsored by the National Park Service and held in Asheville, NC, May 4–6, 2004: Kim Steiner and John Carlson, eds., *Restoration of the American Chestnut to Forest Lands: Natural Resources Report NP/NCR/CUE/NRR—2006/001* (Washington, D.C.: Dept. of the Interior, 2006). Available online at http://chestnut.cas.psu.edu/nps.htm.

217 *"Where there are mountains, there are chestnuts":*
Quoted in Davis, *Where There Are Mountains,* 11.

218 *"faking nature":*
Robert Elliott, "Faking Nature," *Inquiry* 25 (1982): 81–93. Elliott elaborated on the argument in a later book titled *Faking Nature* (London: Routledge Press, 1997).

218 *American philosopher Eric Katz extends the argument:*
Eric Katz, "The Ethical Significance of Human Intervention in Nature," *Restoration and Management Notes* 9 (1991): 90.

219 *If the only nature that matters:*
Andrew Light, "Ecological Citizenship: The Democratic Promise of Restoration," in *The Humane Metropolis: People and Nature in the 21st Century,* ed. Rutherford Platt (Amherst: University of Massachusetts Press in association with the Lincoln Institute of Land Policy, 2006). Available online at http://faculty.washington.edu/alight/papers/Light.Ecological_Citizenship.pdf. Light articulates an ethic that encourages an appreciation and awareness of nature wherever it may be found—starting with one's own backyard.

219 *When we take on the far more challenging task of restoring a native landscape:*
William Jordan, *The Sunflower Forest: Ecological Restoration and the New Communion with Nature* (Berkeley: University of California Press, 2003), 72.

220 *species have come and gone:*
Scott Wiedensaul is the source for the grim statistics on species loss in his book, *The Ghost with Trembling Wing: Science, Wishful Thinking and the Search for Lost Species* (New York: North Point Press, 2002), 34–35.

220 *we are now losing an estimated fifty thousand species a year:*
Stephen R. Kellert and Edward O. Wilson, *The Biophilia Hypothesis* (Washington, D.C.: Island Press, 1993), 36–37.

220   *"the greatest extinction spasm":*
      Ibid.

220   *U.S. government inspectors now intercept about fifty-three thousand*
      pathogens:
      Richard Mack, *Predicting Invasions of Nonindigenous Plants and Plant*
      Pests (Washington, D.C.: National Academy Press, 2002), 15.

221   *to the tune of approximately $137 billion a year:*
      Yvonne Baskin, *A Plague of Rats and Rubbervines* (Washington, D.C.:
      Shearwater Books, 2002), 4.

221   *The fight to contain the exotics:*
      Ibid. See also Faith Campbell and Scott Schlarbaum, *Fading Forests II:*
      Trading Away America's Natural Heritage (Washington, D.C.: Healing
      Stones Foundation, 2002).

221   *more than twenty exotic pathogens and 360 harmful nonnative insects:*
      Ibid., 7–14.

221   *Generally they have arrived through one of three routes:*
      Ibid.

221   *The casualty list includes:*
      Ibid. See also Web site run by the U.S. Forest Service and relevant Michi-
      gan agencies on the emerald ash borer: http://www.emeraldashborer
      .info/.

221   *The most worrisome disease to surface:*
      Chronology of sudden oak death based on stories in the *San Francisco*
      Chronicle between 1998 and 2006; Susan Freinkel, "If All the Trees Fall
      in the Forest," *Discover* 23 (Dec. 2002): 67–72; and interview with Steven
      Oak of the U.S. Forest Service Southern Appalachian office, June 2006.

223   *Many cultures contain a notion of a cosmic tree:*
      Nathaniel Altman, *Sacred Trees* (San Francisco: Sierra Club Books, 1994),
      30.

223   *The woolly adelgid has caused such a severe decline:*
      Quoted in Campbell and Schlarbaum, *Fading Forests II*, 78.

224   *The losses they produce accumulate over time:*
      Phyllis Windle, "The Ecology of Grief," *Orion* (Winter 1994): 22.

224   *"One of the penalties of an ecological education":*
      Leopold, *Round River*, 165.

224   *the oak trees . . . are themselves in the midst of a major die-back:*
      Oak decline is attributed to a variety of factors having to do with the
      natural and human-mediated ways in which oaks have come to domi-

nate the southern Appalachian forests. Oaks were prominent in the understory of chestnut-dominated forests. When the blight killed off the chestnuts, several species of oaks quickly took their places. Over the course of the last century, this generation of oaks has been able to grow to maturity with relatively little disturbance, thanks to fire-control programs, the formation of national parks, and reduction in timber harvests. You'd think it would be good for the oaks, but the problem is that the southern Appalachian mountains are now covered with forests in which all the oaks are seventy to ninety years old and vulnerable to oak-decline, a disease that afflicts older trees and is associated with stresses such as drought or insect defoliations. The impact of the disease is magnified by the fact that so much of the southern Appalachian forest is vulnerable to it. According to one inventory, there are vulnerable trees in more than half of the 17.4 million acres containing oak forests in the southern Appalachian mountains. Steve Oak, "From the Bronx to Birmingham: Impact of Chestnut Blight and Management Practices on Forest Health Risks in Southern Appalachian Mountains," *Journal of the American Chestnut Foundation* 11(1) (Fall 2002): 32–42.

224 *"When you have tree species after tree species disappearing":*
Craig Lorimer, quoted in Freinkel, "If All the Trees," 73.

225 *Windle discusses her sorrow:*
Windle, "The Ecology of Grief," 20.

225 *As the late Stephen Jay Gould pointed out:*
Stephen Jay Gould, quoted in David Orr, "Love it or Lose It: The Coming Biophilia Revolution" in Kellert and Wilson, *The Biophilia Hypothesis,* 425.

226 *returning the tree to the forest can help redeem a host of human errors:*
The subsequent list of potential benefits comes courtesy of an interview with Marshal Case, July 2006.

ACKNOWLEDGMENTS

I came to this book with little background in any of the areas I knew it had to cover. Given that near-vertical learning curve, I am deeply indebted to the scientists who provided such excellent tutelage, generously sharing their time, expertise, and even in some cases their homes with me. For their patience, good humor, and sufferance of endless questions, I am particularly grateful to Sandra Anagnostakis, Dennis Fulbright, Gary Griffin, Lucille Griffin, Fred Hebard, Charles Maynard, William Powell, and Philip Rutter. But this book would have been thin, indeed, were it not for the contributions of the many other experts I spoke with, including Patrick Angel, Marshal Case, Hill Craddock, Jane Cummings-Carlson, Donald Davis, John Elkins, Albert Ellingboe, Sara Fitzsimmons, Michael French, Hugh Irwin, Douglass Jacobs, Richard Jaynes, Thomas Kubisiak, William MacDonald, Rex Mann, Scott Merkle, Greg Miller, Donald Nuss, Fred Paillet, Scott Schlarbaum, Ronald Sederoff, Paul Sisco, and Kim Steiner. With such fine teachers, I can only say that any mistakes by now are mine alone.

The chapters on the chestnut's role in southwest Virginia could not have been written without Ralph Lutts, whose crash course in the region's history and meticulous documentation of the chestnut trade saved me years of work. My gratitude goes too to Annette Hartigan, research librarian at the Great Smoky Mountains National Park Archives; to the Pennsylvania State Historical Archives; and to Rhoda Switzer, keeper of Flippo Gravatt's archives at Scientists' Cliffs, Maryland.

I am also deeply appreciative of all the chestnut aficionados who shared their thoughts, experiences, and love of *Castanea dentata* with me. That includes Charlotte Barnhart, Annie Bhagwandin, Ruth Jean Bolt, Herb Darling, Danny Honaker, Bob and Ann Leffel, Carl Mayfield, Early McAlexander, Bernard Monahan, Clint Neel, Kathy Newfont, Barry Price, Susan Lea Rudd, Joe Schbeig, Donald Willeke, Jim Wilson, Arlene Wirsig, Coy Lee Yeatts, Dayle Zanzinger, and the many others I met in my travels over the past three years.

Writing may be a solitary process, but happily it's not been a lonely one, thanks to my allies in North 24th Writers: Allison Bartlett, Leslie Crawford, Frances Dinkelspiel, Katherine Ellison, Sharon Epel, Katherine Neilan, Lisa Okuhn, Julia Flynn Siler, and Jill Storey. Their individual and collective editorial gifts helped sharpen my writing and thinking in countless ways. Susan West helped me cut a clear narrative path—and get the science right—in early drafts of many of the chapters. My sister, Lisa Freinkel, provided insightful readings on several key portions, pushing me always to figure out what it was about this story that really mattered.

From start to finish, the faith of my literary agent, Ted Weinstein, in this project was a continuing source of help and comfort. I am also grateful for the guiding hand of my editor at the University of California Press, Blake Edgar.

Support comes in many forms. A grant from the Alicia Patterson Foundation made it possible for me to research many portions of the book without dragging my family into bankruptcy. My mother, Ruth Freinkel, and brother, Andrew Freinkel, helped keep me going with that equally crucial moral support. And a weeklong retreat courtesy of Leslie Landau and Jim Shankland allowed me to get the final chapters done. Thanks, too, to Eli, Isaac, and Moriah Wolfe for their encouragement and willingness to absorb way more information about chestnuts than they ever wanted to know, and for always helping me to keep life in perspective. Above all, thanks to my husband, Eric Wolfe, who has been my infallible compass for all that makes the American chestnut—and the world—worthy of wonder.

INDEX

Addington Mining Inc., 214
agrobacterium, 160–61
Alabama, 75, 81
Allegheny chinquapin trees, 14, 230
Allegheny Mountains, 18, 61
American Association for the Advancement of Science, 52
American Chestnut Cooperators' Foundation (ACCF), 191–95, 198, 265
American Chestnut Foundation, 5, 132, 145–50, 151, 154; backcross breeding program of, 142 *fig*, 148, 152, 163, 171, 173, 179, 184–85, 196–202, 210–14; breeding protocols adopted by, 210–14; genetic engineering program of, 152, 158, 162, 173–75; journal of, 258; Meadowview research farm of, 148, 150, 179–80, 183–87, 199; organizational affiliations of, 174–75, 216–17; state chapters of, 146, 152, 160, 162, 173–74, 180, 186, 191, 197, 210–12, 267
American chestnut trees: benefits of, 226–27; evolutionary development of, 13–14; genome of, 171, 262; geographic range of, xi, 1, 15, 117, 197, 267–68; multiple threats faced by, 196, 198–99; post-blight specimens of, 1, 9–

10, 68, 81, 105, 109, 117–18, 122, 187–88, 207, 268; reintroduction of, 207–8, 226; restoration of, 206–7, 209–10, 213–14, 221, 226–27; taxonomy of, 14
Anagnostakis, Sandra, 68, 112–14, 116, 118–19, 120, 125–26, 143, 179n, 211, 214, 250
Angel, Patrick, 214–18
anti-blight measures: branch cutting, 30, 45, 62; burning, 30, 37, 63; hypovirulence (biocontrol), 111–28, 132, 144, 145, 155, 183, 190, 197, 206; mudpacks, 152; pseudoscientific, 42–43; quarantine, 42, 46, 51, 52, 54, 56, 58, 63, 66, 69; spraying, 30–31, 37, 45, 62; tree cutting, 37, 49, 50, 57, 63, 69, 79, 80, 81
antimicrobial genes, 157–58, 175
Appalachia, 1, 4, 16, 17–27, 41, 46, 52, 147, 172, 187, 188, 206, 222, 224; chestnut blight in, xi, 72–84, 86–88, 225, 271; chestnut trade in, 20–24, 76, 83–84, 233; mining industry in, 214–17, 226, 268; oak decline in, 270–71; socio-economic change in, 84–86; timber industry in, 21, 24–27, 79–80, 87
Appalachian Regional Reforestation Initiative (AARI), 215–18

277

Text:	11/15 Granjon
Display:	Granjon
Compositor:	BookMatters, Berkeley
Indexer:	Andrew Joron
Illustrator:	Bill Nelson
Printer and binder:	Maple-Vail Manufacturing Group